*TRANS*ACTIONS, *TRANS*GRESSIONS, *TRANS*FORMATIONS

*TRANS*ACTIONS, *TRANS*GRESSIONS, *TRANS*FORMATIONS

American Culture in Western Europe and Japan

Edited by

Heide Fehrenbach

and

Uta G. Poiger

Berghahn Books

NEW YORK • OXFORD

Published in 2000 by

Berghahn Books

Editorial offices:
604 West 115th St., New York, NY 10025 USA
3, NewTec Place, Magdalen Road, Oxford, OX4 1RE, UK

Library of Congress Cataloging-in-Publication Data

Transactions, transgressions, transformations : American culture in Western
Europe and Japan / edited by Heide Fehrenbach and Uta G. Poiger.
    p.   cm.
Includes bibliographical references and index.
    ISBN 1-57181-107-9 (hc. : alk. paper). – ISBN 1-57181-108-7
(pbk. : alk. paper)
    1. Europe–Civilization–American influences. 2. Japan–
Civilization–American influences. 3. Popular culture–United States.
4. Popular culture–Europe. 5. Popular culture–Japan.
I. Fehrenbach, Heide.   II. Poiger, Uta G., 1965– .
D1065.U5T7 1999   98-47360
303.48'24073–dc21   CIP

British Library Cataloguing in Publication Data

A catalogue record for this book is available from the British Library.

Printed in the United States on acid-free paper.

CONTENTS

LIST OF ILLUSTRATIONS

Figures

ACKNOWLEDGMENTS

This volume traces it origins back to a colloquium convened by Volker Berghahn at Brown University on "The American Cultural Impact on Germany, France, Italy, and Japan, 1945–1995: An International Comparison" in April 1996. We would like to acknowledge the following institutions and programs for contributing essential funding and support to the event: The Goethe Institut Boston, and at Brown University: the Thomas J. Watson, Jr. Institute for International Studies, the Herbert H. Goldberger Lectureships Fund, the Wayland Collegium, the Bologna Program, and the Brauer-Swearer Fund. Our thanks to Ian Condry for suggesting and securing the cover photo of Japanese rapper Crazy-A (a.k.a. Akira), and to Crazy-A and Crown Records for their kind permission to reproduce it for this book.

Most importantly, we would like to thank Volker Berghahn for providing the inspiration and organizational impetus for the colloquium, and for being such a generous and supportive mentor in our professional and intellectual lives.

Heide Fehrenbach and Uta G. Poiger

NOTES ON CONTRIBUTORS

Botond Bognar is Professor of Architecture at the University of Illinois. Since the early 1970s he has been researching Japanese architecture. He has lectured extensively on the topic in the United States, Canada, Europe, Japan, and Australia and has written several books and numerous articles, including *World Cities: TOKYO* (1997), *Togo Murano: Master Architect of Japan* (1996), and *The Japan Guide* (1995). His latest publication, *NIKKEN SEKKEI 1990–2000: Building Future Japan,* will be published by Rizzoli International in 2000.

Ian Condry received his Ph.D. in anthropology from Yale University in 1999, and currently teaches at Union College in Schenectady, NY. His dissertation, an ethnography of the Japanese hip-hop scene, is based on fieldwork in Tokyo nightclubs and recording studios. His research interests in political economy, mass culture, and new media focus on the intersection of culture and commerce in the context of globalization.

David W. Ellwood is Associate Professor of International History at the University of Bologna and Professorial Lecturer in European History at the Johns Hopkins School of Advanced International Studies, Bologna Center. His major publications include *Italy 1943–45: The Politics of Liberation* (1985), *Re-building Europe: Western Europe, America and Postwar Reconstruction* (1992), and the edited volume *Hollywood in Europe: Experiences of a Cultural Hegemony* (1994). He has written extensively on the political, economic, and mass-cultural relations between the United States and Europe, with particular reference to World War II, the Marshall Plan, and the theme of Americanization. From 1995 to 1999, he was President of IAMHIST, the International Media and History Association.

Heide Fehrenbach is Associate Professor of History at Emory University. She is the author of *Cinema in Democratizing Germany: Reconstructing National Identity after Hitler* (Chapel Hill, 1995) and is currently at work on a book-length study entitled *Race in German Reconstruction: African American Occupation Children and Postwar Discourses of Democracy, 1945–1965.*

Peter Krieger is an art historian specializing in twentieth-century architectural history and theory, urban political iconography, and Mexican architecture, and is the author of various publications on twentieth-century architecture and urban planning . He completed a doctoral dissertation on architecture and urban planning in 1950s Hamburg, and has served as consultant to the Hamburg Landmark Preservation Commission; as architectural critic for various architectural and design magazines; and as university lecturer on modern architectural history at the universities of Hamburg and Bremen in Germany. In 1997 and again in 1998–99, he has been Visiting Fellow at the Instituto de Investigaciones Estéticas at UNAM, Mexico; since 1998 he has also been Visiting Professor at the Faculty of Architecture, Graduate Studies, UNAM, Mexico.

Richard F. Kuisel is Professor of History at SUNY-Stony Brook. His books include *Seducing the French: The Dilemma of Americanization* (1993) and *Capitalism and the State in Modern France* (1981). His current research focuses on the rivalry between France and the United States over commerce and culture.

Franco Minganti is Professor of American Literature at the University of Bologna. He has edited or translated several volumes and is the author of *X-Roads: Letteratura, jazz, immaginario* [X-Roads: Literature, Jazz, Imagination] (1994) and of *Modulazioni di frequenza: L'immaginario radiofonico tra letteratura e cinema* [Frequency Modulations: The Radiophonic Imaginary in Literature and Cinema] (1997). His research focuses on popular genres and their reception; media, fiction, and technology; and Americanization in Italy.

Mary Nolan is Professor of History at New York University. She is the author of *Social Democracy and Society: Working-Class Radicalism in Duesseldorf, 1890–1918* (1981) and *Visions of Modernity: American Business and the Modernization of Germany* (1995).

James Petterson is Assistant Professor of French Literature at Wellesley College. He is a specialist of contemporary French poetry and of intellectual movements in France preceding and following World War II. Recent articles include "Théophile de Viau: In turba clamor, in foro silentium," *Dalhousie French Review* (1998). His book *Post-War Figures of L'Ephémère*, forthcoming from Bucknell University Press, is an in-depth study of the poet-editors of the French literary journal *L'Ephémère*. He is currently working on a book-length project entitled *Poetry Proscribed: The Trials of Poetry in France.*

Uta G. Poiger is Assistant Professor of History at the University of Washington at Seattle, where she teaches German history, gender history, and historiography. Her book *Jazz, Rock, and Rebels: Cold War Politics and American Culture in a Divided Germany* will be published in 2000 by the University of California Press.

Takayuki Tatsumi is Professor of English at Keio University in Tokyo. A specialist of the American Renaissance, postmodern fiction, and literary theory, he has published numerous articles in Japanese and English. His books include *Cyberpunk America* (1988), *A Manifesto for Japanoids* (1993), and the coedited anthology *Storming the Reality Studio* (1991).

INTRODUCTION

Americanization Reconsidered

Heide Fehrenbach and Uta G. Poiger

In 1995 tube stops in Central London featured a McDonald's advertising poster that addressed its audience with a slogan in German
"Schmeckt wie daheim" (tastes just like at home) against a background of a Big Mac and fries. This ad was likely designed to enable
multiple readings. The non-English slogan drew the attention of all
viewers regardless of national origin to McDonald's global presence,
and at the same time the slogan connected McDonald's with home
for German tourists (or more specifically for South German tourists,
since *daheim* is a word commonly used only in Southern Germany).
Thus the ad made McDonald's—and by extension American products, since McDonald's has come to stand symbolically for America—
at once something ubiquitous and something "nativized." America
and Americanization, the ad seemed to say, not only connect cultures outside of the United States to one another but also are part of
local culture.

This volume focuses on what has been the United States' most
controversial export in the twentieth century: American culture.
Any discussion of American culture abroad immediately raises the
specter of "Americanization," a term fraught with political baggage.
As a result, scholars increasingly use Americanization as a descrip-
tive rather than an analytical category. To be sure, even in the
1990s some have attempted to employ a definition of Americanization that equates it with economic modernization and political

and cultural democratization; in other words, they use modernization theories–which have rightly been widely questioned–in order
to give Americanization positive meaning.[1] Others identify cultural
Americanization as a negative tool of American imperialism.[2] Most
recent studies, however, express much uneasiness with both definitions. They instead understand Americanization as describing the
transfer of goods and symbols from the United States to other
countries and focus on how societies abroad have taken up and, in
the process, transformed these influences. In focusing on the reception of American culture abroad, the present volume follows this
trend. At the same time, it suggests that Americanization can and
should be retained as an analytical tool–one, however, in need of
thorough contextualization.

If Americanization is not to be equated with either modernization
or imperialism, it surely has to be understood in the context of
modernity. Using the term "modernity," rather than "modernization," allows us to disentangle modern phenomena, such as urbanization or the rise of commercial culture and mass consumption,
from the positive values of progress that modernization theorists
often attach to such processes. In our view, modernity has ambiguous meanings, and in exploring the links between Americanization
and modernity, we also recognize that Americanization is neither a
uniform nor a unifying phenomenon. This volume suggests nonetheless that the study of Americanization is useful in two ways. First, in
terms of chronology, research on Americanization can in fact identify periods of intense American cultural impact abroad, often closely
connected with American economic and political interests. Some
scholars argue that this impact reached its high point in the three
decades after 1945 and has since declined; others see continued
American domination in a global world.[3] Second, and just as important, since American influences provide a significant reference point
for virtually all modern societies, they allow for comparisons between different "recipients"–be they different nations or groups
within nations. These consumers of American culture have by no
means been passive. Attention to the complex processes by which
societies adopt, adapt, and reject American culture makes it clear
that these encounters say more about those who have been "Americanized" than about the United States. It is precisely a focus on the
complexity of these processes that makes comparisons between
Americanizing nations meaningful.

American culture–and by that we mean images and products
ranging from American movies and music to fashion and architecture, made by industries based in the United States–has, by offering

alternative modes of identification, been crucial in the shaping of new identities. This dynamic has existed since the nineteenth century, but was especially important after 1945, when Western Europe and Japan confronted the legacies of fascism and world war, the cold war and decolonization.

Reactions to American culture abroad have not only been about defining differences between America and "import" nations, but also about delineating differences within these nations along the lines of gender, sexuality, generation, class, race, and ethnicity. Authorities in Western Europe and Japan frequently used normative notions of gender difference, for example, to reject American imports and to contain consumer behavior—especially that of female consumers, who were specifically targeted by American and native advertising and marketing strategies. This rejection, moreover, often went hand in hand with associating American culture with sexualized femininity and hypermasculinity—in short, with a lack of respectability. Thus the consumption of American culture has been denounced as a threat to stable social, sexual, and familial relations and, by extension, to national health and integrity precisely because it has been perceived as encouraging alternative individual and group identities that challenge normative *national* models of femininity and masculinity.[4] This is not to argue, however, that such fears have no foundation in social experience. If we shift our attention from cultural prescription and regulation to the social and psychological meanings of consumption for individual women and men, we find that identity, image, and gender ideals have been historically bound to the consumption of commodities, at least in this century, and that this consumption has led to the articulation of alternative, often transgressive, behaviors and models of identification. In postwar Britain, for example, young female filmgoers "read" Hollywood starlets in opposition to the much more modest model of British womanhood during the postwar years of austerity, due to the former's "abundant femininity,... glamour and desirability." Copying the hairstyle, dress, or demeanor of a favorite Hollywood star allowed women to counter the realities of rationing with little extravagances and a personal style that altered their self- and public images and aided in the production of new forms of femininity.[5]

In addition, some of the most popular American cultural imports have been adapted from the cultures of various American racial and ethnic minorities, and have been employed by nations to confront and reformulate their own notions of racial difference. This is an understudied subject, even though reactions to American culture have always been about constructing and reconstructing differences within recipient nations–and have therefore played a significant role in the process and politics of communal self-definition. Much of American culture–like ragtime, jazz, rock 'n' roll–has been rooted in African-American culture, and audiences within the United States and abroad have often felt titillated and/or repelled by what they perceive as racial transgressions contained in these varieties of American culture. German opponents of jazz in the interwar years, for example, associated the music with black musicians, Jewish promoters, and sexual lasciviousness, and combined anti-black and anti-semitic sentiments to reject jazz as "un-German." Yet even as ideas about biological racial hierarchies (that were so central to the development of modern national identities in Western Europe, the United States, and Japan since the nineteenth century) lost credibility in the aftermath of fascism, efforts to articulate notions of national identity based on cultural and racial differences have continued. Juxtaposing black and white has been but one variant of a broad array of racial hierarchies that contemporaries have constructed between, for example, Jews and non-Jews, whites and Asians, or Japanese and blacks.[6] Subcultures within import nations have at times been able to use American culture to question such visions of racial purity. However, American forms have also been adopted abroad to send intensely racist messages. The uses of American culture are thus malleable and underwrite no particular political agenda or communal vision. In other words, American culture abroad has been neither automatically racist nor anti-racist, but has taken on complex and varying meanings in constructions of racial (and other) hierarchies within consuming nations.[7]

A central unifying theme to the essays in this volume is the issue of identity and, more precisely, the role that American culture and its consumption has played in the negotiation, and continual renegotiation, of such identities. Far from having fixed identities, social groups are historically fluid and highly unstable; their boundaries and self-definitions are both contingent and contested. As anthropologist Richard Handler has reminded us, "To talk about identity is to change or construct it, despite the dominant epistemology of identity, which specifies immutability."[8] In order to capture the mutable, multidirectional, and often highly contested social and cultural processes involved in identity construction, we have chosen to entitle this collection "*trans*actions, *trans*gressions, *trans*formations."

In speaking of American culture, we have consciously omitted the terms "mass" and "popular" from our title, since committing to one or the other would imply in a sense committing to a particular set of meanings. To be sure, the American exports that this volume covers were mass distributed (movies, music, fashions, books) or designed to be used by many people (as in the case of urban planning). However, in the debates of the past twenty years, "mass" culture has come to imply a top-down manipulation of consumers by capitalist interests and industries, whereas "popular" culture has come to mean a culture that originates at the grassroots level with some possibility for the dissemination of an "authentic" folk culture from the bottom up. Instead, we believe that both meanings need to be held in tension and in fact exist contemporaneously. Both help us understand the complex transformations and transgressions that have characterized Western European and Japanese encounters with American culture.[9]

By including Western Europe and Japan in this volume, we address "Western" as well as "non-Western" experiences vis-à-vis American culture. At the same time, comparisons between Japan and various Western European nations make the divisions Western/non-Western problematic, since they reveal the attendant conceptual short-circuit entailed in employing such an easy opposition. Neither can we assume the existence of a uniform West (of Western Europeans nations and the United States), nor should we simply affirm alleged differences between the West and its "others," in this case the West's Far East, or between Japan and its "others," that is, Japan's "Occident." Marilyn Ivy, among others, has recently urged that it is important to recognize the close temporal links of Japanese and Western modernity and postmodernity.[10] For example, Japan, like its Western European counterparts, industrialized rapidly since the nineteenth century, and became an imperial power. In pointing to the links between Japanese, American, and European modernity, we do not mean to relocate Japan into an expanded definition of the modern West and at the same time establish new boundaries between an allegedly modern world of colonizers and a nonmodern world of the colonized. While our focus in this volume is on industrialized ("First World") countries, the questions and dilemmas we engage are of significance beyond Western Europe and Japan.

In this introduction we intend to locate interpretations of American culture and Americanization historically and to raise issues that might be useful for readers to consider as they read the essays on American culture in different national contexts. Ultimately, we hope that this volume will contribute to the project of constructing comparative frameworks that recognize both similarities and differences in the development of modern nations.

American Culture, Nation-States, Modernity

Although this volume concentrates on the post–World War II period, American culture has had a much longer presence and pedigree in Western Europe and Japan. To be sure, Europeans imagined and reimagined America since Columbus, and the Japanese did the same after the opening of Japan in the mid-nineteenth century. While American culture's appearance abroad predated the era of aggressive expansion by American business interests into international markets, cultural importation and interaction intensified in the late nineteenth century and became the object of sustained official, business, and public concern by the second decade of this century. Thus, Americanization cannot be understood outside of the rise of modern nation-states, consumer capitalism, and mass culture.[11]

In large measure, the modern meanings of American culture abroad were forged during a period of protracted national crises in Western Europe and Japan: World War I and the ensuing interwar years of social and economic malaise for Western Europe; and for Japan, the economic downturns and uncertainty after the World War I boom in 1920 and after the great earthquake of September 1923. American companies sought and received official American assistance in propagandizing the war effort by exporting domestic wares and, after victory, in asserting American interests in a new world order.[12] At least for Europe, this historical context conditioned subsequent receptions, mediations, and meanings of American cultural products. In particular, it encouraged the invention of a rhetoric of national defense against American incursions—one that persists and retains its persuasive powers to this day. American culture's enhanced presence on European soil after 1918 was viewed as an advertisement for the United States' expanding political, commercial, and economic might by victors and vanquished alike. Europeans perceived the U.S. presence as a threat as they struggled to rebuild markets, reinstate political and social order, and recapture international standing following the disruptions and destruction of war. For example, many Germans on both the right and the left came to see the Dawes Plan, which pumped U.S. capital into Germany, as part of American economic imperialism.[13] In this climate, issues of culture were never merely expressions of a commercial, apolitical tertiary sphere, but were implicated in various European attempts to reassert postwar national-political sovereignty and economic interest, to maintain domestic social stability and international prestige, and to shape a cohesive national identity at home and exercise influence abroad. Thus the twin tasks of national reconstruction and (inter)national reassertion set the stage for the semiotic reception of American culture in Europe.

The second postwar period was again characterized by similar conditions and concerns, following as it did another protracted and highly destructive period of technologized war. Nonetheless, this time around there were several significant differences. One primary difference was the unambiguous political intervention and ongoing military presence of the United States in strategic areas of Europe and Asia. This presence was particularly jarring in Germany, Austria, and Japan, associated as it was with the national traumas of defeat and the foreign imposition of democratic political forms, but these were hardly the only countries worried about the increased American presence. The Marshall Plan demonstrated and cemented American economic might, while the military pacts struck in the wake of the cold war–NATO in Europe and bilateral security pacts between Japan and the United States and the Philippines–provided for continued American troop presence in several European and East Asian countries. Initially, then, the American cultural impact was experienced–and in fact bureaucratically organized–as a complement to the more overtly political policies of the American military governments.[14] As advocates for national protectionism complained, the United States' unprecedented political and military commitments abroad assisted in paving the way for the unimpeded international expansion of American commercial interests. Thus the American political presence supported and was served by American business abroad–a stunningly successful symbiotic relationship perceived by many, and not just in the formally occupied nations, as a new "imperialism" bent on destroying the cultural traditions, economic health, and political sovereignty of affected nations.[15]

Despite the dramatic appeal of this narrative of American cultural imperialism, it is worth noting that the realities of American cultural penetration and reception never conformed to the morally Manichaean simplicity assigned it (as homogenizing evil empire vs. the charmingly diversified world). That assessment, in fact, was popularized only in the 1970s, some thirty years after the end of the war, and drew upon New Left critiques of American democracy and capitalism.[16] If the imperialist narrative of Americanization provides an inadequate and inaccurate historical analysis of the complexities of cultural interaction, so too does its alternative, which we will call the narrative of democratic modernization.

The narrative of democratic modernization, which dominated post-1945 history until recently, has tended to present postwar Americanization as a benign and beneficial combination of political mandate, economic stimulus, and consumer paradise. Briefly and crudely put, this narrative links the export and international application of American-style democracy and values with historically unprecedented economic growth, high living standards, and booming consumer societies for adherents abroad. It is a narrative, then, born of the cold war, conditioned by victory over fascism, and based upon presumptive moral and material superiority over communism that stresses (democratic) cooperation and consensus over contest. If the narrative of American imperialism sketches a teleology of decline and the erasure of difference, the narrative of democratic modernization promises a future blessed by progress, prosperity, and peace.[17]

We'd like to question this interpretative teleology in order to highlight the important dilemmas provoked by American imports. The postwar reception of American forms was characterized by an abiding ambivalence, as native officials, elites, and consumers of American products attempted to adjust to dramatically altered domestic conditions and international contexts. This was a time when the bipolar world was emerging, but had not yet stabilized; spheres of influence were contested, and would continue to be as decolonization extended (both geographically and temporally) the need for political resettlements. During this period of uncertainty, a generalized fear developed at all levels of postwar societies that the still neophyte cold war might well turn hot. For a couple of decades at least, Western Europeans and the Japanese had to weigh their resentments regarding burgeoning American political, economic, and cultural influences against pragmatic assessments of national interests within the larger international political context. In this context, the United States often appeared as the only viable guarantor of national survival and economic recovery in Western Europe and Japan. This did not mean, however, that anti-American sentiment was neither articulated nor acted upon. Indeed, hostility toward American culture ran high in the years of reconstruction, as national elites attempted to revive and reformulate national power and identity—often by asserting, policing, and regulating the cultural boundaries and identities of their states.[18] Thus, national expressions of outright antipathy toward American culture coexisted and were consistent with military and economic alliance with the United States. As a result, postwar response to American influence was deeply ambivalent, precisely because of the seismographic uncertainty of the developing postwar political order.

And yet continuities with attitudes toward American culture in the interwar period need to be recognized. American cultural imports, it will be recalled, predated the development of fascist regimes, and certain segments of the European public became avid consumers of American films and fashions prior to the war. Before 1945, then, American products had played a significant role in the construction of modern communal and individual identities abroad; indeed, cultural images of America were often identified with, and came to stand for, modernity itself.

Scholars have identified common characteristics of modernity around the world.[19] In Western Europe and Japan, the major features of mass societies and modernity existed by the 1920s, especially in urban centers. Sites of mass consumption included mass circulation newspapers and magazines, department stores, comic strips, movie theaters, the radio, and tourism. Alongside these arose artistic avant-gardes and critical discourses on mass culture and mass society.[20] Much of the emerging large-scale consumption was based on American developments; and the United States indeed exported technologies for increasing production (e.g., Taylorism) as well as consumption (advertising). In any case, Europeans as well as the Japanese linked the changes that came with modernity to American influences and in fact often saw "America"–that is, the United States–as the source of the modern. It was during these same years that Americanization became a much used term.[21]

For many European and Japanese critics, the United States represented a path of modernity that they feared their own societies would follow. Americanism and Americanization became concepts at the very time that Europeans and the Japanese confronted the homogenizing forces of the nation-state and consumer capitalism. Indeed, as Detlev Peukert has argued for Germany, debates about Americanism and Americanization became part of the "crisis of classical modernity" in the 1920s. On the one hand, this crisis manifested itself in deep uncertainty, feelings of loss, and uneasiness with rationalization often connected to America, and on the other, in exuberant celebrations of progress and Americanism. This sense of crisis, compounded by economic downturns, was crucial to the success of anti-democratic systems in Germany, Italy, and Japan.[22] Debates over the adoption of American models, moreover, were by no means restricted to interwar democracies; they were a central feature of both the emerging Soviet Union as well as fascist regimes. The Soviets, for example, borrowed American production and advertising techniques, even as they were intensely critical of capitalism and liberal democracies.[23]

Nothing, however, suggests the multiple and even contradictory meanings of Americanization better than explorations of responses to American culture in fascist Europe and Imperial Japan. One of the burning–and still under-researched questions–regarding the

American cultural impact on Europe and Japan concerns, in fact, the role of American cultural forms and practices in the articulation of "alternative models" pioneered by authoritarian states under National Socialism, Italian fascism, and in Imperial Japan. What is clear is that nondemocratic governments in the interwar period recognized the need to develop cultural means for the ideological mobilization of their populations to the political goals of the empire-building state—this, after all, was one of the lessons learned during the Russo-Japanese War and World War I. These cultural initiatives, moreover, were consistently and discursively pitted against the successful American variant. American cultural products and practices, however, came to serve as both foil and stimulus. American culture was studied to unlock the mysteries of its "mass" (i.e., transclass, transgender, transnational) appeal, on the one hand. On the other hand, great care was taken to attempt to separate form from function. Interwar authoritarian regimes sought to emulate Hollywood's production values and packaging, for example, but in a way that would foster national consensus over consumer individualism. The problem, then, revolved around the exercise of sovereignty over citizenship: how to invent an attractive ideological alternative to Hollywood that would summon the impressive "centralizing" powers of cultural consumption (and teach audiences to think and respond like "Italians" or "Japanese" or "Germans"), while defusing its pesky "centrifugal" tendencies (that encouraged identification on the basis of subnational groupings such as gender, generation, class, ethnicity).[24]

While more research into these issues is needed, a few observations can be made at this point. First, the success of American commercial culture as a seeming "social glue" at home and abroad meant that it was taken seriously as an ideological challenge and as a political tool by nondemocratic interwar governments and their domestic cultural producers. Despite a rhetoric of rejection, these same groups devoted serious consideration to the question of how to learn from American culture in order to construct a popular mass-cultural alternative that would both serve its political purposes and capture the attractive "export" quality of American culture in facilitating circulation within the expanding boundaries of authoritarian European and Japanese empires. Thus, the state-sponsored cultures of interwar fascism cannot be understood in isolation from American culture, as some wholly "alien" opponent. Rather, fascist culture must be contextualized and considered in relation to the increasingly internationalizing American culture of the period.[25] The relationship between American culture and its authoritarian adversaries was more complex than much of the scholarship would have us believe: if it was grounded in competition with the United States, as it most certainly was, it was also conditioned by a certain fluidity, and even openness, through cultural borrowings, emulations, and reworkings. Thus, intense engagement with American culture helped in large degree to shape the nature of its fascist counterparts.[26] Second, this cultural permeability, while subject to certain real limitations (especially with increasingly autarkic policies during the war), nonetheless had noticeable effects on consumer choice and behavior, at least in Europe. What needs investigation is the relationship between consumer appeal, the pleasures and compensations of consumption, and the range–and political impact–of consumer identifications, in conjunction with a critical assessment of how exposure to and familiarity with American cultural impulses, products, or forms figured in the process (by stimulating consumer desires, for example). This shift in critical focus, moreover, mandates a thoroughgoing reconsideration of the claims and assumptions of Americanization's narrative of democratic modernization since it demonstrates the possibility of adopting and employing American cultural forms for nondemocratic ends.

Third, the above discussion calls into question the usefulness of conventional political periodization when considering historical phenomena of cultural influence, interchange, and interaction. After all, cultural economies are highly dependent on political conditions; institutional and legal frameworks that control the import and export of culture rise and fall with political regimes. Thus, one can justly argue that the Allies' triple victory against Italy, Germany, and Japan was of paramount significance in determining the political, economic, social, *and* cultural landscape of the defeated nations. Military defeat brought with it the ultimate demise of fascist and authoritarian models of political, social, and cultural organization. These countries were undoubtedly unequal partners in the transactions with the United States after 1945. By 1946, the "alternative models" competing to influence postwar reconstruction were effectively reduced to two: the American and the Soviet. Nonetheless, one should be careful about facilely declaring a "fresh start" with the emergence of this brave, new bipolar world.

If fascist cultures were far from impervious to American culture, selectively absorbing and utilizing it rather than shutting it out, postwar democratic cultures were similarly hybrid. That is to say, that although the American military governments sought to expunge fascist ideology from subject cultures, the focus of their efforts tended to be narrowly political, thus permitting a great deal of continuity across the "1945 divide" in terms of activity by commercial cultural producers, distributors, performers, and products. While native audiences were bombarded, sometimes under the guise of "reeducation," by a good deal of wartime and postwar American culture with which they were unfamiliar, they also had access to old-time favorites (movies, stars, music) and, in relatively short order, new native products, which *along with American culture* provided fodder for enjoyment, engagement, and identification.[27] One analytical dilemma is to sort out the nature of this interaction and its implications for political sovereignty, citizenship, and identities in the postwar period and beyond. These questions are also of significance for countries other than the Axis powers, countries around the world that were drawn into the orbit of American political, military, and cultural influence by the emerging cold war.

Analytical Dilemmas

Contextualizing Americanization means analyzing it in relation to other processes of modernity, most notably imperialism and decolonization. For the years after 1945, the processes of decolonization and its impact on the colonizers (of significance not just for France, but also for nations like the United States, Japan, and Germany, who no longer had formal colonies) have not quite entered the consciousness of the historians of the metropole, who have paid much more attention to Americanization.[28] Etienne Balibar has provocatively asserted that it was precisely France's identity as a colonizer that allowed the French to interpret the postwar economic and cultural Americanization of France as a form of colonization.[29] Kristin Ross has recently urged us to view the stories of Americanization and decolonization in tension with one another; she has analyzed postwar France as a country that exploited colonial populations on the one hand and increased its collaboration with American capitalism on the other.[30] Melani McAlister has shown that, in the decades since World War II, U.S. producers and commentators have frequently imagined American culture (for example the big-budget biblical epics of the 1950s) as explicitly anti-colonial. At the same time, they, like U.S. politicians, have affirmed a "benevolent supremacy" of the United States over both the formerly (formally) colonized and the former colonizers. This suggest possibilities for varying ways of identifying with and rejecting American culture.[31] It is no wonder then that attitudes abroad toward American culture have continued to be ambivalent, but we need to know more about this reception. The condition of dual positionality described by Kristin Ross (that is, a Janus-faced engagement with two international relationships, simultaneously acting and being acted upon, and all the while renegotiating their own political position) therefore merits careful investigation. Broadening the context in which, for example, bilateral American-French relations are studied—in this case, "triangulating" the interpretative framework—permits a more comprehensive picture of the contributions and social costs involved in forging national indus-trial productivity and consumer societies.

Uncovering the *interplay* of modernization, Americanization, and decolonization—by juxtaposing simultaneous international and na-tional developments—exposes "Americanization" as but one strand, if a very significant one, of the larger historical and political *constellations* that together condition and construct notions of national power, sov-ereignty, community, culture, and identity. This serves as a double reminder: Americanization is only one facet of modernity and Amer-ica only one of its centers. In other words, we need to ask what roles Americanization plays in relation to other sites of constructing nations.

Attention to the international contexts of Americanization (and for the years after 1945 the cold war and decolonization are espe-cially important) is useful for "putting-the-politics-back-in," for it throws into stark relief the highly political uses for which American culture has been mobilized—at the level of both rhetoric and prac-tice. Recurrent appeals to "national defense" against the American cultural or commercial incursions often serve as a deflective device to muddy the proverbial waters and to blur the identities and inter-ests of native protagonists. Scholars have come to this realization only relatively recently and, as a result, have begun to shift attention from a study of the American "thrust" into foreign markets to a con-sideration of the range, nature, and meanings of reception within national contexts abroad. Thus, of late, increased critical attention has been devoted to differentiating official government responses from those of native business elites, cultural elites, and the wide and segmented publics of consumers.

Crucial too in this regard is the need to disentangle the "realities from rhetoric"—or the practice from the ideology—of cultural and commercial exchange. As Thomas Saunders has shown for the interwar period, German film companies often adopted American business practices, sought American investments, and drew upon American aesthetic and technical forms in order to best both foreign and domestic competitors, while at the same time engaging in a rhetoric of national defense and difference in order to forge a *national* cinema by fostering a dependable domestic market for their goods.[32] The reverse is also the case: long traditions of anti-Americanism have often labeled as American that which has no clear American origin. In a world in which words are frequently at odds with deeds, analytical care is required to disentangle the complex methods and motivations of such seemingly contradictory responses to American culture. Parallel to the dominant discourses often promoted by governments and elites, which posit the existence of a unified, essential nation under siege from American influences, much more complex realities exist.

Americanization and Americanism have all too often assumed the existence of a unified, authentic culture now under attack by American goods and images. British elites, for example, rejected American streamlining and American music after 1945, while working-class youth avidly consumed such products, thus exposing the upper-class and high-cultural character of much of what was deemed authentically British.[33] In other words, no unified, authentic British culture existed prior to the American onslaught. It is no wonder that "Americanization" has become a more problematic term at the same time that scholars are also questioning the concept of the "authentic" as a construction of modern nationalism.[34] Indeed, scholars are recognizing that championing the "authentic" has often served to bolster inequality within colonial and postcolonial states as well as within industrialized nations of the First World.

Such frameworks allow for the analysis of encounters with American culture as a series of contests and thus make it clear that Americanization cannot automatically be equated with homogenization. As the examples from the interwar period show, the adoption of American aesthetic styles can in fact be compatible with very different political messages. An appearance of increased homogenization does not necessarily make for a homogenized experience. Americanization is no longer considered a force exercised exclusively through the strong-armed imposition of American industrial, commercial, and organizational forms with clear political results. The essays in this volume reflect this shift in emphasis away from the study of unidirectional "impact" toward a consideration of the complexities involved in the *process* of cultural interaction, which is perhaps better captured by employing the metaphor of "dialogue" for what transpires both between and within national cultures.

One benefit of altering the tropes of Americanization is to permit the conceptual possibility of agency, choice, and change—for all participants in the process. It also allows a vantage point from which to assess the seductive, if simplistic, oppositions recycled in discussions of American international influence for over three-quarters of a century, which have presented the American presence as initiating a battle for autonomy versus hegemony: for the preservation of national particularity, cultural uniqueness, and historical tradition versus social and cultural monotonization and leveling. The upshot of this has been recurring calls for "resistance," particularly by native elites, and an interpretative emphasis on the communal costs of American influence abroad. What is striking about much of this discourse is its overwhelmingly *prescriptive* nature, based as it is upon assumptions regarding the content and function of national culture, and upon often unambiguous judgments about what does and should constitute "culture," what should be consumed, and by whom. The essays in this volume reformulate the issue. Rather than study how American culture "overruns" native cultures, they ask how American culture is employed in the articulation of postwar identities—be they national or subnational, socially sanctioned or socially transgressive. At the same time, they do not elide the realities of American cultural power. First, because the dialogues are rarely symmetrical, and second, because global capitalism and Americanization as facets of (post)modernity do lead to the appearance of greater homogeneity around the world.

It is perhaps due to the influence of postmodernism that scholars are paying more attention to heterogeneity—that is, they have realized that American influences have met heterogeneous nations abroad. As Kaspar Maase has recently suggested, the significant change may not have happened on the level of "real" empirical exchange (say, the numbers of U.S. movies imported into France), but on the level of perception; we are now paying much more attention to contests over meaning. Indeed, the challenge for modern nation-states seems no longer to ensure unity, but rather to manage difference.[35] But there is no simple solution here because celebrating difference can also be a way to maintain unequal relations of power.

Recent scholarship suggests that authenticity and its seeming opposites "imitation" and "assimilation" take on particular importance in Japanese encounters with America and show a complex interplay between Orientalist images of Japan and Japan's self-image. Orientalist images prominent in both Western Europe and the United States are tied in a paradox: they frequently describe Japan as a nation of expert imitators, technologically advanced and bent on economically conquering the world, yet culturally nonmodern.[36] In spite of the Orientalist thrust of these assessments, a similarly essentialized image of Japan as a unique and homogeneous nation, which has taken the United States as the negative reference point and exemplary of the West, has resonated deeply within Japan itself.[37] As scholars have recently suggested, in Japan, more than in other countries, encounters with the foreign have meant a thorough domestication of the foreign. This domestication has apparently been so rapid and successful that, some have proposed, American imports have been much less controversial in Japan than in Western Europe; the Japanese have been less concerned than their European counterparts about the social frictions and moral transformations that American culture has brought, especially with regard to adolescents.[38] In Japan, it seems, the foreign must be successfully assimilated, lest it threaten the (fictional) homogeneity of the Japanese nation. This conclusion seems a bit surprising in a country where in 1943 intellectuals held a roundtable on "overcoming the modern." Yet if it is true that the Japanese have been less worried about American culture since 1945, the implications of such a response are far from clear. Does it mean that the Japanese are acting in a "non-Western" manner and/or is it a sign that they have reached post-modernity more rapidly? It could be that greater Japanese homogeneity has diffused the power of American culture to aid in the articulation of counterhegemonic race, class, or generational identities. Since subcultures are often youth cultures, the lack of outrage might also indicate different attitudes about adolescence. Such comparative conclusions are speculative at this point, but they suggest the complexities and possible national differences in the interactive relationship of Americanization and nation-building. Neither is "assimilation" an unchanging, ahistorical process in Japan, nor is it an exclusively Japanese phenomenon. The actual mix and meanings of the American and the indigenous differ from nation to nation; cultural hybridity exists everywhere, but it takes varying shapes.

In redirecting attention to the reception and consumption of American culture, we need to identify with precision *what constituted American culture* abroad at any given historical moment. This requires inquiries into availability—what was being exported as "American"—and into how these products were both positioned (via marketing strategies, for example) and perceived within the cultural economies of importing nations (and whether, in fact, there were regional variations within national boundaries). But it also requires detailed attention to consumer behavior and consumer choice: which products of those made available were consumed and by what sections of the public? How were the goods treated and in what ways were they consumed? And above all, what were the semiotics of consumption: what *meanings* were attached to the goods and to the manner of their consumption?

An enormous challenge in considering the nature and function of American culture abroad is to avoid the pitfalls of essentializing the consumer as well as American culture. Recent work on consumption has illustrated that American commercial and cultural products have highly mutable rather than fixed meanings, and that such meanings vary—and can be reconstructed—only in relation to historical context. Context, moreover, is itself multidimensional: it extends beyond the geographic to the relational (such as social positioning) and the temporal (such as memory, and the juxtaposition of historical experience and historical interpretation). There is no monolithic "American culture" but only perhaps an endless stream of image-ideals: culturally and subjectively processed varieties of American culture that serve specific yet endlessly evolving functions for consumer populations. The meanings attached to American cultural products abroad, moreover, have no necessary relation to the domestic meanings ascribed to them in the United States. American products abroad are positioned differently, their uses and meanings rescripted through their *recontextualization* and the act(s) of consumption. They are objects of identity and fantasy, both within the cultural economy of "import" nations but also—and this bears stressing—within the cultural economy of the United States itself. Some scholars have argued, in fact, that the need for U.S. producers to fashion their products to cater to a diverse market within the United States helps account for the remarkable exportability and success of American culture abroad.[39] One wonders whether this eye toward marketing to a diverse domestic population has served to enhance the overall semiotic plasticity of the products both at home and abroad.

* * *

The first section of this volume, "Twentieth-Century Modernities," is devoted to essays that stress the historical dimension of the discourses of Americanization and anti-Americanism in Europe. In "America in the German Imagination," Mary Nolan begins by discussing what she correctly calls the elusive concepts of Americanism, anti-Americanism, and Americanization. Within her wide-ranging overview of German visions of America from the nineteenth to the end of the twentieth century, she locates a major change in the 1920s, when German images shifted from a focus on America and especially the American West as an illusory past to America as the embodiment of modernity; Karl May was replaced by Henry Ford. As she points out, Americanism, or "the discourses that imagined or constructed America as a model of economic, social, and cultural development" for Germany, has been compatible with different ideologies ranging from the Social Democrats to the National Socialists. American production methods were admired by various political camps, but consumption proved much more divisive, raising anxieties about the feminization and racial decline of Germany. After 1945, with American occupation and business involvement, Nolan suggests, "Americanism became part of daily life" in West Germany, coexisting with various anti-Americanisms. Nolan concludes by suggesting that at the end of the twentieth century, with the cold war's demise, America may well be losing its prominent role in the German imagination.

David W. Ellwood's essay on "Comparative Anti-Americanism in Western Europe" employs a historical approach in order to survey the various strands of criticism implicit in this "catch-all" designation, indicating that "anti-Americanism" conceals important distinctions between criticisms of America as regards its military or political power, foreign policy, model of modernization, or site of commercial cultural production to name but a few foci of attack. In considering the period since about 1920, Ellwood seeks to identify and chart the alternating periods of emergence, dominance, recession, and recurrence of particular strands of anti-American sentiment. He argues, moreover, that the cold war marked a historical watershed in this regard, since it necessitated the negotiation of a "new equilibrium between Americanization and anti-Americanization." In large measure, Ellwood suggests that the contours of European anti-Americanism conform to more standard political periodization–that the responses of commentators in the press, academia, government, and the arts are conditioned predominantly by American military, foreign policy, and economic initiatives–but maintains that European responses to American "challenges" betray much about European notions of their own communal and cultural exclusivity, which by the 1990s increasingly express an "anxiety about the future of identities in the Old World." In contrast to Nolan, Ellwood thus concludes that the United States continues to be a prime reference point for Europeans.

Botond Bognar reaches back to the nineteenth century to establish the importance and effect of growing interactions between Japanese and American culture in his essay, "Surface above All? American Influence on Japanese Urban Space." Like other contributors to this volume, Bognar recognizes the "uneven" quality of cultural exchange between the United States and Japan, but nonetheless stresses the mutuality of cultural impact, highlighting for example the reciprocal training and employment of Japanese and American architects in both countries. Thus, while nineteenth-century Japan actively imported and applied American and European technologies, in effect choosing a path of modernization equivalent to "Westernization," the Meiji government initiated this process, Bognar suggests, in order to avoid falling victim to colonization. Modernization was perceived and practiced as a way to ensure sovereignty and independence from the West. Japan, moreover, had a much longer history of cultural borrowings (from the Asian mainland), and into the twentieth century has exhibited a knack for appropriating, adapting, and naturalizing outside influences. Here, Bognar's vocabulary is telling, for rather than portraying Japanese receptivity toward American architectural forms and technologies as a matter of hapless passivity, he depicts it as a "proactive process" of conscious selection and domestication—a process, he implies, that provokes much less anxiety than in Europe because of the Japanese ability to "void associable meanings" from abroad and to create more culturally compatible significations in the process of adaption to the Japanese setting. Precisely because of such mutability of meanings, Bognar cautions against the quest to seek the "precise origin of things" and questions the "possibilities of maintaining [discrete] national or cultural or urban identities." Nonetheless, his conclusion, which draws on the work of Western scholars and theorists to attribute a "'traditional' Oriental" structure to Japanese cities distinct from that of Western cities, suggests the tenacity of national-cultural tropes in efforts to locate and articulate comparative difference, yet it leaves open the questions of what constitutes and who should define contemporary urban "Japanese-ness."

The contributions in the second section of this volume, "Drawing Cultural Boundaries, Forging the National," investigate some of the ways in which public responses to American culture have been employed to define nation-states and national cultures. In "Persistent Myths of Americanization: German Reconstruction and the Renationalization of Postwar Cinema, 1945–1965," Heide Fehrenbach considers the impact of American film and film policy on German reconstruction. Dissenting from conventional narratives of the period that posit the ready and relatively uncontested Americanization of West German cinema and audiences, Fehrenbach suggests that cinematic consumption served as a contested terrain for the renegotiation of postfascist German identity. Focusing on the range of West German responses to film culture and Hollywood imports—by state and religious elites, film professionals, film clubs, students, and the more heterogeneous audience of the 1950s—Fehrenbach uncovers multiple (and sometimes competing) agendas and meanings embedded in contemporaries' reactions to American culture, and indicates how these differed according to political disposition, class, generation, and even geography. Instead of a picture of progressive Americanization, what emerges is a portrait of the postwar years as an era when national culture was energetically asserted in the face of encroaching American influence and imports. West German responses—albeit by various protagonists with varying agendas—nonetheless all participated in the postwar revaluation of what it would mean to be German after National Socialism. As such, they were conditioned by, and need to be understood in terms of, the national postwar tasks of political, economic, and cultural reconstruction.

In "No More Song and Dance: French Radio Broadcast Quotas, *Chansons,* and Cultural Exceptions," James Petterson analyzes the function of appeals to cultural exceptionalism in the recent ratification and implementation of the Pelchat Amendment, which mandates that French radio stations devote 40 percent of their programming to "music of French expression." He argues that the propensity of Amendment proponents to invoke themes of cultural distinctiveness and defense, particularly against incursions from the United States and Japan, was a strategy that uncoupled "culture" from "commerce" and masked the very real commercial interests being fought over by long-time domestic antagonists: the French recording and broadcasting industries. Moreover, by defining French music in reductionist terms as music of Francophone linguistic content, the Agreement propagates a narrow and falsely homogeneous image of "French culture" not only by preventing instrumental musicians from cashing in on lucrative copyright payments but also, more tellingly, by excluding artists from France's former colonies who perform in their native tongue. Thus, identifying Americanization as a cultural threat can be a way to avoid acknowledging differences and imbalances of power within a nation-state. As Petterson reminds us, it can also be a way to obscure indigenous economic interests and the diversity of national populations.

The third section of the volume, "Transnational Stylings: American Music and the Politics of Identity," focuses on the adoption and adaption of American music ranging from jazz and rock to rap in Germany, Italy, and Japan. These American music forms have been contested abroad as well as at home, and it is important to remember that initially they were by no means endorsed by either the U.S. government or elites. Because so much American music has roots in African-American culture, consumers and "imitators" of American music in the United States and abroad have had to confront questions of race and of alleged racial differences. These issues are of particular significance in the three nations (Germany, Italy, and Japan) that in the 1930s combined racial utopias with sometimes vehemently racist rejections of American jazz and swing, while at the same time including some forms of jazz in their own music programming. The reception of American music thus point-edly raises the question of similarities and differences between lib-eral democracies and totalitarian regimes.

Focusing on the decade before the building of the Berlin Wall in 1961, Uta G. Poiger, in "American Music, Cold War Liberalism, and German Identities," compares reactions to American jazz and rock 'n' roll in East and West Germany. In spite of many differences in the political alignments of the two states, she finds surprising similarities in the attacks that West German conservatives and East German socialists leveled against American music and the adolescents who avidly consumed it. Both used allusions to gender and racial trans-gressions (Elvis Presley, for example, was depicted as a female striptease dancer with "black blood" in his veins) to portray rock 'n' roll as dangerous, and both criticized rock consumption as a political threat. However, this dynamic changed by the late 1950s when cold war liberals replaced conservatives in positions of power in West Germany and began to use American music, especially what they called jazz, to portray West Germany as modern, respectable, and anti-totalitarian—and to dissociate themselves from the continued repression of such American influences in East Germany.

In his essay "Jukebox Boys: Postwar Italian Music and the Culture of Covering," Franco Minganti likewise focuses on the mid-1950s to mid-1960s, a period of important transitions in consumption regimes that were frequently associated with American models. Like the West German teenagers Poiger describes, Italian *giovani* became a distinct group that increasingly participated in the consumption of fashions and music made possible by economic miracles. In these same years, Italian covers of American hits became popular, reveal-ing the complex dynamics of Americanization. "Covering" rock usually meant changing the content of lyrics dramatically through purposeful and accidental misunderstandings. Italian covers often celebrated images of good boys and girls, thus eliminating the pro-test character of American originals, erasing rock's African-Ameri-can heritage, and assuring consumers that American music and behaviors were respectable. And yet in these same years, other Ital-ian musicians began to combine American vernacular music with European existentialism in openly political and critical songs.

In "The Social Production of Difference: Imitation and Authen-ticity in Japanese Rap Music," Ian Condry rejects the existence of an essential authentic Japanese culture and of authentic American hip-hop, but nonetheless analyzes the function of Japanese rappers' claims to authenticity and "the real." When rap crossed the Pacific Ocean, Condry shows, it evolved from a music of the underclass to one for trendy middle-class consumers, a development that happened earlier in Japan than in the United States and that was fostered by record companies and rappers proclaiming a "global hip-hop culture." Japanese rappers, by transforming the Japanese language in their performances, have set themselves and their fans apart from mainstream Japanese. "Becoming black" by adopting dreadlocks, for example, has become attractive to some Japanese rappers and their audiences mostly as a demonstration of generational difference, but at times also to criticize social injustice within Japan. Some forms of Japanese rap are less misogynist than that of their American counterparts and appear to promote strong women. Condry concludes by reminding us that American and domestically produced rap in Japan (re)constructs differences, be they between the foreign and the local, or between classes, ethnicities, generations, or genders.

The difficulty of delineating the lines between the "American" and the "indigenous" or "native" is a theme that the three contributors in the last section of this volume ("De-essentializing 'America' and the 'Native'") also take up. In "Learning from America: Postwar Urban Recovery in West Germany," Peter Krieger focuses on the cultural transfer of architectural design and technologies between the United States and West Germany. While much of his essay (which should be read in conjunction with Botond Bognar's discussion of similar developments in Japan) chronicles the overwhelmingly ready reception and, to a lesser extent, application by West German architects and city planners of the American international style as a visual manifestation of postwar political democratization and economic recovery, he also notes instances of regional resistance to American architectural trends on the basis of their inappropriateness for the German context. Initially, much of this "conservative" criticism was defused in the first postwar decade because it resembled so closely the arguments against American architectural modernism issuing from socialist East Germany. Thus architectural design was suffused by cold war ideology; West Germans found it an effective way to publicize their postwar political reorientation and to distinguish themselves from their communist foes. By the early 1960s, however, West German architects again invoked American experts, but this time echoed U.S. critics in denouncing the social and psychological implications of American-style urban architecture and housing projects. Architectural assessments were transformed into explicit social critique and a plea to differentiate West Germany from its U.S. ally. While Krieger concentrates on the transatlantic transmission of American ideas, his essay also suggests the muddiness inherent in national attribution and unilateral notions of cultural influence, for attention to social impact in modern urban planning, and indeed functionalist urban architecture, was born of the Bauhaus school of Weimar Germany. Its famous émigré practitioners like Walter Gropius developed the American variety and, as officially sponsored emissaries, personally (re)imported it back to Germany after 1945, illustrating that both the "American" international style and social conscience had a heavily German-accented voice and vision.

In his study "The French Cinema and Hollywood: A Case Study of Americanization," Richard F. Kuisel takes up the tricky question of whether Americanization causes global uniformity. He insists that in coming to terms with the meanings of American culture abroad, scholars have to recognize that both convergence between different cultures and distinctive assimilation by "indigenous" cultures are at work. From the 1920s to the 1980s, French audiences flocked in higher numbers to French rather than American movies, a trend that has since been reversed with the arrival of American "mega-hits," despite continuous protectionist efforts by the French government. At the same time, French cinema has been unable to make major inroads into the American market. By adopting Hollywood genres, French cinema has Americanized itself and yet has retained a distinctly "French" style. Hollywood, in the meantime, has consistently featured French actors, a phenomenon that Kuisel sees as part of the "hybridization" of American cinema itself. French critics have reacted by criticizing standardization, rather than Americanization, in film, and have presented their recent opposition to GATT (General Agreement on Tariffs and Trade) as a defense of cultural pluralism and national identity. In the end, Kuisel insists that a properly nuanced concept of Americanization allows us to recognize the centrality of America in the processes of globalization and transnational convergence.

The temporal and material links between American and Japanese (post)modernity become particularly clear in the contribution by Takayuki Tatsumi, who discusses cross-fertilizations in American and Japanese culture since World War II. In "Waiting for Godzilla: Chaotic Negotiations between Post-Orientalism and Hyper-Occidentalism," Tatsumi makes use of recent postcolonial theory by taking up the complex concept of mimicry and by questioning the existence of an unproblematic Japanese (or American) "original." For the years from 1945 to the 1970s, Tatsumi finds many Japanese authors consciously assimilating American literary styles. More recently, he detects an increasing synchronicity between the forms and narratives that Japanese and American authors employ, a synchronicity that is resulting from cultural transactions between the two cultures (rather than one-sided adoption of American forms in Japan) and that is characterized by the coexistence of American Orientalism (in Japan-bashing) and Japanese Occidentalism (for example, in the preoccupation with "Japanness," *Nihonjiron,* in the 1970s). Finally, Tatsumi locates another shift that began in the 1980s: Anglo-American writers have employed "Japanesque images" (such as the monster Godzilla or the term for Japanese avant-garde styles, "Thomasson") while Japanese writers have reappropriated Orientalist and thus highly distorted American images of Japan in what Tatsumi calls "chaotic transcultural negotiations." Paradigmatic of these changes is the figure of Godzilla, who started out in the 1950s as a Japanese Occidentalist representation of the threat of nuclear devastation brought on by the United States, but who has since appeared in the novels of American authors and has recently been made by Hollywood into a hero for multiple international audiences.

Tatsumi's use of the term "chaotic transcultural negotiations" confirms a conclusion drawn by other postmodern theorists. According to Arjun Appadurai, "the United States is no longer the puppeteer of a world system of images, but only one node in a complex transnational construction of imaginary landscapes."[40] What Appadurai points out for globalization also holds for Americanization (a term he rejects). As he puts it, the "globalization of culture is not the same as its homogenization, but globalization involves the use of a variety of instruments of homogenization (armaments, advertising techniques, language hegemonies, and clothing)." It seems to us that these examples still frequently have American roots, but what interests us here is the dynamic and tension Appadurai describes.[41] Globalization, and Americanization is certainly a central part of this, has contradictory meanings. The analytical dilemmas that we have laid out above cannot be resolved. We cannot, for example, claim that globalization leads to greater homogeneity or conversely to greater differentiation and heterogeneity. Both impulses are at work simultaneously in the often chaotic negotiations between various groups and cultures, which also serves to blur the distinction between self and other. As the contributions to this volume suggest, it is not just with the rise of postmodernism in artistic production or in social theory that the clearly delineated lines between self and other, between the nation and its others, have become problematic. Rather, both the attempts to delineate these lines clearly and their permeability have in fact been part of modernity since its inception. It is ever more important to analyze these contradictory impulses and developments with great attention to historical specificity.

The United States is not simply engaged in a one-way process of disseminating its culture and thereby its hegemonic power abroad. It is important to see the United States as part of a web of transnational interactions, where influences from abroad reach and transform U.S. shores. Research on American constructions of "the other(s)" abroad is increasing, but it is of equal importance to research the impact of goods and images originating outside of the United States on the formation of American identities. A seemingly one-way street needs to be recognized as a web of two-way highways, even if traffic is not flowing evenly in all directions.[42]

Finally, while this introduction certainly calls for more detailed ethnographic research on the reception of American culture, it seems important once again to direct attention to the significance of economics and politics in the study of culture. To use Pierre Bourdieu's formulation, scholars should not neglect economic and political interests, and the means of distribution, that make American cultural imports into "cultural capital," admittedly of changing value.[43] More needs to be known about how decisions to export or import certain items of American culture, and not others, come about. The comparative study of Americanization that is attentive to these issues has much to contribute to the analysis of power relations within and between nations–particularly in an increasingly globalized world, in which the United States continues to play a dominant role.

Notes

1. See Peter Gann and L. H. Duignan, *The Rebirth of the West: The Americanization of the Democratic World, 1945–1958* (Cambridge, Mass., 1992). We thank Yue Dong, Melani McAlister, and Robert G. Moeller for their helpful comments on earlier drafts of this introduction.
2. See, for example, Armand Mattelart, Xavier Delcourt, and Michelle Mattelart, *International Image Markets* (London, 1984); Herbert I. Schiller, *Mass Communications and American Empire* (Boulder, 1992); Jean Jacques Servan-Schreiber, *The American Challenge*, trans. Ronald Steel (New York, 1968); Jeremy Tunstall, *The Media Are American* (London, 1977).
3. For assessments of American power as declining, see Nolan in this volume; Arjun Appadurai, "Disjuncture and Difference in the Global Cultural Economy," *Public Culture* 2, no. 2 (1990): 1–24; Paul Kennedy, *The Rise and Fall of the Great Powers* (New York, 1987); Kaspar Maase, "'Amerikanisierung der Gesellschaft': Nationalisierende Deutung von Globalisierungsprozessen?" in *Amerikanisierung und Sowjetisierung in Deutschland*, ed. Konrad Jarausch and Hannes Siegrist (Frankfurt a. M., 1997), 219–41; David Morley and Kevin Robins, *Spaces of Identity: Global Media, Electronic Landscapes, and Cultural Boundaries* (New York,

1995); Richard Pells, *Not Like Us: How Europeans Have Loved, Hated, and Trans-formed American Culture since World War II* (New York, 1997). On the continued significance of the United States, see, for example, Ellwood and Kuisel in this volume; Frederic Jameson, *Postmodernism: Or the Cultural Logic of Late Capitalism* (Durham, N.C., 1991); Stuart Hall, "The Local and the Global: Globalization and Ethnicities," in *Culture, Globalization, and the World System,* ed. Anthony D. King (Albany, 1991), 19–39; Roger Rollins, ed., *The Americanization of the Global Village: Essays in Popular Culture* (Bowling Green, 1989).

4. See, for example, Victoria de Grazia, "Nationalizing Women: The Competi-tion between Fascist and Commercial Cultural Models in Mussolini's Italy," in *The Sex of Things: Gender and Consumption in Historical Perspective,* ed. Victoria de Grazia (Berkeley, 1996), 337–58; Heide Fehrenbach, *Cinema in Democratiz-ing Germany: Reconstructing National Identity after Hitler* (Chapel Hill, N.C., 1995), 92–117; Alf Lüdtke, Inge Marßolek, and Adelheid von Saldern, eds., *Amerikanisierung: Traum und Alptraum im Deutschland des 20. Jahrhunderts* (Stutt-gart, 1997); Morley and Robins, *Spaces of Identity,* 55; Uta G. Poiger, *Jazz, Rock, and Rebels: Cold War Politics and American Culture in a Divided Germany* (Berke-ley, forthcoming).

5. Jackie Stacey, *Star-Gazing: Hollywood Cinema and Female Spectatorship* (New York, 1994), 57–58, 80–87, 105–25, 205. On the interaction of American and German models of masculinity, see David Bathrick, "Max Schmeling on the Canvas: Box-ing as an Icon of Weimar Culture" in *New German Critique* 51 (Fall 1990): 113–36.

6. See Michael H. Kater, *Different Drummers: Jazz in the Culture of Nazi Germany* (New York, 1992); and the contributions by Condry and Poiger in this volume. For the United States, see, for example, Michael Rogin, *Black Face, White Noise: Jewish Immigrants in the Hollywood Melting Pot* (Berkeley, 1996).

7. On the significance of race in encounters with American culture, see the con-tributions by Condry, Minganti, and Poiger in this volume. See also John G. Blair, "Blackface Minstrels and *Buffalo Bill's Wild West*: Nineteenth-Century Entertainment Forms as Cultural Exports," in *European Readings of American Popular Culture,* ed. John Dean and Jean-Paul Gabilliet (Westport, 1996), 3–12; Catherine M. Cole, "Reading Blackface in West Africa: Wonders Taken for Signs," *Critical Inquiry* 23, no. 1 (Autumn 1996): 183–215; Nina Cornyetz, "Fetishized Blackness: Hip Hop and Racial Desire in Contemporary Japan," *Social Text* 12 (1994): 113–39; Heide Fehrenbach, *Race in German Reconstruction* (Chapel Hill, N.C., forthcoming); Paul Gilroy, *The Black Atlantic: Modernity and Double Consciousness* (Cambridge, Mass., 1993); Morley and Robins, *Spaces of Identity*; Poiger, *Jazz, Rock, and Rebels*; John Russell, "Race and Reflexivity: The Black Other in Contemporary Japanese Mass Culture," *Cultural Anthropology* 6 (1991): 3–25; Tyler Stovall, *Paris Noir: African Americans in the City of Light* (New York, 1996).

8. Richard Handler, "Is 'Identity' a Useful Concept?" in *Commemorations: The Poli-tics of National Identity,* ed. John Gillis (Princeton, 1994), 30.

9. See also John Whittier Treat, "Introduction: Japanese Studies into Cultural Stud-ies," in Treat, ed., *Contemporary Japan and Popular Culture* (Honolulu, 1996), 1–14; Miriam Silverberg, "Constructing a New Cultural History of Prewar Japan," *Boundary 2* 18 (Fall 1991): 61–89; Robin D. Kelley, "Notes on Deconstructing 'The Folk,'" *American Historical Review* 97 (December 1992): 1400–1408.

10. Marilyn Ivy, *Discourses of the Vanishing: Modernity, Phantasm, Japan* (Chicago, 1995); Miriam Silverberg, "Constructing the Japanese Ethnography of Modernity," *Jour-nal of Asian Studies* 51 (February 1992): 30–54; Morley and Robins, *Spaces of Identity,*

167; Masao Miyoshi, *Off Center: Power and Culture Relations between Japan and the United States* (Cambridge, Mass., 1991); Treat, "Introduction."

11. See Mary Nolan, *Visions of Modernity: American Business and the Modernization of Germany* (New York, 1994).

12. See Frank Costigliola, *Awkward Dominion: American Political, Economic, and Cultural Relations with Europe, 1919–33* (Ithaca, 1984); Joan Hoff-Wilson, *American Business and Foreign Policy, 1920–1933* (Lexington, 1971); Ian Jarvie, *Hollywood's Overseas Campaign: The North Atlantic Movie Trade, 1920–1950* (New York, 1992); Frank Ninkovich, *The Diplomacy of Ideas: U.S. Foreign Policy and Cultural Relations 1938–51* (Cambridge, 1981); Emily Rosenberg, *Spreading the American Dream: American Economic and Cultural Expansion, 1890–1945* (New York, 1982); Kristin Thompson, *Exporting Entertainment* (London, 1985).

13. Dan Diner, *America in the Eyes of the Germans: An Essay on Anti-Americanism,* trans. Allison Brown (Princeton, 1996), 56.

14. See, for example, Fehrenbach, *Cinema*; and Fehrenbach in this volume.

15. See Richard Kuisel, *Seducing the French: The Dilemma of Americanization* (Berkeley, 1993); Pells, *Not Like Us*.

16. See John Tomlinson, *Cultural Imperialism: A Critical Introduction* (Baltimore, 1991), 2–3.

17. See especially Duignan and Gann, *The Rebirth of the West*; Michael J. Hogan, *The Marshall Plan: America, Britain, and the Reconstruction of Western Europe* (New York, 1987); Toshio Nishi, *Unconditional Democracy: Education and Politics in Occupied Japan 1945–1952* (Stanford, 1982); and W. W. Rostow, *The Stages of Economic Growth: A Non-Communist Manifesto,* for his articulation of the "Alliance for Progress" program under the Kennedy administration. For a historiographical discussion of this "heroic narrative" of American influence, see Carol Gluck, "Entangling Illusions–Japanese and American Views of the Occupation," in *New Frontiers in American-East Asian Relations,* ed. D. Borg and W. I. Cohen (New York, 1983). For a critique of this paradigm, see also Melani McAlister, *Staging the American Century: Race, Gender and Nation in U.S. Representations of the Middle East, 1945–1992* (Berkeley, forthcoming).

18. See Fehrenbach, *Cinema*; Dick Hebdige, "Toward a Cartography of Taste," in idem, *Hiding in the Light: On Images and Things* (London, 1988), 45–75; Kuisel, *Seducing the French;* Pells, *Not Like Us*; Poiger, *American Culture*.

19. See, for example, Anthony Giddens, *The Consequences of Modernity* (Stanford, 1990).

20. On the connection between mass culture and modernism, see especially Andreas Huyssen, *After the Great Divide: Modernism, Mass Culture, Postmodernism* (Bloomington, 1986). For Japan, see also Marilyn Ivy, "Formations of Mass Culture," in *Postwar Japan as History,* ed. Andrew Gordon (Berkeley, 1993), 239–58.

21. This was particularly the case in Germany. See Alf Lüdtke, Inge Marßolek, and Adelheid von Saldern, "Einleitung," in *Amerikanisierung,* 7. Nolan, *Visions of Modernity;* Silverberg, "Japanese Ethnography," 33–34.

22. Detlev Peukert, *The Weimar Republic: The Crisis of Classical Modernity* (New York, 1987). Also J. Victor Koschmann, "The Nationalism of Cultural Uniqueness," and Mary Nolan, "Against Exceptionalism," in *American Historical Review* 102 (June 1997): 758–74; Kosaku Yoshino, *Cultural Nationalism in Contemporary Japan: A Sociological Inquiry* (London, 1992); and Leslie Pincus, *Authenticating Culture in Imperial Japan: Kuki Shuzo and the Rise of National Aesthetics* (Berkeley, 1996).

23. On the complex meanings of Americanisms in various political and economic systems, see especially Charles S. Maier, "Between Taylorism and Technocracy: European Ideologies and the Vision of Industrial Productivity in the 1920s,"

Journal of Contemporary History 2 (1970): 27–61. On the Soviet Union, see, for example, Kendall Bailes, "The American Connection: Ideology and the Transfer of American Technology to the Soviet Union, 1917–1941," *Comparative Studies in Society and History* 23 (1981): 421–48; Wendy Kaplan, ed., *Designing Modernity: The Arts of Reform and Persuasion, 1885–1945* (New York, 1995).

24. These terms were employed by de Grazia in her perceptive essay, "Nationalizing Women," 337–58.

25. See, for example, Eric Rentschler's discussion, "German Feature Films, 1933–1945," *Monatshefte* 82, no. 3 (1990): 257–66.

26. On this point, see, for example, Victoria de Grazia, "Mass Culture and Sovereignty: The American Challenge to European Cinemas, 1920–1960," *Journal of Modern History* 61 (1989): 53–87; Eric Rentschler, *The Ministry of Illusion: Nazi Cinema and Its Afterlife* (Cambridge, Mass., 1996); and Ruth Ben-Ghiat, "Envisioning Modernity: Desire and Discipline in the Italian Fascist Film," *Critical Inquiry* 23 (Autumn 1996): 109–44.

27. See contributions by Kuisel and Fehrenbach in this volume.

28. On the significance of colonization and decolonization for the metropole, see especially Frederick Cooper and Laura Ann Stoler, eds., *Tensions of Empire: Colonial Cultures in a Bourgeois World* (Berkeley, 1997); McAlister, *Staging the American Century.*

29. Etienne Balibar, *Les frontières de la democratié* (Paris, 1992), 57–65, cited in Kristin Ross, *Fast Cars, Clean Bodies: Decolonization and the Reordering of French Bodies* (Cambridge, Mass., 1995), 196.

30. Ross, *Fast Cars,* 7–9.

31. McAlister, *Staging the American Century.*

32. Thomas Saunders, *Hollywood in Berlin: American Cinema and Weimar Germany* (Berkeley, 1994); also de Grazia "Mass Culture and Sovereignty."

33. Hebdige, "Toward a Cartography of Taste."

34. See, for example, Homi Bhabha, "Of Mimicry and Man: The Ambivalence of Colonial Discourse," *October* 28 (1984): 125–33; Dipesh Chakrabarty, "Postcoloniality and the Artifice of History: Who Speaks for 'Indian' Pasts?" *Representations* 37 (Winter 1992): 2–26; Eric Hobsbawm and Terence Ranger, eds., *The Invention of Tradition* (New York, 1983); Benedict Anderson, "Census, Map, Museum," in *Becoming National: A Reader,* ed. Geoff Eley and R. G. Suny (New York, 1996).

35. Maase, "'Amerikanisierung der Gesellschaft,'" 239–40.

36. Ivy, *Discourses,* 2; Morley and Robins, *Spaces of Identity,* chapter 8; Silverberg, "Constructing Japanese Cultural History," 65.

37. Ivy, *Discourses,* 2. Also, Koschmann, "The Nationalism of Cultural Uniqueness," 758–68.

38. William Kelly suggested this at the conference "The American Cultural Impact on Germany, France, Italy, and Japan, 1945–1995: An International Comparison," Brown University, April 1996.

39. Maase, "'Amerikanisierung der Gesellschaft,'" 237.

40. Appadurai, "Disjuncture and Difference," 4.

41. Ibid., 18–21.

42. See, for example, Gilroy, *The Black Atlantic;* Beth Bailey and David Faber, *The First Strange Place: The Alchemy of Race and Sex in World War II Hawaii* (New York, 1992); Lisa Lowe, *Immigrant Acts: On Asian American Cultural Politics* (Durham, N.C., 1996); McAlister, *Staging the American Century.*

43. See, for example, Pierre Bourdieu, *Distinction: A Social Critique of the Judgment of Taste,* trans. Richard Nice (Cambridge, Mass., 1984).

Part I

TWENTIETH-CENTURY MODERNITIES

– One –

AMERICA IN THE GERMAN IMAGINATION

Mary Nolan

Europeans have been preoccupied with America for the past two centuries. From the fifteenth century onward, there were many new worlds "discovered" by Europeans and many old ones explored, analyzed, and ultimately colonized–but only one, the United States, has consistently been an object of obsessive discourse and analysis. Only one, the United States, was regarded as a model to be embraced, selectively appropriated, or emphatically rejected. America served as a screen on which Europeans projected fantasies and fears; it provided visions of the past and the future against which Europeans could position themselves. It represented an other, which was yet not completely other, against which Europeans could try to define their particular identities and elaborate their universalistic claims, an other in relationship to which Europeans could not make unequivocal assertions of difference and superiority in the ways they attempted to do toward Asia and Africa. Germany was a latecomer to the debates about the Americas and the United States, as it was relatively late in so many other areas. But despite this–or because of it–Germans have been more intensively and continuously involved in imagining and reimagining America than have other Europeans.

America assumed such prominence in German and European discourses and debates and ultimately in economic, cultural, and to a lesser extent political practices, for many reasons. America represented a past many Europeans assumed they had once shared, an illusory past, occurring in some ill-defined and vaguely imagined era before civilization and capitalism, modernity and complexity. In John Locke's formulation, "In the beginning, all the world was America."[1] Or at any rate, all the European world thought it might have been. America was one of many non-European canvases on which Europeans of liberal and Enlightenment persuasion painted images of uncorrupted, natural man—or men closer to that state than any to be found in Europe.

By the nineteenth century, the United States came to stand not only for the Old World but for the New as well. Indeed, the very designation "America," which had once referred primarily to Spanish America, came to refer to the U.S. alone. It embodied the New World's most complex and appealing as well as problematic elements. America's size and diversity, its natural resources and scenery evoked images of exoticism, limitless space, and perhaps limitless possibilities for individual self-development and discovery, as well as social transformation. Its mix of indigenous peoples, European immigrants, and blacks brought as slaves provided the raw materials for debates about identity and citizenship, for speculations of a sort much favored in the nineteenth and twentieth centuries about stages of civilization, racial hierarchies, and human nature. For a nation like Germany, which was a late and relatively unsuccessful imperialist power, colonies did not adequately supply alternative discursive arenas in which to debate these questions.

Of greater importance, America alone possessed unprecedented economic power and potential that underlay, and in the twentieth century dominated, Europe's images of and discursive and practical negotiations with America.[2] America had natural resources and productive capacities in excess of any European country, its technology and organizational forms were more advanced, and it was unencumbered by a feudal past of a sort recognizable to Europeans. America seemed, in short, economically promising or threatening, depending on one's perspective, and above all economically modern, whatever that might mean—and it meant quite different things to different groups within Germany.

American economic modernity was accompanied by new cultural forms that were more open and democratic but also ostensibly more homogeneous, superficial, and feminized. America was seen to have pioneered new definitions of masculinity and femininity and to exhibit new variants of domesticity and family life, and new understandings of sexuality. For Germans issues of modernity and materialism, technology, and *Kultur* were politically fraught, and attention to America was correspondingly intense.[3]

America was both fascinating and frustrating because it had built a contradictory society and culture on the basis of European colonists and immigrants, who had brought but then transformed European institutions, practices, and values. It seemed deceptively familiar at the same time that it was appealingly—or appallingly—foreign.

The different Americas that Germans constructed in different eras reveal as much, if not more, about Germany and particular Germans as they do about the United States.[4] But German images of America were not based solely on inventive projection or distant observation; rather, they were built on interactions derived from intensive reading about and travel to the U.S. and from American economic and political interventions. America provided the models that Germans selectively appropriated and modified, and a language that they spoke with different class and gender accents. What people read, where they traveled, which consumer goods arrived, and which music was played shaped images of America. The inclusions and omissions, emphases and silences of the resulting discourses about America are more illuminating than the representativeness of the artifacts, the comprehensiveness of the itineraries, or the accuracy of the impressions.

German discourses about the United States position themselves along a spectrum of positive, mixed, and negative assessments of American society and culture, and of the possibility of emulating aspects of them. Americanism, anti-Americanism, and Americanization, terms at once analytical and polemical, designate these positions. Before we can explore the many Americas imagined by Germans, we must unpack these elusive, elastic, and contentious concepts.

I

It is easier to suggest what Americanism is *not* than to define what it *is* with precision. Americanism does not refer to a fixed and coherent image of America, a clearly delineated discourse, or an unchanging model, economic or political, let alone cultural. The frontier, the Fordist assembly line, the flapper, and the Frigidaire, for example, have all figured prominently and sometimes even simultaneously in constructions of Americanism. Efficiency and indulgence, admirable productivism and debilitating materialism, open egalitarianism and mindless homogenization are among the many oppositions that have structured German efforts to define and judge America.

Americanism refers neither to an external and involuntary imposition of American institutions, practices, and values on a European populace that was either coerced or seduced or both. Nor does it refer to a slavish, total, and unconsidered embrace of America as an—or rather as *the*—economic or cultural model.[5] Neither spinelessness nor mindlessness are useful analytical categories for exploring the complexly negotiated relations between Germany and America.

Americanism is most usefully understood as the images and discourses that imagined or constructed America as a model of economic, social, and cultural development. The substantive content of this American model, its essential parts and functional mechanisms, its benefits and costs, its winners and losers were both disputed by different groups in any given period and changed in discourse and reality over the course of the twentieth century. During Weimar, for example, the model centered around streamlined production, while in the Federal Republic it focused on the consumption of standardized products. In some visions, capitalists were projected as the main beneficiaries of Americanization, in others, the working class; in still others, there was an ostensibly classless and genderless optimization of everyone's interests. Culture as consumption and culture as entertainment and leisure, culture as compensation for the rigors of rationalized Americanism or as an integral, disciplining element of it were some of the clashing interpretations.[6]

Americanism was and is associated with a variety of other concepts that attempt to capture the fundamental socioeconomic and cultural transformations of the twentieth century—rationalization, Taylorism, Fordism, mass consumption, mass culture, modernization, and modernity.[7] During Weimar, industrialists and right-wing engineers, stressing efficiency, performance, and calculability, saw Americanism as the embodiment of rationalization and Taylorism, while Social Democrats depicted Americanism in terms of rationalized Fordist mass production and consumption. Throughout the twentieth century, Germans linked Americanism to modernization and modernity, but certainly did not agree upon the definitions or evaluations of these two related but by no means identical phenomena.

Americanism did not assume a uniformly positive assessment of all aspects of American society, polity, or ideology but rather an openness to things seen as central to the American model. Americanism rested on the belief that, in the words of one Weimar observer, "America was a good idea."[8] But like so many good ideas, it was partial and contradictory, its sweeping theoretical claims on its own behalf were open to conflicting interpretations, and its practical implementation was open to criticism. Ambivalence, not unequivocal enthusiasm, characterized Americanism and its proponents both during Weimar and after 1945.

What was common to all brands of Americanism, however, was the insistence that America was a model to be reckoned with, a phenomenon in relationship to which one of necessity had to chart one's development and define one's identity. Underlying Americanism was not Locke's belief that "In the beginning, all the world was America." Rather, it was the simultaneous hope and fear that in the end all the world would *become* America.

Americanism's openness involved economy and society, culture and–with more reservations–gender. The omission of politics is deliberate. To be sure, domestic and international political considerations profoundly shaped the adoption of both Americanism and anti-Americanism, but by and large Germans did not see American governmental institutions, political parties, ideologies, and political culture more broadly as either central to America as a model of modernity and prosperity or as worthy of emulation. Yes, Weimar Germans debated Wilsonianism, refugees "exiled in Paradise" revised earlier critiques of American democracy, and post-1945 West Germans of necessity grappled with the imposition of American conceptions of democracy, political parties, and anti-communism.[9]

Yet, especially during Weimar and from left to right on the political spectrum, Germans assumed that the economic and social lessons that they might learn from America would further their own distinctive political projects at home. Thus, Weimar Social Democrats thought their version of Americanism would help democratize the economy and society and promote social policy, while conservative and nationalist industrialists believed that their understandings of the American model supported their efforts to limit democratization and the welfare state.[10] America was perceived as potentially more destabilizing to Germany's economic practices, social hierarchies, and cultural values than to its political institutions, even though, in fact, America reshaped Germany's political arena as much as, if not more than, any other realm.

From 1917 on, Americanism and anti-communism, anti-Americanism and communism were mutually constitutive of one another, and German images of America were shaped by the Russian Revolution, the subsequent deepening of ideological divisions within interwar Europe, and the cold war.[11] To be sure, many in Weimar Germany were both anti-American and anti-communist, but for those on the left the choice was between the Russian and the American models of modernity. After 1945, anti-communism, whether propounded by Social Democrats or Christian Democrats, entailed at the very least reluctant Americanism.

Proponents of Americanism did not restrict themselves to analyzing America: they urged Germans and Europeans to adopt selected elements of the American model and combine them with valued national practices and commitments. The goal was to become Americanized while remaining oneself.[12] Shared by many across the spectrum of political positions and social classes both in Weimar and after 1945, this goal tended to unify as long as it remained abstract and to divide once it came to specifying what was concretely meant by Americanization on the one hand, and being German on the other.

The German fascination with America long predated the twentieth century, but Americanism as a conceptual framework for understanding Germany, America and modernity, as a social and economic program, and as a cultural stance emerged only in the interwar years. As we will see, nineteenth-century German images of America were pervasive, popular, and often rather positive, but America was not seen as the embodiment of modernity. German and European dominance, development, and difference were assumed or asserted, often through familial metaphors that depicted Europe as the parent and America as the child. America was growing but still not mature, clever—even precocious—but definitely not wise. It might move along roads Europe had traveled or might carve out its own path, but it would not draw others in its wake; at most, its influence would be limited to other colonies or former colonies. Americanism could only develop once such comforting assumptions were undermined, once the child not only grew up and left home, but tried to make its own home a model for the rest of the world.

This definition of Americanism is in many respects highly unsatisfactory, for its meanings remain underspecified, ambiguous, and contested. Yet, these very definitional flaws help us understand the appeals of Americanism. The elasticity and capaciousness of the category meant that it could express a variety of expectations and aspirations. Americanism was a language that enabled people to communicate or think they were communicating, while permitting them to say very different things with the same words. Americanism could thus be instrumentalized to serve conflicting goals and was compatible with a variety of otherwise incompatible political positions—with Weimar Social Democracy as well as with the technocratic visions of engineers and the profit-making calculus of capitalists. It was compatible as well with Leninism in the Soviet Union, Ludwig Erhard's social market economy, and the modernization program of French businessmen, engineers, and government officials in the Fourth Republic.[13] Americanism was not what the American state, American business, or the American culture industry imposed, but what Europeans tried to imagine and negotiate out of the capacious and elastic American model; out of concrete American interventions, which were numerous and influential, but by no means all determining; and out of internal European and German desires and debates.

Ironically, it is easier to define anti-Americanism than Americanism. There is a numbing repetitiveness and striking continuity about anti-Americanism that is missing in Americanism.[14] The tropes, which first appeared at the turn of the century, did not change once firmly established in Weimar. There were criticisms of materialism, standardization, and homogeneity; laments about the lack of culture, education, and spirituality; persistent fears about a feminization of the public sphere and about the American woman; and a deep conviction that Europe remained the home of Homo sapiens, while in America a clever but shallow *Homo faber* dominated.

Anti-Americanism was not simply the flip side of Americanism, a devaluation of all that Americanism held dear. Rather, it reflected a set of anxieties that were shared to some degree by even the most enthusiastic proponents of Americanism. Anti-Americanism stressed the costs of rationalization and Fordism, of mass consumption and mass culture, while ignoring possible benefits and dismissing the possibilities of picking and choosing elements of Americanism and inserting them in a different context, where they might have different implications. The proponents of Americanism sometimes ignored these costs—in the 1920s, for example, labor overlooked the weakness of American trade unions, while capital paid little attention to American industrial relations—and neither asked about the place of racism in the American economic and social model. Sometimes advocates of Americanism embraced what its opponents emphatically rejected, seeing, for example, the position of American women in the 1920s or the character of American youth culture in the 1950s as positive and emancipatory.[15] Sometimes advocates of Americanism acknowledged that the costs of emulation were real but asserted that they were necessary to achieve greater gains. From the 1920s on, both social democracy and communism accepted the Taylorist and Fordist transformations of work in order to enhance productivity and ultimately consumption, even though this eroded skill and diminished job satisfaction for an elite of male workers.

Many different and incompatible versions of Americanism were advocated, but only some elements of the American model were actually transplanted to Germany. Americanization refers to the adoption of American forms of organizing production and consumption, to technology and techniques of management and industrial relations, to consumer products and forms of marketing, to cultural goods and the institutions of mass culture. In studying Americanization, the objects of analysis are relatively clear and straightforward, but understanding what functions and meanings these objects had and have within the European context is most definitely not. Americanization is not a linear narrative of Europe becoming just like America but rather a complex tale of how Europe has incorporated elements of the American model and redefined both them and the European contexts into which they were brought. Americanization was the result of ongoing debates about Americanism and anti-Americanism, and it is to those debates and their outcomes in Germany that we will now turn.

II

In the late eighteenth and nineteenth centuries, books and articles, novels and poems about American were published in abundance by adherents of the Enlightenment and by romantics, by 1848 liberals, and by conservatives. Scarcely a major German thinker failed to offer reflections on America: there was Goethe's famous "America, you have it better," and Heine's initial enthusiasm for America's liberty and equality, followed by growing disillusionment with its hypocritical practice of slavery and its social and cultural monotony.[16] Whereas Hegel was troubled by the dominance of private economic interests over a common interest in America, by the proliferation of religious sects, and by the general absence of a state in the European sense, Marx remarked more favorably about the development of American capitalism, with all the contradictory progressive and regressive elements it entailed. In the century's early decades, the romantic poet Nikolaus Lenau produced a widely read litany of complaints about America that mixed cultural criticism, economic fears, and unhappy travel experiences.[17] At century's end, Kafka produced a nightmarish portrait of an America dominated by bureaucracy and modern business, and characterized by alienation and impotence.

But none of these authors or approaches is what first comes to mind when reflecting on nineteenth-century German images of America. Rather, it is Karl May, one of Germany's most prolific authors and certainly its most popular nineteenth-century novelist. The most famous and influential of May's forty-odd adventure stories, which were set in a variety of exotic locales, are those dealing with the American "Wild West" and Native Americans, referred to, of course, as Indians. There were short stories produced in the 1870s, fictional "travel reports" published in the 1880s, and, most importantly, the many tales of his Indian hero, Winnetou, and his white blood brother, Old Shatterhand, written from the 1890s through the first decade of the twentieth century. It has been claimed that "[i]n the German imagination, the Far West is the most enduring and popular of all the myths about America."[18] Certainly, it was the image embraced most unequivocally, and Karl May was pivotal in shaping it.

May's novels were not based on accurate information about American Indians, although he did read some of the available literature on Native American tribes and on the conquest and settlement of the West. Nor were the novels based on actual encounters with Indians—or any other Americans, for that matter. May first went to the U.S. in 1908, long after his reputation had been established and most of his Wild West novels had been published. May's novels drew on the conventions of the already popular Western genre of which James Fenimore Cooper was the prime exemplar.[19] How much he borrowed generously from the information, plots, and characters of other Western writers is a disputed issue among May scholars, but original and accurate or not, May has been unbelievably popular for the past century.

May's novels conveyed an image of America as first and foremost a place of nature in all its complexity—physical nature, man in struggle with nature, man in a quasi state of nature. The state and capitalism, urbanization and industrialization, society and culture of a nineteenth-century European sort were missing or present only on the margins of these tales, as threats to the people and ways of life that were central and valued. May did not depict the Far West, the uncivilized West as a utopia. There were good and bad Indians, as well as even more numerous bad whites; even noble Indians were doomed.

But May's American West was a simpler and more open world, where interactions were direct and honest and heroic adventure could occur in exotic settings. It was a place where values and the individuals embodying them were more noble—though not originally, to be sure, even in the Winnetou stories. Winnetou was first depicted as a rather wild and crafty figure, bent on revenge for the wrongs done him and his people, prone to violence, and altogether "too Indian."[20] As May developed his central figure, Winnetou became a noble savage, representing the best of his race and the unspoiled character of the New World. He advocated reconciliation and even converted to Christianity.[21] The noble savage was the best

Christian—or did he become noble because he ultimately became Christian? The ambivalence is never resolved in May's narratives.

May did not so much project Teutonic myths onto the American West as invent an illusory past for both America and Germany, a past set in a timeless, ahistoric present. The condition of Indians and their projected future were not explained with reference to the American state's policy of systematic expulsion and extermination. Nor were the economic imperatives and racism that underlay such policies explored. The very timeless and decontextualized character of his stories enabled May to raise those older Enlightenment themes about human nature, about society before state and modernity. And in good Enlightenment fashion, nature was seen as noble and ad- mirable—and tragically doomed by inexorable progress. America was an elusive past for which one might long, but it was neither the future toward which Germany might be heading nor a model that should be emulated.

Elements of America as the future do, however, appear in May— on the margins in some readings, in a central position in others. The America of noble Indians and the uncivilized (in the best sense of the term) West are threatened by another America: a Yankee America of profit-hungry capitalists, markets and materialism, technology and modernity. Noble man had to struggle not only against nature, but against the depraved business world.[22] Some of the key tropes of anti- Americanism made their appearance even before Americanism did.

A veritable army of scholars have speculated on why May's nov- els have proven so popular. In part, they were simply good adventure stories of a sort enduringly appealing to young readers. Physically, ethnically, and culturally, May's America was so different from nineteenth- and twentieth-century Germany that readers young and old, male and female, could project both a range of adventures and an ensemble of virtues impossible to imagine in Germany.[23] Amer- ica was epic fiction, not a life one might actually lead. In so far as America was an illusory past, it was one very prominent object of German nostalgia for lost clarity and simplicity, for a world unclut- tered by the accoutrements of modernity. Anti-modernism shaped May's vision of America, and that vision in turn appealed to the anti-modernism so prevalent in a Germany experiencing rapid industrialization and urbanization, intensive social transformation, and bitter political conflict.

Others writing contemporaneously with May presented more complex and varied images of America, featuring not only "limitless prairies, bold adventures and simple people," but depicting as well skyscrapers, Wall Street and one dimensional businessmen.[24] One thinks here of Friedrich Ratzel's sketches of major American cities, the reflections of Wilhelm von Polenz on *The Land of the Future*, the ruminations of the psychologist Hugo Munsterberg on Germans and Americans, the travelogues of Edwin Rosen and Arthur Holitscher.[25] What is striking about these works is their multiplicity of images, lack of focus, encyclopedic range, and indiscriminate curiosity. Women and marriage, schools and hospitals, Broadway theater and small-town musical culture, sweatshops and steel mills, Niagara Fall and the Grand Canyon, immigrants and Indians–all are touched upon, none analyzed in depth. In these works, America is no longer an illusory past, but it is not yet a model of modernity. American wealth, prosperity, and technology sometimes arouse desire, while mass society and mass culture inspire dread, but overall America is a fascinating collection of curiosities, whose relevance to German identity and development is not clearly articulated. That was to change in the interwar years.

III

America loomed large in the German imagination of the 1920s, assuming new contours and characteristics. While anti-Americanism elaborated the same critiques with updated examples, Americanism emerged full blown for the first time. Debates about the emulation of or capitulation to American economic and cultural forms were accompanied by enthusiastic but selective borrowings, hesitant appropriations, and unwanted infiltrations of practices and products, values and fantasies.

Weimar images of America were no longer Western and rural. Rather, the quintessential America was situated in cities–in Detroit with its speeding automobile assembly lines; in Chicago with its stockyards, Sears and Roebuck, and skyscrapers rising out of the prairies; or in Pittsburgh with its integrated steel mills, producing day and night. America was located in Los Angeles, with its new conceptions of urban space and housing and that mecca of mass culture, Hollywood. Or America was to be found in New York's soaring skyscrapers and glittering boulevards, its avant-garde, multiracial culture and "American tempo," although not in New York's technologically backward and small-scale manufacturing economy.[26]

America no longer represented nature, but rather its physical appropriation, social transformation, and economic development, built on new technologies, ways of organizing production, and approaches to management and marketing. For Weimar Germans,

America conjured up images of vast, sleek factories, filled with the most modern machines. Materials were efficiently delivered to speeding assembly lines, which turned out standardized, inexpensive goods, for either further production or consumption. American levels of productivity and profit, the sheer abundance and diversity of goods, astonished and provoked wartorn and relatively impoverished Germany.

America was imagined first and foremost as a system of production and an ideology of productivism. To be sure, the American regime of production provided new products that were central to new forms of mass consumption, and its productivist values of speed, standardization, efficiency, and calculability were elevated to the highest virtues not only of work but also of life. Images of America could not be limited to the world of production, but it was American production methods that Germans, who otherwise agreed on very little, admired and sought to imitate. The consumptionist and cultural implications of the American model, by contrast, proved much more divisive. Social Democrats embraced the American model intellectually and strategically; they admired the magnitude and modernity of America's production facilities, and saw American production methods as the best means to raise German wages, consumption patterns, and wealth to American levels. German engineers and scientists studying production methods mixed professional admiration and political considerations in their assessments. Americans purportedly enhanced productivity by optimizing technology, factory organization, and job execution rather than exploiting the individual worker, and thereby offered a means of resolving social conflict within the factory that did not limit technological progress or profits. German industrialists were much more ambivalent about American production methods. While they wanted to increase efficiency, exports, and profits, they were reluctant to invest in mass production technologies and were determined to curb wages, social benefits, and consumption for workers. Whatever vision of modernity was advocated, a full or partial Americanization of production was seen as its essential foundation and as a flexible basis on which a variety of social programs and political institutions might develop.[27]

In the interwar years, the romantic, fictional Indian Winnetou was displaced by the matter-of-fact millionaire businessman Henry Ford as the symbolic center of German imaginings of America.[28] Nothing captures better the shift from America as nature to America as production. The productive innovations of Ford's Highland Park and River Rouge factories were universally admired; engineers, capitalists, and trade unionists alike waxed poetic about the wonders of

Fordist production, claiming repeatedly to have been deeply moved by its beauty and efficiency, grandeur and harmony.[29] There was no consensus, however, about whether Fordism as a system of production required mass consumption and, as a result, high wages and innovative marketing mechanisms. German industrialists insisted it did not, arguing for the adoption of specific Fordist technological and organizational innovations without any transformations of wage structures or consumption patterns. The less powerful but economically more perceptive Social Democrats insisted that America had not only solved the problems of supply and production, but had accurately recognized the centrality of demand and consumption. Fordism seemed to provide capitalism with a solution to both problems.[30]

In the 1920s America was no longer seen as Germany's illusory past, as immature or exceptional. Rather, it was advanced, and Germans could find their future written there, or at least one possible future, an indubitably modern one. Weimar Germans no longer imagined America in order to speculate on what human nature might once have been, but rather to celebrate or anguish over what men and women in modernity were or might well become. Imagining America no longer provided a welcome escape from contemporary economic problems, cultural crises, and gender conflicts; it confronted these issues in their most extreme forms.

Weimar Germans developed their understandings of America in multiple ways. Many traveled to the U.S., visiting its industrial heartland, commenting on culture in New York and perhaps Hollywood, and visiting homes and families. Many more read Henry Ford's bestselling autobiography or one of the innumerable travel reports and more scholarly commentaries, published as books or as articles in a wide variety of popular, professional, and political journals.[31] Still others saw American movies or listened to American jazz or watched the Tiller girls dance review, whose female "movement machines," seemed to embody America's obsession with technology, collective discipline, and rationalization.[32]

The vast majority of Germans did not encounter either Americans or American consumer goods to any significant degree. Consumer durables had barely penetrated the German middle-class market, the number of automobiles per capita was far below not only the United States but France and England as well, and radios were relatively rare. Neither the German home nor transport nor leisure were transformed as they were being transformed in America and would be in Europe from the 1950s on. Indeed, even those Germans who preached the virtues of and economic need for mass consumption were unclear as to what exactly was to be consumed. Cars seemed impossibly expensive, but little emphasis was placed on household items, such as vacuum cleaners, washing machines, and refrigerators. Among Social Democrats, trade unionists, and feminists, advocacy of consumption remained abstract, fear of the seductions of consumer culture was strong, and pleas for individual housewives and workers to be rationalized, disciplined, and responsible were numerous.[33]

The emergence of Americanism intensified anti-Americanism, one thrust of which was directed at the costs of the production model so widely admired. For some, Fordism, with its assembly lines, standardization, mechanization, and deskilling, was simply impossible given Europe's relative lack of markets and investment capital. For many others in capitalist and right-wing engineering circles, Fordism was culturally and economically objectionable, for it threatened Germany's specialized "quality work," on which exports depended, and eroded the "joy in work" and loyalty to firm and factory community that purportedly existed.

The critique of economic Americanism was not limited to its impact on labor relations, product lines, and the culture of production; Americanism threatened culture on every level–tradition and *Kultur*, definitions of masculinity and femininity, domesticity and national identity. America was held to be excessively materialistic, an accusation at once amorphous and emotionally powerful. American men were single-mindedly devoted to the almighty dollar, obsessed with productive efficiency and profits, rational, practical, ever calculating, but unable or unwilling to devote any energies to *Kultur* or *Bildung* and utterly lacking in *Geist*. The inevitable accompaniment of American materialism was the absence of outstanding cultural and educational institutions and accomplishments; a pervasive lack of interest in art, music, and intellectual pursuits; and the shallowness of spiritual values.[34]

Worse still, American men's preoccupation with the economy, admittedly a key to American economic success, opened the way for a far-reaching feminization of culture and a dangerous empowerment of women. Many of the anxieties about modernity in its American guise were focused on the American "new woman," with her bobbed hair, short skirts, flirtatious manner, love of movies and mass consumption, and claims to economic and sexual independence. But equally troubling were the less flamboyant, autonomous middle-class women who attended college and held jobs, ran local cultural institutions, and managed a modern home, replete with appliances and canned goods. Married they might well be, but not in a form acceptable to German observers like Adolf Halfeld, author of the most widely read anti-American tract of the 1920s. American women, he and many others argued, demanded not only abstract equality but also concrete help with housework and childcare; they lacked the erotic charms of European women, and their materially comfortable, efficient homes were comfortless.[35] The American home, family, and sexuality lacked the proper spirit every bit as much as American public life did.

Americans were simultaneously envied and disdained for their superficial openness and pseudo-egalitarianism. While such attributes were perhaps fitting for a people seen as utterly lacking in intellectual depth and a tragic sense of life, Germans worried that they were less a result of America's exceptional past and privileged present than of modernity in its American form. Worse, superficiality and pseudo-egalitarianism might take root in German soil.

Weimar anti-Americanism repeatedly critiqued the standardization and homogenization so central to Fordism. Sometimes mass production was linked to low quality, at other times to stifling conformity that outweighed any benefits of quality at low price. Even Social Democrats, who so enthusiastically proclaimed the benefits of Fordist mass consumption, anxiously counted the different types of bedsteads and alarm clocks, dishes and dress styles that they encountered when traveling through America, happily concluding that efficiency and reasonable diversity could coexist.[36]

American mass culture was seen to reflect and reenforce those aspects of American life that made even proponents of economic Americanism anxious. Movies and jazz music, which were consumed in the most unmediated form and which offered enticing images of consumption, sexuality, and youth culture, were subject to the harshest criticism. So too were those allegedly least immune to the seductions of Americanized mass culture and consumption, indeed most implicated in promoting them—namely, women.

The impassioned Weimar debates about Americanism led some alarmists to fear that "… not socialism but Americanism will be the end of everything as we have known it."[37] But the American model of modernity—prosperous, functional, materialistic, and bereft of tradition, domestic comfort, and *Kultur*—did not become the German reality in the 1920s. Americanization was contained both by Germans' poverty and limited consumption and by German capital's reluctance to embark on a full Fordist restructuring of the economy. America's economic involvement in Germany took the form of loans more than direct investment or multinational production; its political interventions were sporadic, and its military presence nonexistent. When the depression hit America every bit as hard as

Germany, the allure of Americanism as an economic model and emancipatory vision diminished rapidly.

National Socialism further discredited Americanism, even as the Nazi state remained fascinated with American technology and mass consumption and Hitler admired and honored Henry Ford and sought to Germanize Fordism. German industry continued to rationalize production piecemeal along American lines, while retaining, as it had in Weimar, flexible specialization and "quality work."[38] Elements of Americanization–from productivity wage systems, to the people's radio, to study trips to American factories–coexisted with a strident anti-Americanism that made previously latent anti-semitism and racism central to its attacks. America was depicted as decadent and weak but also dangerous because it was dominated by Jews and permitted racial mixing.[39] Nazi reactionary modernism departed from its Weimar predecessor in yet another way. Instead of viewing rationalization and Americanization as a necessary prelude to renewed national strength, Hitler and leading Nazis insisted that territorial expansion was a prerequisite for German Fordism.[40]

IV

After 1945, the American occupation, the Marshall Plan, and the cold war fundamentally shifted the terrain on which Americanism and anti-Americanism battled. Germans no longer invented America from afar or on the basis of limited firsthand experience; America came to Germany. There were hundreds of thousands of military personnel, a smaller but no less influential army of European Recovery Program officials, hundreds of cultural representatives in America Houses, and businessmen in abundance.

In the postwar decades, Americanism came to represent an economic model and a way of life centering around and mediated by mass consumption, commodified leisure, and mass culture. Fordist production, so central to the images of the 1920s, was assumed to be inevitable and was implemented at varying pace in different industries, but rarely debated publicly. At issue, rather, was the Fordist "consumption regime."[41]

No one person looms large in the post-1945 German imagination of America as Henry Ford did during Weimar. It was not personalities, such as Elvis or Kennedy, who commanded center stage, but rather commodities. The Coke bottle occupied pride of place, with blue jeans not far behind. A variety of consumer durables, from the automobile to the washing machine, refrigerator, and vacuum cleaner, were not necessarily made in America—or with secret American ingredients, as Coke was—but they symbolized Americanism as a lifestyle and value system. Americanism became part of everyday life, and the commodities associated with it came to shape social relationships.[42] In Germany, the consumer goods themselves were mediated by Americans, especially GIs.

From the turn of the century onward, consumption haunted German anti-Americanism. Mass consumption was seen as both product and promoter of materialism with all its attendant vices; consumption required a restructuring of wages, social hierarchies, and cultural values, and threatened to subvert traditional gender roles. After 1945, such concerns did not disappear but were displaced by new discourses about the costs and benefits of Americanism, which simultaneously legitimated and disciplined mass consumption. One such discourse, embraced by Ludwig Erhard, endorsed consumption as essential to economic recovery and the proper functioning of the social market economy. Capital, previously so insistent on the impossibility of mass consumption in Germany, gradually came to accept the necessity of Americanizing not only production techniques and management practices but product lines and purchasing power as well.[43]

A second discursive strategy was to reimagine or Germanize the practice of consumption—or rather its practitioners. The potentially irrational female German consumer became the object of disciplining and surveillance by market researchers and educators. As the primary controllers of household income, women were to become critical, rational, and cost-conscious consumers, who would promote economic recovery and modernization while maximizing family welfare.[44] Women, long considered susceptible to the dangerous allures of Americanism, were expected to negotiate its adoption. They had been assigned this role in Weimar, when the rationalized housewife was to mediate American models of modernity by Taylorizing her own work and eschewing consumption. In the Federal Republic, she was to consume, but without sacrificing the needs of her children to her own selfish desires, as American women reputedly did.[45] The German Democratic Republic developed its own variant of the discourse of restrained and responsible consumption, and there, too, disciplined consumption was women's work.[46]

Yet a third discourse accepted American modes of consumption while blaming the problems of modernity on outside "others." Maria Höhn's study of the Rhineland-Palatinate in the 1950s traces how a massive American military presence transformed a rural agrarian economy into a modern locus of military-related production, service, and mass consumption. The local population took new jobs, rented rooms to GIs—and the women who worked for and lived with them—consumed new goods, saw American movies, and heard jazz. But locals also perceived and loudly lamented threats to morality, domesticity, and *Heimat*—the homeland, not *Kultur*, for this was impoverished rural Germany. They resolved their ambivalence by blaming those threats not on an abstract and all-pervasive Americanism, but on particular outsiders (*Fremde*) who abused modernity and Americanization. Reflecting both Weimar and Nazi tropes of anti-Americanism, the targets were, first, women who worked for or were sexually involved with soldiers, regardless of whether that sexual relationship was a common-law marriage, a casual affair, or prostitution; second, black GIs—race was always specified; and third, Jewish bar owners, who provided the spaces that facilitated the ostensibly dangerous liaisons between black Americans and single German women. One could not control Americanization, but one could try to control German women's sexuality.[47]

Finally, although West Germans remained concerned about materialism, they no longer associated it exclusively with Americanism. Catholics and conservatives, who had seen America as materialism incarnate, now linked materialism to both National Socialism and communism.[48] Redefinitions of American materialism and consumption were inseparable from the all-pervasive cold war anti-communism. Consumption, rational and disciplined to be sure, was detached from materialism and associated with freedom, prosperity, and a beneficent capitalism. Materialism, with its connotations of narrow economism, a lack of culture, and loss of values, was associated with socialism and authoritarianism, with a regimentation that existed in the East, not in America. Mass consumption was reconceptualized and legitimated even before it existed widely in the 1960s.[49] The quantity and variety of goods as well as the purported quality of consuming practices were offered as proof of the superiority of Americanized capitalism over materialistic socialism. For its part, the communist East criticized American materialism as decadent, praised austerity as proof of moral superiority, and promised greater consumption in the future.[50]

In the Federal Republic, Americanization came to be seen as inevitable, but it did not go uncriticized. Multiple anti-Americanisms flourished: those in which nostalgia for *Heimat* and laments about *Kultur* and modern women predominated; those that perpetuated the anti-semitism and racism of Nazi critiques; and those of the left that rejected neither the productivism of interwar Americanism nor the consumerism of post-1945 models, but rather attacked economic and military American imperialism.[51] In contrast to earlier periods, these anti-Americanisms coexisted with a pervasive Americanization of German life.

Americanization was associated with specific goods—Coke, cars, jeans, rock 'n' roll, and household consumer durables. Did Americanism and Americanization create a West Germany that was essentially similar to America in production, consumption, and mass culture? Or did American hegemony and German emulation and negotiation result in a version of modernity or consumer society that had its origins in the American model but developed its own distinctive identity? Coke, for example, was the best-selling brand name among nonalcoholic drinks by the end of the 1940s, but did consuming it make one more American and was that the intent?[52] Was the car the quintessential symbol of the American way of life, "an ideology on four wheels"?[53] Or did the development of the Volkswagen create a car culture that both partook of the American model and differed from it? The scholarship cited above as well as the essays in this volume suggest how complexly negotiated the adoption of American products and practices were. Even as they transformed Germany, they were themselves redefined and repositioned. Rather than exploring these processes, I want to conclude with some speculations about the future of Americanism, anti-Americanism, and Americanization.

V

As the twentieth century ends, so too does the long-standing German and European preoccupation with America, outbursts of anti-Americanism notwithstanding. Neither Americanism nor anti-Americanism have the purchase they enjoyed for the past century or more. Nor is Americanization in its previously recognizable forms central to the social and cultural transformations now occurring.

The demise of Americanism is intimately related to the end of the American century so grandiosely proclaimed in the 1940s. America no longer commands undisputed economic hegemony; the Fordist model of mass production, high wages, and mass consumption has exhausted itself in America and elsewhere. America no longer symbolizes the "fantasy of timeless, even, and limitless development" that it did in the 1950s and 1960s.[54] Benjamin Barber has argued that American economic and cultural hegemony will be rebuilt on the basis of American dominance of "the infotainment telesector." English is, after, all the language of the Internet, and America dominates rock music and movies.[55] The global economy of the 1990s is a far cry from the wartorn and prostrate world system of the late 1940s, however, and it is far from clear whether American control, democratic decentralization, or highly concentrated international capitalism will triumph.

Ironically, the end of the cold war and the elimination of any alternative to capitalism, American style or other, has further weakened both Americanism and anti-Americanism. Every commodity and cultural practice need no longer be coded American or Russian, capitalist or communist. To define their own identity, Germans need no longer position themselves between East and West; even as they strive to define themselves in relationship to a variety of Eastern "others," Slavic and Muslim, they need not align themselves with America.

Can America feature as prominently in the German imagination when its economic and political hegemony has eroded? Can American mass culture alone sustain the vigorous discourses of Americanism and anti-Americanism that have thrived in the twentieth century? Or, as a 1996 *New York Times* article that described Germans in Leipzig building tepees and dressing as Native Americans suggested, will the romanticized American West resume its previous privileged place in the German imagination while anti-Americanism is redefined as ecological anti-modernism?[56]

Notes

1. John Locke, *Two Treatises of Civil Government*, vol. II, chap. V, sec. 49, cited in Dan Diner, *America in the Eyes of the Germans: An Essay on Anti-Americanism* (Princeton, 1996), 3.

2. For an extensive discussion of the German preoccupation with economic America, see Mary Nolan, *Visions of Modernity: American Business and the Modernization of Germany* (New York, 1994).

3. For an introduction to the vast literature on Americanism, modernity, and anti-modernism, see Jeffrey Herf, *Reactionary Modernism: Technology, Culture and Politics in Weimar and the Third Reich* (New York, 1984); Detlev J. K. Peukert, *The Weimar Republic: The Crisis of Classical Modernity* (New York, 1987); and John Willett, *Art and Politics in the Weimar Period: The New Sobriety, 1917–1933* (New York, 1978).

4. For an introduction to visions of America in different periods, see, in addition to Diner, *America*; Frank Trommler and Joseph McVeigh, eds., *America and the Germans* (Philadelphia, 1985); Peter Berg, *Deutschland und Amerika, 1918–1929* (Lübeck and Hamburg, 1963). Alf Lüdtke, Inge Marßolek, and Adelheid von Saldern, *Amerikanisierung: Traum und Alpentraum im Deutschland des 20. Jahrhunderts*

(Stuttgart, 1996); and Ralph Willett, *The Americanization of Germany, 1945–1949* (London, 1989).

5. My emphasis on Americanism and Americanization as contested and negotiated phenomena, as attitudes and processes that European countries both partially accepted and partially rejected and that they sought to alter in terms of their own culture and identity is shared by such authors as Lüdtke, Marßolek and von Saldern in the introduction to their *Amerikanisierung*, 7–33, and Richard Kuisel, *Seducing the French: The Dilemma of Americanization* (Berkeley, 1993).

6. See Nolan, *Visions of Modernity*, 58–82, 108–120.

7. For introductions to the history of Taylorism, see Judith Merkle, *Management and Ideology: The Legacy of the International Scientific Management Movement* (Berkeley, 1980); for Fordism, see Nolan, *Visions of Modernity*, 30–57; for mass consumption, see Victoria de Grazia, ed., *The Sex of Things: Gender and Consumption in Historical Perspective* (Berkeley, 1996).

8. Hans A. Joachim, "Romane aus Amerika," *Die neue Rundschau* 41 (September 1930): 397–98, cited in Anton Kaes, "Mass Culture and Modernity: Notes toward a Social History of Early American and German Cinema," in *America and the Germans*, vol. 2, 323.

9. See Berg, *Deutschland und Amerika*; Anthony Heilbut, *Exiled in Paradise* (New York, 1983); Jeffry M. Diefendorf, Alex Frohn, and Hermann-Josef Rupieper, eds., *American Policy and the Reconstruction of West Germany, 1945–55* (New York, 1993).

10. Nolan, *Visions of Modernity*, 50–54, 71–81.

11. Both the Bolsheviks in Russia and the German Communists embraced Taylorist and Fordist ideas, even as they rejected America as a social and cultural model. See Nolan, *Visions of Modernity*, 54, 81–82; Kendall E. Bailes, "The American Connection: Ideology and the Transfer of American Technology in the Soviet Union, 1917–1941," *Comparative Studies in Society and History* 23 (July 1981): 421–48; and Hans Rogger, "*Amerikanizm* and Economic Development in Russia," *Comparative Studies in Society and History* 23 (July 1981): 381–420.

12. The dilemma of Europe vis-à-vis America was similar to that of colonized countries vis-à-vis Western modernity. For the latter, see Partha Chatterjee, "Colonialism, Nationalism and Colonized Women: The Contest in India," *American Ethnologist* 16, no. 4 (1989): 622–33.

13. Kendall Bailes, *Technology and Science under Lenin and Stalin: Origins of the Soviet Technical Intelligentsia, 1917–1941* (New York, 1978); Erica Carter, "Alice in Consumer Wonderland: West German Case Studies in Gender and Consumer Culture," in *Gender and Generation*, ed. Angela McRobbie and Mica Nava (London, 1984), 191–94; Kuisel, *Seducing the French*, 70–102.

14. Diner, *America*, 14–17, stresses both the continuity of themes in anti-Americanism and the peculiarly intense variants that developed in Germany. Reinhold Wagnleitner argues for the similarity in anti-American tropes across Europe in *Coca-Colonization and the Cold War: The Cultural Mission of the United States in Austria after the Second World War* (Chapel Hill, N.C., 1994), 26–27. See also Emil-Peter Müller, *Antiamerikanismus in Deutschland: Zwischen Care-Paket und Cruise Missile* (Cologne, 1986), 22.

15. Nolan, *Visions of Modernity*, 120–27.

16. Diner, *America*, 38–41.

17. Ibid., 9, 46; Müller, *Antiamerikanismus*, 56–57; Wagnleitner, *Coca-Colonization and the Cold War*, 15, 20.

18. Beeke Sell Tower, "*Asphaltcowboys* and *Stadtindianer*: Imagining the Far West," in *Envisioning America*, ed. Beeke Sell Tower (Cambridge, Mass., 1990), 18–19.

19. Manfred Durzak, "Winnetou und Tecumseh: Literarische Ikone und historisches Bild," in *Karl Mays Winnetou: Studien zu einem Mythos*, ed. Dieter Südhoff and Hartmut Vollmer (Frankfurt a.M., 1989), 160–67.

20. Peter Uwe Hohendahl, "Von der Rothaut zum Edelmenschen: Karl Mays Amerikaromane," in *Karl Mays Winnetou*, 214–25.

21. For discussions of the transformation of Winnetou's character, see Franz Kandolf, "Der werdende Winnetou," in *Karl Mays Winnetou*, 179–95; Horst Wolf Müller, "Winnetou: Vom Skalpjäger zum roten Heiland," in *Karl Mays Winnetou*, 196–213.

22. Hohendahl, "Von der Rothaut zum Edelmenschen," 219–21; Diner, *America*, 45–46.

23. Tower, "*Asphaltcowboys*," 19.

24. Südhoff and Vollmer, *Karl Mays Winnetou*, 149–50.

25. Arthur Holitscher, *Amerika, Heute und Morgen* (Stuttgart, 1913); Wilhelm von Polenz, *Das Land der Zukunft* (Berlin, 1903); Friedrich Ratzel, *Sketches of Urban and Cultural Life in North America* (New Brunswick, N.J., 1988); Edwin Rosen, *Der deutsche Lausbub in Amerika* (Stuttgart, 1912).

26. Nolan, *Visions of Modernity*, 22–29.

27. Ibid., 26–54, 59–82.

28. Ibid., 32–36.

29. Ibid., 30, 36–37.

30. Ibid., 50–54.

31. Ibid., 18–22, 32–39.

32. Fritz Giese, *Girlkultur: Vergleiche zwischen amerikanischem und europäischem Rhythmus und Lebensgefühl* (Munich, 1925), 82–95, 119–22.

33. Nolan, *Visions of Modernity*, 115–20, 211–26.

34. Ibid., 98–99, 108–27.

35. Adolf Halfeld, *Amerika und der Amerikanismus: Kritische Betrachtungen eines Deutschen und Europäers* (Jena, 1927).

36. Nolan, *Visions of Modernity*, 110–13.

37. Gunter Dehn, *Proletarische Jugend* (Berlin, 1929), 39, cited in Peukert, *Weimar Republic*, 178.

38. Tilla Siegel and Thomas von Freyberg, *Industrielle Rationalisierung unter dem Nationalsozialismus* (Frankfurt a.M., 1991). See also, Rüdiger Hachtmann, "'Die Begründer der amerikanischen Technik sind fast lauter schwäbisch-allemannische Menschen': Nazi-Deutschland, der Blick auf die USA and die 'Amerikanisierung' der industriellen Produktionsstrukturen im Dritten Reich," in *Amerikanisierung*, 37–66.

39. Diner, *America*, 89–103. Adelheid von Saldern, "Überfremdungsängste: Gegen die Amerikanisierung der deutschen Kultur in den zwanziger Jahren," in *Amerikanisierung*, 213–44.

40. Phillip Gassert, *Amerika im Dritten Reich: Ideologie, Propaganda und Volksmeinung, 1933–1941* (Stuttgart, 1997), 92–94, 159–62.

41. The term is from Victoria de Grazia, "Changing Consumption Regimes," in *The Sex of Things*, 11–24.

42. Ralph Willett, *The Americanization of Germany, 1945–49*, 10–15, 99–114. For a study of Americanization and consumption in post–World War II France, see Kristen Ross, *Fast Cars, Clean Bodies: Decolonization and the Reordering of French Culture* (Cambridge, Mass., 1995).

43. Volker Berghahn, *The Americanization of West German Industry, 1945–1973* (Oxford, 1986). For a discussion of Erhard, see A. J. Nicholls, *Freedom with Responsibility: The Social Market Economy in Germany, 1918–1933* (Oxford, 1994), 151–247.

44. Erica Carter, *How German Is She? Postwar West German Reconstruction and the Consuming Woman* (Ann Arbor, 1997), 1–106; Erica Carter, "Deviant Pleasures? Women, Melodrama, and Consumer Nationalism in West Germany," in *The Sex of Things*, 359–80.

45. Robert G. Moeller, *Protecting Motherhood: Women and the Family in the Politics of Postwar West Germany* (Berkeley, 1993), 216.

46. Ina Merkel, "Eine andere Welt: Vorstellungen von Nordamerika in der DDR der fünfziger Jahre," in *Amerikanisierung*, 248–51, and idem, "Mental Traditions and Historical Change of Consumer Mentalities Illustrated on the Example of the DDR or About the Failure of the Counter-Modernity on the Battleground of Consumerism," unpublished manuscript. For a discussion of how East and West sought to create a disciplined, responsible response to American popular culture as well as mass consumption, see Uta G. Poiger, "Rock 'n' Roll, Female Sexuality, and the Cold War Battle over German Identities," *Journal of Modern History* 58, no. 3 (September 1996): 577–616; and idem, "Rebels with a Cause? American Popular Culture, the 1956 Youth Riots, and New Conceptions of Masculinity in East and West Germany," in *The American Impact on Postwar Germany*, ed. Reiner Pommerin (Providence, R.I., 1995).

47. Maria Höhn, "GIs, Veronikas and Lucky Strikes: German Reactions to the American Military Presence in the Rhineland-Palatinate during the 1950s," (Diss., University of Pennsylvania, 1995).

48. Maria Mitchell, "Materialism and Secularism: CDU Politicians and National Socialism, 1945–1949," *Journal of Modern History* 67, no. 2 (June 1995): 255–77.

49. For consumption in the 1950s, see Michael Wildt, *Am Beginn der Konsumgesellschaft: Mangelerfahrung, Lebenshaltung, Wohlstandshoffnung in Westdeutschland in den fünfziger Jahren* (Hamburg, 1994).

50. Merkel, "Mental Traditions."

51. Diner, *America*, 107–49; Michael Ermarth, "*The German Talks Back*: Heinrich Hauser and German Attitudes toward Americanization after World War II," in *America and the Shaping of German Society, 1945–1955*, ed. Michael Ermarth (Providence, R.I., 1993).

52. Ralph Willett, *Americanization of Germany*, 103–5.

53. The quote is from George Ball, cited in Benjamin R. Barber, *Jihad vs. McWorld* (New York, 1995).

54. Ross, *Fast Cars*, 38.

55. Barber, *Jihad vs. McWorld*, 59–87.

56. "Germans in Their Tepees? Naturally," *New York Times*, 2 April 1996, A 4.

– Two –

COMPARATIVE ANTI-AMERICANISM
IN WESTERN EUROPE

David W. Ellwood

The Question of Definition

Ideologies, Prejudices, Identity Crises

Why do expressions of antipathy to the United States in all their forms attract an "ism" in their categorization? There is a contrast here with the fate reserved for those other nations so often the objects of scorn, derision, repudiation, or even sustained criticism, which suggests the presence of forces stronger than simple lexical convenience. Anglophobia, anti-German feeling, and Japan-bashing have at various times been prominent currents of sentiment in international life, but none have attained the distinction of quasi-ideological status implied in that categorical "ism" attached to hostility toward the United States.

A clue to the nature of the phenomenon may be provided by consideration of the exalted label used to signal the distinctiveness and uniqueness of America's national life and experience: "exceptionalism." A cultural norm whose principal function is to identify a different, more acceptable, non-European variety of nationalism, "exceptionalism" when rendered explicit and codified for emulation and admiration becomes "Americanism," a summation, as Seymour

Some elements of this article appeared previously in "The American Challenge Renewed: U.S. Cultural Power and Europe's Identity Debates," *Brown Journal of World Affairs* (Winter/Spring 1996–97).

Martin Lipset explains, of the central principles of "the American Creed."[1] In this sense, "anti-Americanism" may represent a mirror image of the creed, united historically by way of a common ideological thrust, or rather separated by it in the sense of Wilde's famous *mot* on Britain and America as two nations separated by the barrier of a common language.

Behind its pseudo-ideological authority, its provocative associations, and its lexical facility, the true usefulness of "anti-Americanism" as a category of thought or behavior lies surely in its catch-all nature. Conveniently but misleadingly, it hides the important distinctions between those intent on attacking America the nation, the government, the foreign policy; those who find repugnant whatever or whoever is American: the way of life, the symbols, objects, products, and people; and the critics of Americanism, those who reject the explicit values and ideals of the United States in their distinctive normative form. Those who fail to note such differences risk creating the mirror image of the behavior they denounce. Seen from the solemn pages of the *Annals of the American Academy of Political Science*–which devoted its issue of May 1988 to the phenomenon–anti-Americanism simply suggests "a persistent pattern of gross criticism of the main values enshrined in the U.S. Constitution,"[2] or a "hostile caricature" of the ideals and behavior of the American people. An enduring characteristic of elite behavior throughout Continental Europe in this view, anti-Americanism is inspired by envy and sustained by impotence.

A historical rather than a moral or ideological judgment provides a different perspective, throwing into relief some of the internal contradictions of the phenomenon. Expressing in the same issue of the *Annals* an outlook widely held among analysts of the subject in Europe at that time, Marie-France Toinet explained what was the "important thing about the French fascination and rejection of Americanism …":

> … the French are not so much holding a debate about the United States but about themselves, about their society, their goals and their methods. It is, so to say, a Franco-French debate, where American arguments– often half-baked–are just an excuse or a pretense. The French hold the United States up as a mirror to look, in fact, at themselves.[3]

But the most lucid denunciation of the confusion over anti-Americanism's motivation and definition had already been offered by one of Britain's most celebrated writers of the 1950s, J. B. Priestley. Responding to accusations of anti-Americanism directed by U.S. reviewers at his 1955 American travelogue *Journey Down a Rainbow*, Priestley denounced the willful compounding by his critics of everything

America was and stood for with their specific preferences in politics and foreign policy:

> It is as if when friends from New York arrived outside our door [in London], I did not invite them until I had made sure they were in full agreement with our policy in Cyprus and were enthusiastic admirers of Eden, Butler and Macmillan....
>
> When Mrs. Smith tells Mr. Smith that his trousers are baggy and he needs a haircut, nobody accuses her of being anti-Smith.[4]

An Evolving Antagonism

The Early Phase: Stereotypes and Experiences

Just as positive visions of America in all their complex European forms accompanied the growth of the new nation from its earliest days, so did a mounting backlash of criticism and hostility. Herbert Spiro of the *Annals* was quite certain: "Anti-Americanism has been endemic among the ruling classes in continental Europe since 1776 at the latest."[5] The commercial materialism, social fragmentation, lack of culture, and sheer artificiality of the American experience were well-established stereotypes even before Dickens and Tocqueville produced their classics of description and analysis in the 1830s to 1840s. But although wincing at their criticisms—in a fashion Tocqueville famously presented as a form of cultural insecurity and which was repeatedly confirmed by later observers—no American of the time is known to have accused these writers of "anti-Americanism."

As long as subsequent commentators and historians confined their attention to negative imagery of the United States produced by European writers—whether based on direct observation or hearsay—they were never in short supply of stereotypes. But when the play of images among elites gave way to shared experience on a mass scale, a qualitatively different process of attraction and repulsion was set in motion. Late nineteenth-century emigration was of course the first of these shared experiences. The historian Paolo D'Attorre notes that in the work of Italian Catholic writers close to the world of the emigrants, the idealized promised land of the first rural emigrants progressively gave way to a much more contradictory and ambiguous judgment. At the turn of the century, negative judgments prevailed by far over positive ones, says D'Attorre, a mixture of "snobbish scorn and hostile diffidence" characterizing the tone of commentary, with "explicit anti-Americanism" very much in evidence. But no one thought of calling it such at the time.[6]

"The Future in America"[7] —And the Arrival of a New Power Presence

Then, from the era in which American industry, media, entertainments, business, and diplomacy began to exert a discernible effect in Europe, that is, the final decade of the nineteenth century, the questions of elite imagery and collective emigrant experience were obliged to give way to the need to come to terms with a concrete force or challenge whose permanence no one doubted. As C. Vann Woodward put it:

> The future intruded in the shape of missionaries, evangelists, salesmen, advertisements and movies. It took the form of new brides in the oldest of families, new faces in the highest society. It also appeared at lower social levels in strange attitudes and ideas, new ways of thinking, new styles of living, and alien values. Europeans began to hear these innovations from the mouths of their own children and with increasing apprehension and dismay.[8]

As awareness of the country's new strength grew, theorists of America's destiny began to express the view that the United States would and should supplant the European empires, especially the British, and hence should prepare consciously to organize the projection of its power. What Woodrow Wilson contributed to the debate, as America prepared to enter World War I, was an original conviction that to this power should be added a moral mission: "manifest destiny" would be redefined (again) to offer the benefits of America's historical beliefs and experience in such a way that they might become a model for the salvation of the world.

Universalism, moral exceptionalism, altruism—all were identified with Wilson's project. Yet, as Henry Kissinger has pointed out, the pretense that they might become the operational standards for conducting international relations everywhere was "largely incomprehensible to foreign leaders."[9] Wilson's vision was effectively disabled by his Allied partners in Paris in 1919. But did the president's exasperation with his European interlocutors stretch to the point where he accused them of anti-Americanism? Surely not.

The visionary status of Wilson's project was destined to endure, and to inaugurate a new era of "isms" in the Western world's international affairs. As the logic of his methods was escalated and intensified to the point of aberration by the totalitarianisms, so the accusation of "anti-Americanism" began to alight ever more frequently on those who, in bad or good faith, felt driven to mount a sustained criticism of whatever America produced, represented, believed in, or did.

The Modernization Challenge

It was no coincidence that when in the 1980s historians began systematic analysis of European antagonisms to the United States, they should have concentrated first of all on the interwar period. While D. L. Le Mahieu offered a wide-ranging study of the British elite structure of thought in which the new anti-Americanism flourished, David Strauss's analysis of the French case and Michela Nacci's study of fascist Italy both concentrated on anti-Americanism as such. This they understood as a symptom of the deep crisis of modernization in national societies produced by the combined effects of the permanent arrival after 1918 of mass production, mass democracy, and mass communication, together with postwar distress.[10]

Taylorism, Hollywood, jazz, dance halls, cafés, retail chains, new forms of advertising, leisure pursuits, and role models swept through postwar Europe with extraordinary efficiency and ruthlessness, and greatly antagonized traditional elites engaged in the very difficult business of reconstituting their power and legitimacy after the catastrophe.[11] Starting from this vantage point, the 1980s approach to anti-Americanism firmly established that the full twentieth-century flowering of the stereotypes, prejudices, and semi-ideological denunciations gathered together in the concept took place in the 1920s, that it went beyond the question of imagery to invest the entire range of America's incarnations as a power presence in Europe's new mass society, and that cycles of alienation were established that have persisted to the present.[12] It was apparent that the more that ideology was exalted by the totalitarian regimes, the more that criticisms of America took on a militant, comprehensive aspect throughout Europe, independent of the ebbs and flows of America's prestige in popular culture, as well as of U.S. actions in foreign and economic policy.

From World War II to Vietnam: Domination and Its Discontents

Nevertheless, until the outbreak of World War II, relative disinterest characterized reactions within the U.S. to European anti-Americanism. Explicit *official* preoccupation with the phenomenon began to appear only after the end of that conflict,[13] when the meaning of America's presence in Europe had been transformed, and all concerned had begun to realize that the new situation of limited sovereignty in a superpower world would bring unprecedented resentments, and would require a different sort of opinion management (this was one of the many purposes of NATO and Atlanticism). Although not studied as such at the time, the years of the cold war were also readily identifiable as a period when a new equilibrium between Americanization and anti-Americanism had to be constructed, not least because the eager adoption of an American-style standard of living by many sections of European society failed to silence the strident rejection by others of the United States' conduct in international affairs, first in the cold war and then in the Third World.[14]

In this way a fourth historical source of antagonism—Washington's foreign policy—was added to imagery, shared experience, and modernization pressure as driving forces of anti-Americanism. Henceforth, the specific expressions of the phenomenon would usually be composed of some if not all of these elements. In the France of the 1950s, notes Richard Kuisel, "foreign policy acted as a volatile variable that caused abrupt swings in popular appreciation of the United States while raising the specter of foreign domination." In fact, a comprehensive fear of hegemony began to haunt the French during the first postwar decade. Up to a quarter of interviewees in opinion polls (but especially those on the militant left) expressed "negative feelings that ranged from apprehension or irritation to antipathy and dislike."[15]

In Italy a more contradictory set of forces was at work in these years. The "political anti-Americanism of the Left coexisted with an undying, though now more discriminating, passion for American culture," comments Alessandro Portelli. This the rebellious new generations of the late 1950s and 1960s came to see as a source of inspiration in their defiance of traditional mores and patterns of authority. But the right also felt heartened and threatened simultaneously:

> … the same forces which were turning Italy into a political satellite of the United States were also vociferously worried about the invasion of American cultural artifacts, undermining our humanistic civilization and our classical culture—as well as our rural, Catholic way of life.[16]

The Vietnam War was the crucial factor that transformed the role of foreign policy in European anti-Americanism. The growing demand of public opinion to condemn official U.S. behavior for its ruthlessness, arrogance, and ideological absolutism was accompanied by an awareness that American society was deeply split on the war, and that the more Washington administrations insisted on the ideological stakes in Vietnam, the more America's *credibility* (key word of the era) as a model society and set of values was compromised. Tracing the rise through the Vietnam years of a new conception of American "imperialism" in Dutch opinion—in liberal and denominational circles as well as on the left—Rob Kroes notes that the experience left a lasting residue of pacifism and disaffection from

U.S. security policy in that society. Yet it did foster admiration for America's capacity to express an effective oppositional culture in a time of crisis.[17]

The Euromissiles Crisis and the End of the Cold War

The 1980s resembled the decade of the 1960s in that both periods saw official concern over anti-Americanism reach exceptional heights on both sides of the Atlantic. Consciousness of this parallel may well have been one of the impulses feeding the new intellectual urge to try to approach the issue afresh with "dispassionate exactitude."[18] A group of French scholars insisted that the "Vietnam syndrome" in their nation's anti-Americanism was by that time long gone, while France's military-strategic independence–"that indisputable triumph of Gaullism"–insulated it very beneficially from the agonized "Euromissiles" debate going on elsewhere in those years.[19] The group, used to experimenting at the time with the concept of "collective mentality," concluded that the phenomenon was an expression of "passion, instinct, irrationality," and hence a sort of "psychopathology," fostered in part by the Americans themselves out of Tocquevillean insecurity and narcissism. Fitful and exceptional compared to the nation's historic enmities with the English and then with the Germans, French anti-Americanism was not a serious cultural phenomenon.[20]

But while historians and sociologists outside France began to ponder the implications of these judgments, politicians and diplomats insisted that in times of international tension and crisis like the mid-1980s cultural preoccupations were swept aside, and attacks were once more aimed directly at American foreign policy and at all the forces supposedly driving it. As the U.S. ambassador in London wrote in early 1987:

> America the violent, America the crass, America the inept have all become everyday images in Europe. Professors at prestigious universities and writers in influential journals, creative artists and prominent politicians embellish and transmit the message....
>
> Little wonder then that opinion polls in Western Europe often indicate a low regard for American policies and a deep suspicion of American motives.[21]

Against the background of the old Euromissiles dispute, the new Reagan militancy in the East-West confrontation, U.S. rearmament, the "Star Wars" project, the 1986 attack on Libya, and other episodes, peace movements swelled in Western Europe. The full repertory of criticism, complaint, and denunciation that had developed over two centuries was consciously deployed to express the sense of fear and impotence felt by many in the Old World (particularly in West Germany). Within the State Department anxious paper-writers worried that "the latest swell of anti-Americanism in various parts of Europe may surpass even that of the Vietnam War era," and that "there is a definite trend in the willingness of Europeans to equate morally the two superpowers."[22] In response, faithful allies in such countries as Britain offered comprehensive programs of action to fight the threat.[23]

Then, miraculously, within less than five years, all this sentiment would be defused and forgotten. Following the collapse of the historic Soviet enemy, the old connections based on security and Atlanticism quickly began to fade in significance, reappearing in the public eye only in times of crisis such as the Gulf War and the Bosnian conflict. On what authority, then—besides history—might America's now uncontested superpower status and leadership function rest? In a sense, the old imperial questions of power and the resentments it inevitably gives rise to, of success and the envy it always provokes, not only persisted but had become more obvious. However, it was the long-term role of the United States as creator and seller of uniquely appealing models and myths that gradually began to attract attention once again. No longer held up as a society to be emulated or reviled, no longer organizing the now-uniting-now-dividing common response to the "Red Threat," the question of American hegemony gradually reappeared after the end of the cold war in its 1920s form. By the mid-1990s, the modernization challenge was back, dividing the Europeans and evoking in some of them—opinion-makers, writers, commentators, "intellectuals"—many of the Old World's most characteristic anti-Americanist reflexes.

The Patterns of Intellectual Anti-Americanism

Defenders of Civilization

As already seen, the original interwar anti-Americanism, articulated by critics of the new modernity, was an expression of aristocratic disdain for the emerging realities of mass-produced popular culture. Such attitudes persisted at the highest levels of society in some countries like Britain until at least the mid-1950s. Relatively mild examples of anti-Americanism are found in a 1951 essay collection, edited by the philosopher Bertrand Russell, on the impact of American culture in Europe. The Anglo-American historian J. E. Morpurgo, for instance, took up the attack on Hollywood, accusing the industry of having reinvented and amplified the most decadent aspects of traditional European culture, Americanizing hedonism and self-indulgence in order to retransmit them as new forms of mass shared experience, easy to acquire, easy to enjoy.[24] In the early 1920s, this elite outlook had ensured the rejection of the American model of commercial radio at the time of the BBC's foundation. During the debate on the introduction of privately run commercial television in 1956–Britain being the first nation in Europe to make this choice–its continuing influence was crucial in guaranteeing that the American experience in this field would *not* be emulated.[25]

But the cold war gave birth to a much sharper, more ideological critique of the United States and its works, expressed primarily by militant left-wing sources. The Italy of the 1950s, for example, produced Pier Paolo Pasolini, a violent denouncer of the era's new conjunction of cosmic fear and hedonistic materialism, who combined elements from Catholic ethics and communist propaganda in his own highly personalized rhetoric. Pasolini's contribution to the 1963 television documentary film *Anger*, on the fear of atomic war, declaimed at one point, against a background of the finale of the 1956 Republican convention: "When the classical world has finally been worn out, when all the artisans and peasants have died out, when industry has set up an unstoppable cycle of production and consumption, then history will have ended for us."

In a mirror-like contribution from the far right to the same film, Giovanni Guareschi, author of the *Don Camillo* comedies, developed his own condemnation of the "lonely crowd" and the "live now, pay later" mentality. Over pictures of violence at a rock 'n' roll concert in France, Guareschi concluded: "The frantic search for material goods, the lack of faith in the future, the disintegration of the family, these are the roots of our discontent and anguish."[26] Shortly afterwards, in an interview with *Le Monde*, the left-wing political scientist Maurice Duverger dissociated himself from what he called the fashionable, idiotic anti-Americanism of the time. But, he insisted, "the domination of the American economy, the invasion of the American mentality–all that is very dangerous."[27]

Today's historians explain reactions such as these in terms of the role politicians, opinion-leaders, and intellectuals (in particular) have traditionally assigned themselves as the mediators and explainers of novelty, as the definers of acceptable modernity in each local context. Conserving the "fundamentals" of culture and identity in this way, say the British critics David Morley and Kevin Robbins, "… is about sustaining cultural boundaries and boundedness. To belong in this way is to protect exclusive, and therefore, excluding, identities

urge to annihilation are part of the American sub-culture, the negative side of the national and imperial history of that democracy."[36]

But the Gulf moment soon passed away, and with the social democratic left in Europe relieved by the double victory of Bill Clinton, the residual undertow of anti-Americanism most noticeable in the mid-1990s was more likely than not to be radically conservative in origin. Outside Germany, figures such as Le Pen in France (but not the *LePenistes*), Enoch Powell in Britain, the ex-Communist writer Saverio Vertone in Italy all could be found expressing varieties of criticism normally associated with the principal elements of the "anti-Americanist" tradition.[37]

The Question of Power

The Forms of Power

Following Secretary of State James Baker's declaration of 1989, after the fall of the Berlin Wall, the political leaders of the United States began to assert that "America is a European power," and they found no resistance to this claim, which had never been stated so boldly in the era of the cold war. By the mid-1990s the U.S. power that most Europeans were obliged to come to terms with were the local manifestations of America's unique, unflagging capacity to invent, produce, and distribute mass culture. U.S. films and television programming occupied 80 to 90 percent of European markets; the McDonald's empire planned to open eighty franchises per year in France alone;[38] Blockbuster Video and Foot Locker shoe stores (with their definition in English) were springing up in every city center; the "colonization of the subconscious"–a famous quote from the 1975 Wim Wenders film *Kings of the Road*–was visible in the presence of American icons throughout European car, food, and fashion ads.

From its financial and telecom services (expanding everywhere), to the EuroDisney theme park (1992), *Jurassic Park* (1993), Windows '95 and the "Coke Olympics" (1996), the "American challenge"–first identified as a new form of threat by the glamorous French media entrepreneur Servan Schreiber in 1967–was returning with renewed vigor. Servan Schreiber's pioneering and far-sighted bestseller denounced what he saw predominantly as business imperialism: the drive of the biggest U.S. corporations to set up bases in the member states of the European Economic Community, taking advantage of the new integration drive to outperform local competitors and overwhelm national markets and national economies.[39] As elements of this process reappeared impressively in the wake of the Single

European Act of 1992 and the Maastricht Treaty,[40] the institutions and leaders of the renamed European Union struggled to respond. Compared to 1967, though, the stakes seemed higher. With conflicts over communal, national, and supranational loyalties becoming ever more prominent in European politics, so the debate over the new American challenge encountered the rising wave of anxiety about the future of identities in the Old World, whether individual or collective. As a result, by the end of the twentieth century, explicit resistance to America took the form not so much of rejection of whatever the United States stood for, produced, or did, but of struggle against the perceived *inevitability* of the destiny of convergence and homogenization on the American pattern.

In the week before the U.S. presidential election of 1996, a new survey of French opinion on America was published by *Le Monde*. Entirely ignoring the aftereffects of the cold war and Washington's behavior in the international arena, the questions posed were limited to the old categories of imagery and America's modernizing impact on French popular culture. Negative sentiments prevailed now, and were seen to be on a rising trend from at least 1988, the date of an identical inquiry. *Le Monde*'s reporter commented:

> No matter that CNN is present in many public places, that young French people sport Nikes, jeans, and baseball hats, that New York is a top destination for French tourists, America as such provokes at best indifference rather than enthusiasm.... America's image deteriorates in parallel with the success of its popular culture in France.

No less than 70 percent of interviewees deplored the "excessive" cultural influence of the United States on their television screens; 59 percent felt likewise over the cinema. Yet the sample was unmoved by the penetration of the English language into their lives. Perversely repudiating their government's militancy over the question, 54 percent of the group saw nothing to be worried about. A rising concern, however, was American-style fast food: 30 percent judged its presence excessive, a figure up from 10 percent in 1988. French people were just as inclined to consume what America was offering as to deplore themselves for doing so—concluded *Le Monde*: "Hypocrisie ou sentiment de culpabilité?"[41]

Dependence and Defiance

Stanley Hoffmann's 1964 intuition that "(t)he more European societies become alike in their social structures and economic makeup, the more each national society seems to heighten its idiosyncrasies,"[42] had become, thirty years later, the focal point of a vast confrontation over identity, diversity, and convergence in which a part-real, part-imaginary United States often served as the supreme counterpoint against which each society sought to define its sense of itself and its future.[43]

This explains why, with each of the major Western European nations undergoing a fundamental identity crisis of some kind, their reactions to U.S. power and hegemony after the cold war focused so often on the mass culture challenge in their midst. Yet the behavior on display in Britain, Germany, France, and Italy could scarcely have been more diverse. Much of British political and media culture–"bemused by America, terrified of Europe" as the Royal Shakespeare Company was once described–seemed to seek as comfortable an accommodation with whatever the U.S. offered as could profitably be arranged. At the other extreme, as already seen, prominent German commentators raised ever higher the pitch of their hostility to America's alleged impact on their historical inheritance. For its part, France had by now developed a well-established tradition of cultural protectionism, based on the claim of the "exceptionalist" status of French civilization in European history beginning with the crowning of King Clovis in A.D. 996. The Italians, by contrast more open and relaxed, disputed whether fascism, communism, or Catholicism had done more to condition their national identity and their lack of what they saw as a healthy sense of patriotism. Their problems were thought to be entirely historical and internal: no blame was attached to America.[44]

Yet in Italy, too, radical conservatives denounced the Americanization of politics–particularly in the rise of the Berlusconi phenomenon–and conflict persisted over the allegedly noxious effects of the spread of the McDonald's fast-food network, and the meaning of Coca-Cola's ubiquity.[45] Although Coca-Cola continued to attract its share of scorn throughout Europe–a Glasgow writer accused the company of "attempting to hijack the festive season" when in 1995 it sponsored the city's Christmas lights[46]–its selection as a target for generalized abuse of American commercial intrusiveness was much diminished compared to the late 1940s, when in France and elsewhere it had been a *cause célèbre* in the great battles of the left against U.S. hegemony in all its forms.[47] To a lesser extent, this role had been imperceptibly imposed upon the McDonald's chain, which continued to find opposition to its presence from fashionable Hampstead in London to the banks of the Seine, from Florence to Cracow, opposition not directed at other hamburger vendors. The fact that conservative islanders were simultaneously resisting the "rape" of

Bermuda by the company demonstrated once again that left and right, intellectual and "lay," versions of modernist anti-Americanism continued to converge in ways that even extended Europe's attitudes to its old domains. The McDonald's experience also showed that relatively small symbols of American economic power, because of their visibility, ubiquity, and dynamism, were still the ones expected to bear the most disproportionate burden of the resentments felt by local citizens and consumers, who attempted to pit their influence against that of corporations once merely "multinational," now turned "global."[48]

Americanisms and Anti-Americanisms

In 1992 Paul Hollander, an author long based in America, offered the first comprehensive survey of international anti-Americanism, comparing it with the version he perceived to be historically prevalent in the United States itself. Hollander characterized the Western European expression of the phenomenon as "a blend of envy of American power, contempt for American culture, and apprehension about American military might and presence." The product of "a great variety of attitudes, beliefs and circumstances … it tends to acquire an irrational dynamic of its own that springs from the need of human beings to explain and reduce responsibility for the misfortunes in their lives."[49]

Heavy with moralistic denunciations of the mindsets, susceptibilities, rancors, and resentments seen to pervade European—especially intellectual—judgments on the United States, the book seemed to reflect the unhappiness of the mid-1980s era, rather than its time of production in 1992. Grievances definable as legitimate were unidentified in Hollander's analysis. Attitudes, it appeared, would only be allowed to acquire the features of a "rational dynamic" when they conformed to America's moral principles and perceived practices. The causal connections between the "circumstances" and the shameful "beliefs" remained unexplained.

More perceptive observers had no difficulty in demonstrating how underlying contradictions in the workings of the transatlantic power relationship could produce conflicting sentiments in public opinion. The American political scientist Andrei Markovits pointed to the unintended effects of American monetary policy in Germany's recent history. He noted that in an exported-oriented economy like Germany's, for instance, the dollar, whether too high or too low, was universally blamed for the nation's economic ills, and that this attitude too fed anti-American sentiment. "Thus, as in so many aspects of America's presence in West German reality," wrote Markovits in

1989, "the United States remains betwixt and between: While still needed it becomes increasingly unwanted."[50]

Repeatedly throughout the century, critics denouncing the social uniformity and standardization they perceived reflected the pressure of American-inspired technological innovation, another pattern of grievance that had established itself in the 1920s and tended to reappear in subsequent decades in cycles of unpredictable duration and intensity.[51] In antithesis, a French observer commented in 1958, "the champions of diversity like to invoke, in their *apologia* for Europe, its cathedrals [that "trump card" of anti-Americanism], the old masters of Flanders and Umbria, Purcell or Palestrina, Kant or Saint Theresa d'Avila."[52] Forty years later, antiquarianism–the presentation of the European alternative as historical museum or theme park–had gone decisively out of fashion. Diversity's champions, however, were more alert than ever, and they now included American intellectuals and opinion-makers who could not be accused of patronizing nostalgia or romanticism, or of inciting scorn for their native land.[53]

Certainly the Europeans could not match the worldwide spread of Hollywood, satellite television, the computer revolution as symbolized by the Internet and the Microsoft empire, or the combination of commercial and technological power that promised to fuse computer and telecommunications technology under the auspices of global combines controlled from America. These challenges of the 1990s renewed ancient feelings of impotence that belied the denunciations of "irrationality" and "psychopathology" so often applied to alleged anti-Americanism.

The classical version of that phenomenon had always reflected a resentment of the *combined, cumulative* effect of America's capacity to project its power in so many ways at any given time, and its unflagging ability to invent new opportunities to do so according to circumstances. An exemplary case of this latter mechanism at work in the 1990s was the appearance of the reality and myth of the CNN worldwide television network, alongside the projection of America's military power at the time of the Gulf War of 1991. Some European observers reacted by denouncing what they saw as a totally standardized, supra-national "picture-producing system."[54]

Ubiquity versus intrusiveness, globalism versus homogenization; hegemony versus hubris: however structured, the power question is inescapable in any historical discussion of anti-Americanism, just as it has become in political and sociological treatments. Yet without the preceding baggage of images and stereotypes, the accompanying experience of world wars and cold wars, or the development of an exceptional modernizing dynamism, the ascendancy of U.S. power would never have provoked or attracted the resentments, envies, and antagonisms that anti-Americanism has traditionally expressed. Talking of a "cultural backlash" visible in the world today against America's historic urge to present itself as a nation with a missionary destiny, Samuel P. Huntington notes: "What is universalism to the West is imperialism to the rest." Even within the familiar confines of the transatlantic relationship, the same association between sentiments, ideas, and force has often been at work in the course of Europe's American century.[55]

Notes

1. Seymour Martin Lipset, *American Exceptionalism* (New York, 1996), 31.
2. Herbert J. Spiro, "Anti-Americanism in Western Europe," *Annals of the American Academy of Political Science* (May 1988): 122.
3. Marie-France Toinet, "French Pique and *Piques Françaises*," in ibid., 137; see Richard Kuisel, *Seducing the French: The Dilemma of Americanization* (Berkeley, 1993), chapter 1.
4. J. B. Priestley, "Who Is Anti-American?"(1957), in *Essays of Five Decades* (London, 1969).
5. Spiro, "Anti-Americanism," 124.
6. P. P. D'Attorre, "Sogno americano e mito sovietico nell'Italia contemporanea," in *Nemici per la Pelle*, ed. D'Attorre (Milan, 1991), 16–18.
7. H. G. Wells, in *The Future in America* (New York, 1906), was among the first to suggest in what ways America's present was likely to signal Europe's future social development.
8. C. Vann Woodward, *The Old World's New World* (New York, 1991), 80.
9. Kissinger's masterly treatment of Wilson is to be found in his *Diplomacy* (London, 1995), chapter 2; citation at 44.
10. D. L. Le Mahieu, *A Culture for Democracy: Mass Communication and the Cultivated Mind in Britain between the Wars* (Oxford, 1988); David Strauss, *Menace in the West: The Rise of French Anti-Americanism in Modern Times* (Westport, Conn., 1978) concentrates on the years 1917–32; M. Nacci, *L' anti-americanismo in Italia negli anni trenta* (Turin, 1989); see Emilio Gentile, "Impending Modernity: Fascism and the Ambivalent Image of the United States," *Journal of Contemporary History* 28 (1993).
11. The classic account is Frank G. Costigliola, *Awkward Dominion: American Political, Economic and Cultural Relations with Europe 1919–1933* (Ithaca, 1984).
12. An outstanding guide to the French case is the 1986 collection *L'Amérique dans les têtes: Un siècle de fascinations et d'aversions*, ed. Denis Lacorne, Jacques Rupnik, and Marie-France Toinet (Paris, 1986; proceedings of the Paris conference of December 1984).
13. For the French experience, see Kuisel, *Seducing the French*, 24–25.
14. See Stanley Hoffmann, "Europe's Identity Crisis: Between the Past and America" (1964), in Hoffmann, *The European Sisyphus: Essays on Europe 1964–1994* (Boulder, Colo., 1995), in particular 29; this is one of themes of Ellwood, *Rebuilding Europe: Western Europe, America and Postwar Reconstruction* (London, 1992), chapter 12.

15. Kuisel, *Seducing the French*, chapter 2; citations at 30, 31.
16. A. Portelli, "The Transatlantic Jeremiad: American Mass Culture and Counter-culture and Opposition Culture in Italy," in *Cultural Transmissions and Receptions: American Mass Culture in Europe*, ed. R. Kroes et al. (Amsterdam, 1993), 129.
17. Rob Kroes, "The Great Satan versus the Evil Empire: Anti-Americanism in the Netherlands," in *Anti-Americanism in Europe*, ed. R. Kroes and M. Van Rossem (Amsterdam, 1986), 34–35.
18. M. Cunliffe, "The Anatomy of Anti-Americanism," in ibid., 20.
19. Denis Lacorne and Jacques Rupnik, "La France saisie par l'Amérique," in *L'Amérique dans les têtes*, 16.
20. André Kaspi, "En guise de conclusion," in ibid.
21. Charles Price, "The Risks for Europe in Anti-American Sentiment," *The Guardian*, 22 March 1987.
22. Kenneth Dillon et al., "Anti-Americanism in Europe: An Old Problem Takes Ominous New Shape," unpublished paper, n.d., but probably Spring 1987. I am grateful to Dr. Stephen Low of the Association for Diplomatic Studies and Training for showing me this paper.
23. J. P. Shea, *Countering Anti-Americanism* (London, 1986).
24. J. E. Morpurgo, "Hollywood: America's Voice," in *The Impact of America on European Culture*, ed. Bertrand Russell (Boston, 1951).
25. Valeria Camporesi, "There Are No Kangaroos in Kent: The American 'Model' and the Introduction of Commercial Television in Britain, 1940–1954," in *Hollywood in Europe: Experiences of a Cultural Hegemony*, ed. D. W. Ellwood and R. Kroes (Amsterdam, 1994).
26. P. P. Pasolini and G. Guareschi, *La Rabbia,* Rome, 1963; retransmitted by RAI 3, 29 May 1992.
27. Cited in R. Kuisel, *Seducing the French*, 191.
28. Cited in Duncan Petrie, "Introduction: Change and Cinematic Representation in Modern Europe," in *Screening Europe: Image and Identity in Contemporary European Cinema*, ed. D. Petrie (London, 1992), 12.
29. Ellwood, "Introduction: Historical Methods and Approaches," in *Hollywood in Europe*, 2–18.
30. Thomas Elsaesser, "German Postwar Cinema and Hollywood," in ibid., 287–89; on *Io e il Duce, La Stampa*, 17 April 1985; *Corriere della Sera*, 23 April 1985.
31. *La Stampa*, 19 May 1993.
32. *International Herald Tribune*, 30 May 1994.
33. Michael Ermarth, "German Unification as Self-Inflicted Americanization: Critical Views on the Course of Contemporary Development," unpublished paper, 1.
34. The nature of this search and its relationship to present-day debates over German identity is effectively explained in Dieter Oberndörfer, "Germany's Liberal Democracy in the Making–The Challenge of Identity," Johns Hopkins University Bologna Center, Occasional Paper no. 3, November 1996.
35. *Washington Post/Guardian Weekly*, 3 February 1991.
36. *Il Manifesto*, 16 February 1991; this far-left daily more than doubled its sales during the Gulf War.
37. Comments on Le Pen and his followers in *Le Monde*, 30 October 1996; Powell cited in *The Economist*, 26 February 1994; Saverio Vertone, *La trascendenza dell'ombelico* (Milan, 1994), chapter 2.
38. Fast-food case cited in "Europe on the Road," Channel 4 (GB), 3 August 1996.
39. J. J. Servan Schreiber, *Le défi américain* (Paris, 1967), U.S. edition, *The American Challenge* (New York, 1969).

40. *Business Week,* 7 October 1996.

41. Alain Frachon, "L'image des Etats-Unis ne cesse de se dégrader en France," *Le Monde,* 31 October 1996.

42. Hoffmann, "Europe's Identity Crisis," 18.

43. This is what C. Vann Woodward calls America's function as the "Silver Screen in the West"; *The Old World's New World,* chapter 2.

44. I have treated these cases in more detail in "The American Challenge Renewed: U.S. Cultural Power and Europe's Identity Debates," *Brown Journal of World Affairs* (Winter/Spring 1996–97).

45. The leading conservative writer Marcello Veneziani believed that left and right had embraced "Americanization" as a solution to their ideological bankruptcy after the end of the cold war: "Volevate l'America," *Il Messagero,* 16 April 1996.

46. Janice Forsyth, *The Scotsman,* 23 December 1995.

47. Richard Kuisel dedicates an entire chapter to the Coca-Cola affair in his *Seducing the French,* chapter 3.

48. Bermuda case in *The Independent,* 13 March 1996.

49. P. Hollander, *Anti-Americanism: Critiques at Home and Abroad 1965–1990* (New York, 1992), chapter 8; citations at 369, 410.

50. Andrei S. Markovits, "Anti-Americanism and the Struggle for a West German Identity," in *The Federal Republic of Germany at Forty,* ed. Peter H. Merkl (New York, 1989), 50–51.

51. Contemporary examples include reference in an interview with Sir I. Berlin, *New York Review of Books,* 21 November 1991; Portelli, "The Transatlantic Jeremiad," 134; German case of 1920s analyzed in Mary Nolan, *Visions of Modernity: American Business and the Modernization of Germany* (New York, 1994), especially chapter 6; Gramsci might be chargeable with anti-Americanism for his famous essay on "Fordism and Americanism," written between 1929 and 1933. But the analysis is probably too narrowly focused on attacking the European ruling classes to attract the full condemnation; English edition *Antonio Gramsci: Selections from the Prison Notebooks,* ed. Q. Hoare and G. Nowell Smith (New York, 1971).

52. Léo Moulin, "Anti-Americanism in Europe: A Psychoanalysis," *Orbis* (Winter 1958): 455.

53. James Fallows, "The Information Revolution: New Strains for Europe, America, Asia," *International Herald Tribune,* 16 May 1994.

54. Interview with leading French media and history specialist Marc Ferro in *Le Monde,* 10–11 February 1991.

55. S. P. Huntington, "The West: Unique, Not Universal," *Foreign Affairs* (November/December 1996): 40.

– *Three* –

SURFACE ABOVE ALL?

American Influence on Japanese Urban Space

Botond Bognar

To most short-term Western visitors of Japan, Japanese cities, and most especially Tokyo, seem profoundly Westernized or, more precisely, Americanized. Indeed, in many respects Japanese cities are as modern as their counterparts in the United States or anywhere else in the First World and carry most attributes of a highly developed contemporary urban culture. Japan is not only one of the most urbanized countries, but also one of the most advanced consumer societies, with cities offering the same high-quality products, facilities, and services as in New York, Chicago, London, or Paris. For example, today in Japan one finds the same brand-name and designer stores, supermarkets, and mega-malls as in the States, and the increasingly large public atria in corporate office complexes appear as frequently as in the United States.

Moreover, in Japan there are a growing number of high-rise buildings and skyscrapers that make certain urban districts, such as Shinjuku in Tokyo, reminiscent of New York (see Fig. 3.1). Advertisements, billboards, and signs flooding Japanese cities are, more often than not, also rendered in English, and many cultural institutions are similar to those in the United States. Golf and baseball are as popular, and perhaps even more so, as in the States. Movie theaters and playhouses feature the latest Hollywood films and

FIGURE **3.1** Shinjuku high-rise buildings, which evoke the New York City skyline. (Photo: Botond Bognar)

Broadway shows; museums and concert halls present the same world-class events as New York's Museum of Modern Art or Carnegie Hall. For better or for worse, Japanese urban life and culture are influenced by the "same" commercial culture that characterizes much of American cities today. To mention but the most obvious ones, McDonald's, Burger King, Dunkin' Donuts, Kentucky Fried Chicken, Baskin-Robbins, and other fast-food outlets dominate the Japanese urbanscape more than in America; indeed the first Disneyland outside the United States was built in Japan. The presence of these commercial enterprises appears to leave no question about the degree to which the Japanese cultural and urban landscape has been influenced by its American counterpart. Yet, at closer investigation, the extent and nature of the "Americanization" of Japan's urbanscape turns out to be a much more complex issue than indicated by hurriedly drawn first impressions.

* * *

Today the United States and Japan, the two most powerful economies in the world, depend on each other to a large extent. A smoothly functioning and friendly relationship between the two countries is essential for the progress not only of the two, but also of the rest of the world. Beyond close political and trade relations, there is a significant and growing interaction between the two cultures. In our postmodern age of information and global economy this is not surprising, but it should be noted that such interactions have been uneven; the disparity between Japan and the United States in this regard, although diminishing, continues to prevail even today. Even if one considers the popularity of Japonism (that is, the initial, though often merely superficial, impact of Japanese art and architecture on the United States and Europe after Japan's opening to the West in the mid-nineteenth century) and the West's continued fascination with the remote and "esoteric" Orient, it is safe to say that Japanese culture has been more extensively shaped by its American counterpart than vice versa.[1] If it is true that Japan exports far more products and manufactured goods than it imports, then it is also true that Japan imports vastly more information about or from the United States than the other way round.[2]

While maintaining a friendly relationship remains the cornerstone of both Japan's and the United States' foreign policies, there have been ongoing frictions that have marred or at least problematized their relationship throughout the years. Interestingly enough, such frictions today are more pronounced within the spheres of economy, trade, and politics than that of culture, even though these conflicts actually often stem from prevailing cultural and social differences. American cultural influence on Japan and Japanese urban space historically has also been tied to American political interests. Americans have used this influence to facilitate Japan's postwar democratization, to secure Japan's assistance in combating communism in the Far East, and ultimately to establish the economic, political, and military presence of the United States as a dominant power in Asia. Yet Americans have also regarded Japan as a rival of the United States, particularly in its role as an economic superpower. This ambivalent, not to say paradoxical, relationship between Japan and the United States (and in many respects also between Japan and the West in general) is not new to the postwar world, but began when the two countries established their first official contact with each other about a century and a half ago.

Much of today's Japanese culture is derivative of or responds to American culture. These same complex processes have shaped, directly as well as indirectly, the quality of both Japanese architecture and urban space, that is to say, both the physical and nonphysical aspects of urban setting.[3]

Willingness to borrow and learn from other cultures has a long history in Japan. Prior to the country's encounter with the United States and the West in the mid-nineteenth century, Japanese culture had already been profoundly influenced and shaped by other Asian cultures. While Japan had never been occupied or colonized by foreign powers, and so was never forcibly subjected to the value systems and political will of others, the Japanese as an island nation actively sought contact with continental cultures and civilizations in order to enrich their own. During this proactive process that continued with varying intensity from the mid-sixth century until 1639 (when the country was closed to external influences), elements of foreign cultures–in this case, mainly Chinese and Korean–were imported into Japan and, after a time of coexistence with the native culture, were assimilated or "Japanized."[4] The reopening of the country in the nineteenth century witnessed the resumption of Japan's massive cultural importation, but this time the source was Western cultures and civilization. Among these, American–or more precisely Anglo-American–culture became the most important. Throughout the years, the American way of life has provided the Japanese with a model to emulate and has had a growing influence on Japan and on the quality of its urban space.

In fact, the modern era in Japan was launched with American "assistance" in the middle of the nineteenth century. Until that time, Japan, a feudal society, had been closed to the rest of the world for more than two hundred years. During the Edo Period (1603–1868), the ruling Tokugawa shogunate prohibited any contact with foreign countries or cultures for security reasons. Thus, except for a small trading post in Nagasaki port, where initially only Portuguese and then Dutch and Chinese traders could continue a very limited and controlled operation, Japan was an isolated country. This changed in 1853 when Commodore Matthew Perry, representing expanding American economic and political might, forced Japan through intimidation to open its gates once again to the rest of the world. This first encounter between the two countries was soon followed by the initiation of trade relations and the Japanese-American Treaty of Peace and Amity of 1854.[5]

The opening of the country and the subsequent Meiji Restoration in 1868 signaled the beginning of an unparalleled development in Japan that profoundly affected its society and radically altered the course of both its architecture and its urbanization. One of the first steps by the Meiji government toward a new urban policy was the transfer of Japan's capital from Kyoto to Edo, which was then re-named Tokyo (meaning "eastern capital") in 1868. As a result, Tokyo assumed the status of the premier Japanese city in the country, and increased its already major role in the history of Japan–and now of the world.[6]

During the second half of the nineteenth century, Japan embarked on the road of rapid and sweeping modernization of its economic, industrial, agricultural, educational, and political institutions and infrastructures. Modernization was, moreover, a strategy undertaken by the Meiji government to avoid colonization by Western powers. Yet Japan lacked experience and technological skill as well as experts and professionals to carry out this task; in order to build up the country's infrastructure and institutions, the government had to import professionals along with advanced technologies. Initially, foreign experts, technicians, engineers, scholars, and educators were invited to Japan to do the job. Foreigners arrived from many Western countries, including, most significantly, the United States. In order to modernize the country, Japan followed the example of advanced, industrialized Western countries; thus modernization in Japan became tantamount to Westernization. The United States helped initiate Japan's emergence into the ranks of major industrial powers, a status that the nation had already attained by the turn of the century. Such assistance from the United States continued with some interruptions—most importantly during World War II—when the two nations found themselves on the opposite sides of international conflicts.

The modernization of Japan could not adequately proceed, however, without substantial social transformation, which affected both the social system and urban infrastructure. Following the Meiji Restoration, the modernization of Japanese cities encouraged the growth of capitalism, which helped to undermine the feudal system. In the process, Tokyo became the "engine" of the reform movement and has remained so ever since. There was an urgent need for innumerable new types of urban facilities for government administration, production, commerce, transportation, and culture. A new type of urban model emerged as well, the precedent for which derived from Western examples, both European and American. In 1871, for example, the so-called Iwakura Mission—a large delegation led by the senior minister Tomomi Iwakura and consisting of numerous high-ranking members of the Meiji leadership—embarked on an eighteen-month tour of the United States and Europe to undertake a firsthand examination of Western society. Its goal was to achieve a better understanding of the requirements of economic life, especially factory production, the application of technology to industry and agriculture, and Western modes of mass transportation and communication. The delegation was impressed by the advanced planning and monumental qualities of the urban centers they visited, and upon returning home promoted similar planning initiatives for Tokyo. As a result,

Foreign Minister Kaoru Inoue invited the German architects Hermann Ende and Wilhelm Böckmann to design the new governmental district of Hibiya in central Tokyo. The ambitious and highly monumental plan of 1886 by Ende and Böckmann failed to materialize, however, when Inoue's political downfall in 1887 resulted in the cancellation of the initiative. Only two buildings of the planned urban reconstruction, the Ministry of Justice (1895) and the Supreme Court (1896), were completed, of which only the former stands today.

After the Iwakura Mission, an increasing number of Japanese were sent abroad to acquire training and expertise to be put to good use upon returning home. Study abroad became widespread and continued into the post-1945 era. Beginning in the Meiji (1868–1912) and the Taisho (1912–1926) periods, practically no major project could be started in Japan without first sending the persons in charge to foreign countries to research the Western precedents of the project at hand. One of the most prominent examples of this was the design and construction of the Parliament Building. With its commencement in 1909, delegations were sent to the United States and several European countries to study parliament architecture. The resulting eclectic complex in Tokyo, which still serves the Japanese Diet today, was finally completed after much controversy in 1936 (see Fig. 3.2).

FIGURE 3.2 Parliament Building in Tokyo, 1936. (Photo: Botond Bognar)

It is important to emphasize that, in the radical transformation of their country, the Japanese were not merely reluctant "warriors" but truly active participants and eager learners. Lagging behind the West by about one hundred years in just about every respect, Japan was hungry for Western knowledge, culture, and civilization, and this often meant a wholesale embrace of anything Western.[7]

Initially, the construction of new types of buildings, such as offices, banks, factories, and schools, that had not existed before in Japan were designed and supervised by foreigners, and materials necessary for their construction were often imported from abroad. By around the turn of the century, however, a new generation of Western-educated Japanese architects, spurred by the growing local industrial production, began to assume leadership from their American and European predecessors in the modernization of the country's construction and urban infrastructure. The importation of foreign expertise, especially in the field of technology, nevertheless continued and even intensified. Tokyo became the testing ground of Western ideas in urban design and architecture before they were implemented in the rest of the country.[8]

In architecture, the construction technology first employed in Japanese cities was masonry or brick technology; for example, in 1874 much of the newly developing Ginza area in Tokyo was built in red brick according to designs of the British civil engineer James T. Waters. Waters introduced not only a new construction technology to Japan, but also a form of Western urbanism, insofar as his gaslight- and tree-lined streets strongly reflected the character of Regent Street in London and the Rue de Rivoli in Paris. While the concept of such streets survived and developed further in Japanese cities thereafter, brick technology soon proved to be unsuitable for the island nation, which is prone to frequent earthquakes and fires.

Accordingly, by around the turn of the century, first concrete and later steel technologies were imported, this time primarily from the United States, where the famous so-called Chicago School of Architecture, responsible for the completion of the first skyscrapers, developed the steel frame system for high-rise construction. The well-known American design firm McKim, Mead and White worked on these neoclassical buildings. In this architectural style, technologically advanced mechanical and structural systems, such as the steel frame, were "dressed" in historically inspired façades and decoration, often of European origin. Good examples of this are works by Kingo Tatsuno (1854–1919), a disciple of Josiah Conder, including his Bank of Japan (1896) in Tokyo (see Fig. 3.3), and others by Toshikata Sano, especially his Maruzen Bookstore Building (1909),

FIGURE 3.3 Bank of Japan, Tokyo. Architect: Kingo Tatsuno, 1895.
(Photo: Botond Bognar)

also in Tokyo, which combined American technology with eclectic European styling.

Eventually, the rationality of the new technologies yielded a less historicizing architecture and produced types of building that were entirely novel in Japan. The Marunouchi Building (1923) in Tokyo was the first full-fledged office building in the country. Although it was drawn up by the real estate department of the Mitsubishi Company, the contractor for this large project was the American Fuller Company of Chicago, which also provided its own patented reinforced concrete technology for the construction. Another example is the design and construction of the Sumitomo Head Office and Bank Building in Osaka (1926). Commencing in 1916, this major project by the Sumitomo Eizen Design Office utilized the reinforcing steel frame construction, for which many components and structural elements had to be imported—again from the United States. In fact, some of the structural design for the project was done in Chicago, with the assistance of American experts, by one of the building's Japanese architects, Kenzo Takegoshi, and the structural engineer Miyahiko Ikeda.[9]

For the construction of high-rise buildings, such as the Marunouchi and Sumitomo, the introduction of the elevator and new mechanical systems was a precondition. Such equipment also was imported initially from the United States, where the Otis Company, developer of the modern elevator, revolutionized the fields of both architecture and urbanism. Still, there were limits to the ability of Japanese architects to transfer such technology to Japan. The Sumitomo complex in Osaka, for example, was originally designed as a seven-story structure, but after the devastating 1923 earthquake in Tokyo, the height was reduced to five stories for reasons of safety. The much larger Marunouchi Building was built only eight stories high.

This indicates that the adoption of Western technologies did not necessarily result in high-rise structures comparable to their American counterparts. In Japan, the importation of new, foreign technologies, such as the steel frame, made the first multistory buildings possible and assured against disaster in the event of unpredictable tremors. American technology also provided the means for launching new types of urban buildings, among which the large office building was perhaps the most important. Patterned after American models, these constructions began to alter the urbanscape of Japanese cities in substantial ways by the 1920s. With a total floor area of 60,000 square meters, the Marunouchi Building was not only the largest structure at the time of its completion, but also the first really modern urban complex in Japan—outfitted with the most advanced mechanical equipment and boasting a complete line of shops and other kinds of facilities, such as restaurants and an auditorium on its first and second floors.

The range of commercial services in one structure was perhaps one of the reasons that this building attracted more interest among Japanese professionals than Frank Lloyd Wright's new Imperial Hotel (see Fig. 3.4), which opened in Tokyo in 1923, the same year as the Marunouchi Building. Wright was commissioned in 1911 to design the hotel, and invited to Japan in 1913. By this time Wright had considerable knowledge about Japan since he had already visited the country in 1905, and had become an avid collector of Japanese art, particularly woodblock prints (*ukiyo-e*). He also admired traditional Japanese architecture, which he had first been exposed to at the 1893 World's Columbian Exposition in Chicago, where a replica of the famous Phoenix Pavilion of the Byodo-in Temple (1053) in Uji, Kyoto, was part of the Japanese exhibition. He also viewed a replica of Kyoto's famous Golden Pavilion (1397) at the 1904 Louisiana Purchase Exposition in St. Louis. The subsequent Japanese influence on Wright's design is clearly manifested in the horizontal disposition, the multiple large overhanging roofs, the ornamental patterns, the free-flowing spaces, and the intimate relationship with nature characteristic of his so-called Prairie Houses from around the turn of the century, one of the best representatives of which is the Robie House (1909) in Chicago.

FIGURE 3.4 Tokyo Imperial Hotel. Architect: Frank Lloyd Wright, 1923. (Photo: Botond Bognar)

Note: The hotel was demolished in 1968; its central part, with the lobby, was reconstructed in 1985 in Meiji-mura, a village museum near Inuyama, Aichi Prefecture, where it now stands among the rolling hills of the Japanese countryside.

Based on his experiences with and interpretations of Japan, Wright nurtured a romantic, even exotic, image of this Far Eastern country. Wright's preoccupation with Japanese design, combined with his devotion to richly adorned Mayan-style houses in Los Angeles, his Eldorado visions in architecture, and his unfolding idea of the Broad-acre City, an urban model similar to contemporary suburbia, were evident in his Imperial Hotel design.[10] The resulting two-story building had a horizontal thrust, was built in stone with reinforced concrete elements and a "floating" foundation on piles commonly used in the States, and was excessively embellished with motifs that Wright considered of Japanese origin.

Scandalously over budget, the hotel was officially opened on September 1, the very day the 1923 earthquake hit Tokyo. The hotel was one of the few structures to survive the jolt and subsequent fires due to its reinforced concrete technology. This feature, rather than its architectural design or style, made the building a celebrity. As a result, the engineering–particularly the earthquake-proof reinforced concrete technology embodied in it–was appreciated, and boosted the strongly engineering-oriented faction of Japanese architects.

By contrast, the aesthetics of Wright's architecture and his handling of the project proved to be too idiosyncratic and alien to the Japanese people and to Japanese architectural traditions. Those aspects invited much criticism, and Wright's work had little significant lasting impact on the evolution of modern Japanese architecture and urbanism. As Antonin Raymond, Wright's assistant in Japan in 1919, remarked about the hotel: "[The] design had nothing in common with Japan, its climate, its traditions, its people and its culture.... [Wright's] thoughts were entirely concentrated on the expression of his own personal imaginings."[11]

Raymond–who broke with Wright in 1920, one year after joining him to work on the Imperial Hotel–immediately established an office in Tokyo (in addition to his New York office) and, working in Japan until his death in 1976, proved ultimately to be more influential than his early mentor. Beginning in the early 1920s, he promoted a line of "American" design, which was closer to Le Corbusier's modernism than to Wright's work. Thus, although Raymond was to blend Japanese elements into his designs later on, he first forwarded the cause of international modern architecture in Japan that was both European and American in origin. He also helped train numerous modern Japanese architects, among them such future masters as Junzo Sakakura (1904–1969) and Kunio Maekawa (1905–1986), who worked in his office at different times in the 1930s.[12] Raymond also played a significant role in the development of early postwar architecture in Japan, and built the Tokyo headquarters of the American Reader's Digest Publishing Company in 1951. The two-story building was designed according to the latest American standards with the most advanced materials, technologies, and mechanical equipment, such as steel, glass, and glass block, as well as central heating, air conditioning, and fluorescent lighting. The first of its kind in Japan, the building attracted the attention of Japanese architects and engineers and launched a new direction in modern urban complexes in Japan.

Paradoxically, Wright along with other visiting foreign architects in Japan, including Raymond and particularly the German Bruno Taut (1880–1938), had another kind of influence: they helped the Japanese "rediscover" their own traditional architecture, which in the frenzy of rapid modernization was either forgotten or discounted as something irrelevant to the future. Thus, Western architects were instrumental in rekindling a sense of appreciation in the Japanese for their own historical architectural traditions.

The influence of these architects coincided with new intellectual developments in Japan that marked a turn away from seemingly unconditional Westernization. During the political uncertainties of the 1920s and 1930s, there emerged a growing sentiment in some academic architectural circles to advocate a combination of "Western learning with Japanese spirit" (*wakonyosai*)–that is, the intent to continue the acquisition of the technological and engineering prowess of the West, while adhering to the aesthetic values and sensibilities of Japanese culture. A prominent representative of this ideology was Toshikata Sano. His followers were engineering-oriented architects who became leaders in universities, industrial schools, and even the Architect Association. Yet the patriotic spirit of *wakonyosai* spread beyond this circle of engineering oriented architects; most Japanese architects of the 1930s espoused similar, if not particularly well-defined, ideas.[13] The first "movement" of resistance to wholesale modernization cum Westernization, and hence to Americanization, was thus in ideological conflict with the budding movement of Japanese modern architecture, which at this time drew more inspiration from international than domestic sources.

This traditionalism, which favored a literary or formal return to Japanese or other Asian architectural styles, received a substantial boost during the mid- to late 1930s, when increasingly chauvinistic and militaristic governmental circles demanded for political reasons that major new structures be designed in a manifestly "Oriental" or pan-Asian style. Many public projects were designed with large, tiled, "traditional" roofs yielding what has become known as Imperial Crown style (*teikan-yoshiki*). Such architectural and urban complexes of Imperial Crown style were constructed with the latest Western technologies and outfitted with modern mechanical equipment, but then were "dressed" to meet the official requirement. Despite such formal, if only superficial, styling and a tendency toward monumentality, many of these buildings represented remarkable architectural qualities. Hitoshi Watanabe's (1887–1973) Tokyo Imperial Museum in Ueno (1937) and Daiichi Seimei Insurance Building in Tokyo (1938) are emblematic of this architecture.

* * *

Japan's loss in the Pacific War in 1945 meant another significant American "impact"–albeit a destructive one–on Japanese urbanism. American firebombings of Tokyo and other major cities, along with the two atomic bombs dropped on Hiroshima and Nagasaki, dealt a devastating blow to both the population and the infrastructure of

most urban areas in Japan. In Tokyo the extent of damage far surpassed that caused by the Great Kanto Earthquake of 1923: more
than 710,000 homes (about 50 percent of all residences) and approximately 96,000 people perished, with an additional 71,000 people
missing or seriously injured. Material reconstruction and the resumption of urban life commenced and progressed under American
occupation.[14] Although the Americans created and enforced entirely
new conditions for political and social institutions in Japan, they did
not directly intervene in the process or program of (re)urbanization.
In rebuilding Japan as a new, democratic society, the Japanese were
"free" to engineer the fate of their cities. Grand plans, such as the
War Damage Rehabilitation Plan (1945) and the National Capital
Region Development Plan (1955) were drawn up.[15] Aimed as much
at rebuilding as at redesigning cities, these plans adhered to Western
or American models.

Implementation of these plans, not unlike the Earthquake Reconstruction Plan of about two decades earlier,[16] was delayed due
to excessive costs, and in the end was only partially carried out.
Since these postwar plans failed to satisfy the urgent need for shel-
ter of most of the population, citizens were prompted to rebuild
their homes themselves. The overall result was that most cities, first
and foremost Tokyo, were rebuilt with their prewar, largely Edo
Period (1603–1868) urban structure and have thus retained their
densely built and labyrinthine fabric, along with a chaotic system of
narrow roads.

The reconstruction of Hiroshima and Nagoya proceeded more or
less along new plans; their different circumstances encouraged the
development of different strategies in urban planning.[17] Adopting the
concept of the American parkway, Nagoya, which had a tradition of
relatively successful land readjustment policy since the 1920s, led the
way. As part of the War Damage Rehabilitation Plan, twenty-four
American-style, 100–meter wide boulevards were planned in various
Japanese cities. Ultimately, only four were realized, two of which
were in Nagoya. The Japanese imported Frederick Law Olmsted's
idea of a vehicular scenic highway for pleasure located outside of
built-up areas, and applied it to the construction of wide promenades
within central urban areas. Despite efforts to the contrary, however,
the density and assortment of Japanese architecture remained for
the most part unchanged from the prewar period.

As the volume of reconstruction work surpassed the capacity of official urban planners and engineers, a number of young architects and
urban designers began to receive commissions to prepare new plans
for some of the destroyed cities. Kenzo Tange's (b. 1913) involvement

in Hiroshima is a prominent case in point.[18] He and his group of designers prepared a detailed and comprehensive scheme that centered on the famous Peace Park Project (1946–1955). Hiroshima, as one of the victims of the two atomic bombs dropped on Japan, gained an important symbolic character as a "peace city"; its reconstruction received American approval for special treatment.[19] Tange's proposal, by aspiring to modernist Western urban planning principles, was a comprehensive and monumental plan with an extensive system of wide urban avenues, roads, parks, and plazas, and a scheme that divided the city into seven functional zones: residential, industrial, commercial, cultural, recreational, administrative, and communication (transportation). Introduced at the 1951 Congrès Internationaux d'Architecture Moderne (CIAM) in Britain, the plan was prepared and presented more for the appreciation of an international audience than for actual domestic use. While praising Tange's plan for its modernist ideas, Western urban planners had little idea that much of Tange's concept, including the Peace Boulevard, was less a direct reference to Western monumental planning than the result of the necessity to provide building evacuation routes and fire barriers in case of future emergencies. The actual reconstruction of the city, which proceeded according to the administrative plan of 1949, integrated the main elements of Tange's plan yet largely deviated from the overall scheme. Only the symbolic part of the project was realized, and this was limited to the construction of Tange's designs for the Peace Boulevard and the Peace Park with the Atomic Memorial Museum (see Fig. 3.5). As a result, Hiroshima, too, has succumbed to the typically chaotic developments of the Japanese city, which have engulfed the few symbolic edifices of the plan.

The Hiroshima Project, like many other urban redevelopment plans in Japan since the Meiji Restoration, reveals that urban planning has also been guided by the intention to exhibit Japan's progress and parity with the West.[20] In addition to the abovementioned examples, one might add the urban renewal project for Tokyo in preparation for hosting the 1964 Olympic games, the first time that the games were held in Asia, or the urban preparations related to hosting the World Expo in 1970 in Osaka and the Marine Expo of 1975 in Okinawa. The most recent such showcasing is exemplified by numerous urban developments on reclaimed land, such as the ones in Osaka, Yokohama, and Tokyo. The most conspicuous of these remains the Tokyo Teleport Town, a new urban district developed on a large landfill area in Tokyo Bay. Launched in 1987, this ongoing urban project was designed as a model city of the twenty-first century. The Tokyo Teleport Town was scheduled to host a World City

FIGURE 3.5 Drawing of Hiroshima Peace Park. Architect: Kenzo Tange, 1955.

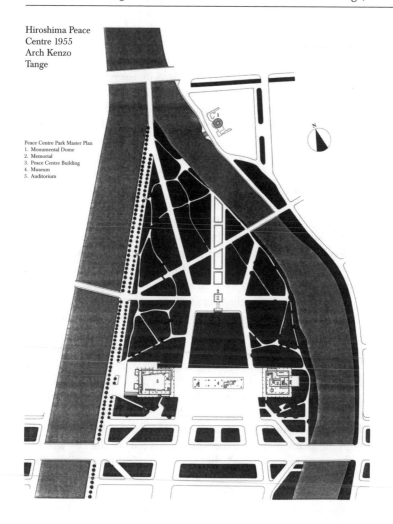

Hiroshima Peace
Centre 1955
Arch Kenzo
Tange

Peace Centre Park Master Plan
1. Monumental Dome
2. Memorial
3. Peace Centre Building
4. Museum
5. Auditorium

Exposition, "Urban Frontier–1996," in which Japan intended to display to the rest of the world its vision of the "future" in urban infrastructure, amenities, technologies, and entertainment. However, the "Urban Frontier" Expo had to be canceled due to cost overruns and the onset of economic recession; the Teleport Town project now proceeds with substantially reduced plans and at a much slower pace.

During the early postwar years, the difficulties in realizing new urban development projects in Japan were due to complex circumstances, which included an absence of both professional experience and traditions of implementing large-scale urban plans, the enormity of the task at hand, time pressures, the disorganization of planning authorities, lack of sufficient funds, and perhaps also a certain lack of faith in such large-scale plans. In addition, the razed or extensively damaged cities lost their infrastructure, and most of their historic and prewar buildings as well. The loss in Tokyo was especially severe as a large number of urban structures, including historic monuments, had already been destroyed in the Great Kanto Earthquake of 1923. In this sense, the capital of Japan, more than any other urban area in the country today, is a "brand new" city. In Tokyo, as in many other Japanese cities, no significant historic monuments remain, and with only a very few structures surviving from the pre-1923 era, there is no "old town" either. Its layout, however, is in many sections still that of the pre-Meiji period, and thus Tokyo does not have a "new" or "Western" feel.

Beyond the destruction of Japanese cities, there was another, equally significant, if indirect, American impact on Japanese urban space, which commenced in the late 1940s. In the aftermath of the lost war, Japan was indeed very much impoverished; the country, along with its cities and industries, was in ruins. In order to foster Japan's transition toward a genuinely democratic society–a foremost American interest–the American government realized that it needed to help the Japanese to recover their economy. Initially "help" was unofficial and limited to the flourishing black market, which channeled a substantial amount of American goods into the country, often through the occupying army. Some urban areas developed into busy markets for such goods; one well-known example is the area near Ueno station in Tokyo called *Ameyoko-cho*, or American alley. Although the black market is long gone, this part of the city still features more than four hundred cut-rate shops advertising and selling goods of American (and other) origin. Indeed, after the war, things American gained widespread popularity. This is largely attributable to the presence of the occupying American forces and civilian staff, and, after the end of the occupation in 1952, to the large number of Americans living in Japan as part of the armed forces stationed in the country in the wake of the cold war.

Japan's democratization was carried out by occupation forces and with strict American control. Even the new Japanese constitution, enacted in May 1947, was drafted by the occupying powers and thus strongly reflected their policies toward Japan. This document, adopted by the Japanese with almost no modification, was modeled after the constitutions of the United States and of Britain. Democratic Japan demanded new structures such as the prefectural government office and municipal office or city hall. A government program in 1955 called for the construction of innumerable such buildings in cities all over the country, creating the possibility for the evolution of a new public space. Kenzo Tange's Tokyo City Hall (1957) launched a line of innovative urban architecture and was instrumental in ushering in a new and highly successful stage in Japan's modern architecture, which soon attracted international attention. This "new Japan style" of architecture was represented by Kenzo Tange, Kunio Maekawa, Junzo Sakakura, and a new generation of Japanese architects in the 1950s and early 1960s. It successfully blended a basically modern Western "international" design with certain reinterpreted elements of traditional Japanese architecture. In addition to the Tokyo City Hall, the Hiroshima Peace Center and Museum (1955), also by Tange, and the Tokyo Metropolitan Festival Hall (1960) by Maekawa should be mentioned as noted examples.

After World War II, the United States became one of the most important centers of modern architecture. Many European pioneers of the modern movement, such as Walter Gropius, Mies van der Rohe, Josep Lluis Sert, Richard Neutra, Marcel Breuer, and Eric Mendelssohn, immigrated to the States in the 1930s in an effort to escape political repression and to continue their professional activities under very favorable conditions. These men, in addition to American (and American-based) designers such as Buckminster Fuller, Louis Kahn, Eero Saarinen, Philip Johnson, and the architects of Skidmore, Owings & Merrill (SOM), developed into the flag-bearers of modern design during this time. By the 1950s and 1960s, moreover, the United States was preeminent in advancing new technologies, new building types, and new types of design offices. No wonder, then, that America attracted architects from all over the world and that postwar Japanese architects and urban planners, despite their difficult situation at home, were eager to study and work there. During the 1950s, at the height of exchange initiatives, more than three thousand Japanese went abroad to study, mainly to the United States. Among today's most influential Japanese architects who visited the States in the postwar years are Fumihiko Maki (b. 1928), Yoshinobu Ashihara (b. 1918), Minoru Takeyama (b. 1934), and Yoshio Taniguchi (b. 1937).[21] They all brought their American experiences back to Japan, and subsequently produced work characterized by a certain degree of rationality in design, coupled with a concern for the urban realm and the public dimension of architecture. Others, like Kenzo Tange, became sought-after participants in international conferences and gatherings, or embarked on architectural tours to both the United States and Europe.

American assistance in reconstructing Japan's economy gained substantial momentum when the Korean War broke out in 1950. Endeavoring to turn Japan into a bulwark of anti-communist power in Asia, the United States used the country as a military staging area. The Japanese economy became a large supplier of American war machinery, as well as a base for its armed forces. As orders for supplies, along with investment, production, and trade between the two countries, grew rapidly, Japanese industry developed at an unprecedented rate—a phenomenon that by the early 1960s became known as the "Japanese economic miracle." The economic boom in Japan was accompanied by an equally rapid urban expansion, as many people seeking jobs flocked to the cities. Urban developments of this time can be compared to those at the beginning of the Meiji Era. Beyond physical reconstruction, the rate of urbanization in Japanese cities far surpassed prewar dimensions. Tokyo's population, which shrank from 7.32 million in 1940 to a mere 4.39 million during and immediately after the war, rebounded to 9.68 million by 1960. By the late 1960s and early 1970s, about three-quarters of Japan's population lived in urban areas; today this percentage is much higher.

Beginning with the occupation, the Japanese have also adopted (naturalized) many American customs and lifestyles. Christmas, for example, although not an official or religious holiday, is now extensively celebrated—particularly among families and friends who exchange presents—and is a huge commercial success. Department stores started the custom of holding Christmas sales as early as the 1930s; the sales, moreover, conveniently coincide with the distribution of the year-end bonus and the purchasing of year-end presents. Today, beginning in late November, large and small cities, and nearly every public and commercial building, but particularly department stores and shops, are outfitted with lavish Christmas decorations, greetings, or sale ads, lending the urban space a festive "American" atmosphere. In addition, Japanese businesses have marketed American-style weddings set in Christian chapels that have been especially built for such occasions (and nothing else). Such American-style weddings are a growing phenomenon, even if followers of the Christian faith constitute only about a half percent of the Japanese population. Some of the most remarkable examples of such wedding chapels in Japan have been designed by the internationally acclaimed architect Tadao Ando (b. 1941). His Rokko Chapel (1986) and Church on the Water (1988) (see Fig. 3.6) are operated by Japanese-owned resort hotels, where newlyweds can spend their honeymoon as well. Both of these small structures are among Ando's most outstanding works.

FIGURE 3.6 Church on the Water, Hokkaido. Architect: Tadao Ando, 1992. (Photo: Botond Bognar)

These examples indicate that the Japanese give preference to the forms and often the rituals of things borrowed from outside sources without being concerned with the significance of the "original." In the process of being influenced by (elements of) foreign cultures, they give new meaning(s) to the borrowed element—which meaning is often incompatible with that of the original—or else they manage to "void" associable meanings, thereby turning the thing into empty form or ritual. French philosopher and linguist Roland Barthes had this to say about this unique if not particularly new predilection of the Japanese: "[In Japan] an age-old technique permits the landscape or the spectacle to produce itself, to occur in a pure significance, abrupt, empty, like a fracture. Empire of Signs? Yes, if it is understood that these signs are empty and that the ritual is without a god" (see Fig. 3.7).[22]

A more obvious example of "empty signs" is the strange impact of the English language—one of the vehicles of American culture—on Japanese popular culture and on the quality of its urban public space. The Japanese are fascinated with foreign words, but, more often than not, manage to use them in commercials, billboards, neon signs, and other places (such as on T-shirts) in combinations that make little or no grammatical sense. If the words look decorative

FIGURE 3.7 Typical streetscape at Shinjuku, Tokyo. (Photo: Botond Bognar)

FIGURE 3.8 House with 54 Windows, Hiratsuka. Architect: Kazuhiro Ishii, 1975. (Photo: Botond Bognar)

enough, it does not matter if they are misspelled, nonsensical, or completely unsuited to the situation in which they appear or to the product that they intend to promote. The same can be observed in the realm of architecture, where elements of Western architecture are often imported out of context and are hence disconnected from their original significance. The numerous popular love hotels are a case in point; their design mimics and romanticizes the styles of Western chateaux, palaces, castles, and other historically evocative structures. Architect Kazuhiro Ishii's House with Fifty-Four Windows (1975) in Hiratsuka City is just one example among many in which a prominent designer selects a Western architectural element as a theme for his building and plays it out in numerous popular variations. In this case, Kazuhiro Ishii chose the window, which appears in fifty-four varieties in his building (see Fig. 3.8). Late capitalist consumer society and globalizing information technologies of the 1970s and 1980s have accelerated Japanese appropriation of foreign elements, and have effectively turned such appropriation into an art form, while blurring the boundaries between the popular and high arts as well as between American and Japanese cultures.

Since the United States and Japan are the two largest consumer societies, it is no surprise that the American influence is the most evident in Japanese mass culture. American fast-food restaurant chains are extremely popular in Japan, and their outlets can be found everywhere in the country. They have been naturalized or domesticated to the extent that younger generations take them as something innately Japanese. As the anecdote goes, small Japanese children visiting the United States with their parents are often surprised to discover that there are McDonald's restaurants in America as well. This taking over the "original" is perhaps best illustrated by the case of the formerly American 7–Eleven store chain, which, after failing in the United States, was purchased by a Japanese company; now the stores are virtually extinct in the United States but are ubiquitous in Japan. One of the latest developments in Japan is the rapid spread of large super- and even hypermarkets. Of course, this is attributable as much to the changing lifestyles, including the spread of suburbia and the car culture in Japan–both American in origin–as to the "direct" importation of its American architectural model.[23]

Following the American example, huge corporate complexes and shopping malls are built with increasingly large atrium spaces in Japanese cities.[24] The architectural firm Nikken Sekkei has designed several of such complexes, including the Shinjuku NS Building (1982), which features a 430-foot atrium, the world's tallest (see Fig. 3.9). The latest such example, the Tokyo International Forum complex, was completed in 1997 according to the designs of the American architect Rafael Vinoly, who is based in New York. The Forum features an enormous glass atrium, which stands apart from other parts of the complex yet is connected to them by bridges and underground levels. This solution provides for a large open public plaza in between the two sections. Not only the atrium, but even more so the open public plaza, which is a missing element in the history of urban development in Japan, introduces a new kind of public space in Tokyo. While their design and use, in most cases, have not been truly successful so far, it remains to be seen how far they will succeed in the future. Most of these atria have been designed as overly monumental and sterile–rather than as complex, dynamic, or sociable–spaces, which do not invite relations with surrounding urban public spaces. As a result, the city-at-large cannot penetrate the space, and the spontaneity of urban life is forfeited to the rationality of control by the corporate or government owner.[25]

However, not every imported aspect of urbanism has taken root in Japanese soil. While Japan has succeeded in many areas–such as industrial production and economic growth, as well as architecture–in emulating and even surpassing its Western counterparts, its urban developments have never really been the same as in the United

FIGURE **3.9** Shinjuku NS Building, Tokyo. Designed by Nikken Sekkei Ltd., 1982. (Photo: Botond Bognar)

States. Although Japanese cities have been rapidly modernizing, Japanese progress has consistently defied a truly Western-type urbanization. Tokyo, as much as other Japanese cities, has effectively retained its premodern, Edo urban structure, and its essence as an Asian city; and the Japanese have retained a predisposition to favor the situational over the predetermined, and to prefer an integration without synthesis. Japanese castle towns (*joka-machi*), predecessors of most contemporary metropolises in the country, were laid out according to pragmatic "plans" or considerations, rather than lofty ideals, and so were more mutable and flexible than their Western counterparts. Feudal warlords or *daimyo*, the rulers of such castle towns, for example, customarily rearranged the urban areas around their castle, moving entire districts of trade or of temple compounds to other locations, mainly for defensive purposes. As the historian Henry D. Smith II has pointed out, in Japan there is "no indigenous tradition of imposing cosmic symbolism on the form of the city; no tradition of using the city as a metaphor for utopian ideals; and no tradition of the city as an autonomous political unit [either]."[26] Today this is apparent in the prevailing organization or spatial matrix and the quality of the Japanese built environment, which have remained, against all odds, largely unaffected by the inroads of Western modernist, and highly rational, urban design principles. Tokyo, although unique in its scale, dynamics, and density of urban events, nonethelesss epitomizes the Japanese course of urbanization; it has continued to develop piecemeal from its parts, according to a "fuzzy logic," to become a conglomeration of an endless variety of "patchwork."

Until about the mid-1970s, such "chaotic" processes of Japanese urbanization were disparaged by both Japanese and Western architects and urbanists; the Japanese city was diagnosed with an illness whose cure was sought in modern Western urban models. The first to recognize the appropriateness of Japanese traditions in their urban theories and practice were the Metabolists, a group of young architects centered around Tange who in the 1960s and early 1970s advocated the need for regular renewal and the interchangeability of certain architectural and urban elements in the city. Deriving their new mode of urbanism from certain tenets of Buddhism and from contemporary structuralist philosophy, they rejected the rigidly functional (and eventually failed) master planning strategies of the modern movement. Instead, they viewed the city as a living entity that is in the process of continuous change, and in which the elements or "cells" can become obsolete or "die," and thus be transformed or replaced while the whole organism goes on living. The Metabolists entrusted the realization of this process to highly advanced industrial

technology, whose progress in Japan not only fostered rapid obso-
lescence within the built environment, but also seemed to offer the
means by which to meet its challenge: the standardization and easy
replaceability of obsolete elements and spatial units. Thus the Metabolist idea of architecture and urbanism was much more dynamic
than that of its high-modernist predecessor. Among the most notable
representatives of this architecture are Kenzo Tange, Kiyonori Kiku-
take, Kisho Kurokawa, and Fumihiko Maki. Although the Metabolist
movement in Japan rejected foreign as well as modernist urban
models in principle, in its execution the resulting architecture was for
the most part heavy and monumental in style and paradoxically
proved to be as rigid, inflexible, and authoritarian as its contemporary modernist counterpart. The movement lost its significance with
the energy crisis and economic recession of the 1970s, which also
revealed the dark side of technology, such as congestion and environmental pollution. The postmodernism of the 1970s and beyond
was often rather anti-technological.

With the advent of the postindustrial, postmodern society and the
age of information technology, the previous perspective of idealist
modern architecture and urbanism began to change rapidly. "Chaotic" Tokyo (or the Japanese city at large) was celebrated by Japanese architects, urban designers, public leaders, and citizens as a new
kind of urbanism, one as valid and as progressive as the models the
Japanese had formerly emulated. In seeking to reestablish an affirmative identity, the Japanese began to measure the Japanese city on
its own terms—not only in comparison with, but also in contrast to,
classical and modern Western models, particularly that of the United
States. Beyond the many undeniable deficiencies and liabilities of
Japanese urban space, such as congestion, high land prices, lack of
natural landscapes, and shortage of affordable housing, Japanese
architects and urban planners now recognize its many advantages
and assets: its energy, innovation, community spirit, flexibility, and
resilience. Indeed, as Japanese and foreigners alike are beginning
to realize, despite all its "negative" aspects, the Japanese city—in
our accelerated world of information, rapidly progressing electronic and digital technology, and new lifestyles—works, and works
amazingly well.

This new and more "liberated" spirit in Japanese urbanism has
elicited from Japanese designers an astonishingly broad spectrum of
interpretations of, and responses to, the city. Debunking many of their
previous aversions toward their chaotic and restless built environment,
Japanese architects have rediscovered its vitality, flux, and hidden but
still-surviving Japanese traditions, which are expressed in perpetual

change and easy adaptability, and are thus constituted by urban events rather than the permanence of the built fabric. In other words, these architects, despite their divergent approaches, share a basic position, namely, that heterogeneous, volatile, and chaotic urban conditions can be understood as a different kind of order rather than as mere anarchy, and can be the source of creative energies and even of poetic inspirations. Indeed, the 1980s saw a radical paradigm shift in Japanese architecture and urbanism that has elicited an appreciation and artistic exploration of the phenomenal and the ephemeral.

The new directions in urban design today draw from an increasingly wide variety of sources, both local and foreign, in interpreting and responding to the phenomena of the rapidly changing Japanese city. Beyond innovative architectural and urban theories, these include, but are not limited to: new social developments and lifestyles; scientific discoveries; the availability and workings of the latest information and media technologies; computers; and futuristic new materials and structures. These are assembled in a range of unique combinations that blur the sharp distinction not only between the traditional and the futuristic, but also between the domestic and the international, and especially between the Japanese and the American. Günter Nitschke put it this way: "In 'A Garden of Microchips,' a metaphor used by Toyo Ito, or in 'Architecture as Second Nature,' one used by Itsuko Hasegawa, or in 'Electronics Garden,' one used by Hiroshi Hara in a recent urban design competition, one finds no more reference to the by now redundant imagery of traditional urban aesthetics, Western or Eastern, of High-Culture or of Gemütlichkeit."[27]

The evolving new paradigm in Japanese design–in which, as in Ito's or Hasegawa's recent architecture, buildings often appear as temporary structures of a high-tech camp for what Ito calls today's "urban nomads"–strives to evoke and construct architecture with an almost immaterial lightness and "transparency" (see Fig. 3.10). It is in this sense that Japanese urban space–in contrast to its American and European counterparts–continues to be much less defined by the physical, permanent, classically stable or immutable entity of its constituent elements (see Fig. 3.11), and thus promises better adaptability to our fast-paced age of information. Since the time of the so-called "bubble economy" in the early 1980s, these developments have elicited much admiration and have become referred to in the international literature as the "new golden age of Japanese architecture." Currently, recognition of new Japanese urbanism and urban architecture comes as much, or even more so, from outside of Japan–and particularly from the United States–as from within Japan.

FIGURE 3.10 External view of the courtyard of "Silver Hut" (Ito Residence) in Tokyo, as seen through the perforated aluminum wall. Architect: Toyo Ito, 1984. (Photo: Botond Bognar)

FIGURE 3.11 Remote view of the Shonandai Cultural Center in Fujisawa City, seen from the southwest. Architect: Itsuko Hasegawa, 1991. (Photo: Botond Bognar)

This recognition is manifested by the extended practices of a large number of internationally renowned European and American architects, who have become active in Japan and have often completed some of their most outstanding works in this country. Steven Holl, Cesar Pelli, Kevin Roche, Mark Mack, Rafael Vinoly, Peter Eisenman, Morphosis, Michael Graves, Frank Gehry, and ROTO Architects are only a few of the many outstanding Americans who have received commissions here. Such heightened interest of these designers in Japan means not only that their works will have an undeniable effect on the local urban culture, but also, and more significantly, that Japanese architecture and urbanism–characterized by highly innovative design and exceptional execution with futuristic technologies– have achieved much admired world-class qualities that have begun to impact considerably other architectural cultures, including first and foremost that of the United States. Particularly since the early 1980s, American architects, urbanists, and students of architecture, among others, have been paying increasing attention to the unique developments and qualities of Japanese architecture and urbanism, as well as the outstanding work of Japanese architects, who have come to be regarded as among the most influential leaders in the world of design today. An increasing number of radio and television programs, books and magazines, lectures and exhibitions have highlighted and continue to feature the latest from Japan's new urban architecture.[28] The changing Western perception of Japan is characterized by the comment of the well-known architect and educator Peter Cook, who asked in 1990: "Where do we go for the most important architectural information? At the moment I think that is Japan."[29]

Another indication of cross-cultural exchange is the steadily increasing number of Japanese architects who win competitions abroad, receive the most prestigious international awards, and are commissioned to design prominent complexes in foreign countries, many of which are in the United States. In addition to Tange, Maki, and Kisho Kurokawa, who have been active in the United States and other foreign countries for some time, Japanese designers Tadao Ando, Arata Isozaki, Toyo Ito, Shin Takamatsu, Yoshio Taniguchi, and the Nikken Sekkei Company, Ltd. are making an international impact. Ando is currently working on the Fort Worth Museum of Art, a high-profile project next to Louis Kahn's Kimball Art Museum in Texas; while Yoshio Taniguchi was recently awarded the job of designing the extension to the Museum of Modern Art in New York. Both architects received their commissions after winning international design competitions. Kazuyo Sejima, a young woman architect from Tokyo, is one of the four finalists for the extension and redesign of the Illinois Institute of Technology in Chicago, which was originally the work of the German-American Mies van der Rohe, one of the giants of modern architecture.

Historically, Japan has been disposed to nurture an urban culture that readily absorbs the influence of others. However, in today's interconnected technological and global economy, Japan has itself become an influential model in the fields of architecture and urbanism. As a result, the relationship between Japan and the United States has become a multidimensional and complex process of exchange. Moreover, in the global context of our interactive contemporary world, it has to be recognized that within this exchange there is as much tendency toward the homogenization of the urban landscape as toward diversity and the cultivation of local identities. Kisho Kurokawa, one of Japan's internationally recognized architects and theorists, advocates what he calls "interculturalism," in which cultures of various kinds, both East and West, would develop by means of a "symbiotic" relationship.[30] One therefore has to be cautious in pinpointing who influences whom and in what respect, or what and where the precise origin of things may be. The possibilities for maintaining national or cultural urban identities need to be reexamined and redefined.

To be sure, it is undeniable that Japanese urban space has been significantly impacted by foreign influences, a process manifested in the innumerable signs of a long-standing American "cultural invasion" in Japan. But it is also clear that this "Americanization" cannot be seen as an overly determining force or as merely a negative phenomenon. American culture and architecture have historically provided, and will continue to provide, a rich storehouse from which the Japanese could draw and appropriate in various ways and for various purposes, while giving new meanings to the incorporated elements in order to shape and enrich their own complex cultural and urban landscapes. Reciprocally, American architects and urbanists increasingly benefit from the influential example of Japan.

In the final analysis, it can be concluded that the Japanese urban landscape has not become Americanized as a result of the American cultural impact. The Japanese city has not been transformed into an American-style city, either in its physical or spatial disposition, or in its feel or meaning. While in many areas some, and in some areas most, of the constituent elements are of American (or other foreign) origin, the overall spatial matrix or organizing system, as well as the semantic field, are unlike the American or any other Western model. Japanese cities retain their underlying or "hidden," and therefore not immediately apparent, Japanese urban

FIGURE 3.12 Cityscape of Shibuya, Tokyo, as seen from the east. (Photo: Botond Bognar)

structure—crowded, ambiguous, chaotically ordered, adaptable, dynamic, and volatile—in which large-scale or radical urban planning efforts have repeatedly failed, and in which the elements, or "parts as episodes," are always more important than the whole, which is therefore bound to remain evasive (see Fig. 3.12).[31] As Henry Smith remarked, "The idea of the city [as much as that of public urban space] in Japanese culture is [historically] elusive ... and the ... patterns of [contemporary] urban growth have done little to clarify it."[32] Despite its various and significant foreign influences—or perhaps, paradoxically, because of them—the Japanese city remains in-(de)finite and continues to constitute both a "traditional" Oriental and at the same time also a radically new postmodern and, potentially at least, more future-oriented mode of urbanism than its American counterpart.

Notes

1. Among the well-known American architects who were influenced by Japanese design, Frank Lloyd Wright (1867–1959) and the Greene brothers, Charles (1868–1957) and Henry (1867–1954), should be mentioned as particularly good examples.

2. In terms of translated books, magazines, and various other printed or non-printed materials, like dubbed films, Japan as early as the 1970s was importing about twelve times more from other countries than they were importing from Japan. H. Watanabe, "The Image Industry: Architectural Publishing," in *Japan: A Dis-oriented Modernism*, special issue of *Casabella*, nos. 608–609 (January–February 1994): 123.

3. It is important to state at the outset of this essay that here space is understood as not merely a physical entity, but also the urban realm in general, which includes urban lifestyles, institutions, the political and economic underpinnings of urbanization, and architecture and its semantic sphere.

4. Japan imported from China, by way of Korea, its writing system; the religions of Confucianism and Buddhism, including Zen; many art forms, such as pottery and ink painting; the culture of tea; city planning; architecture and construction techniques; and aspects of a centralized political and legal system. This began as early as prehistoric times, but intensified after the mid-sixth century A.D., when Buddhism and related arts were introduced in Japan.

5. The Treaty provided for the opening of the Japanese ports of Shimoda and Hakodate to American ships, the supplying of provisions to these vessels, the good treatment of shipwrecked sailors, and the establishment of an American consulate in Shimoda.

6. For further details, see Botond Bognar, *World Cities: TOKYO* (London, 1997).

7. This is not to say that there was no resistance at all to these importations. Indeed, both in the mid-sixth century, the time of the first significant contact with China, and in the mid-nineteenth century, when Japan opened to the West, there were internal forces, or clans, that opposed such "open" policy for Japan, but they eventually yielded to the majority.

8. One notable example is the case of the British civil engineers who helped to construct the first train line between Shimbashi in Tokyo and Yokohama in 1872. Following their own custom back home, these engineers introduced the left-hand traffic in these lines, which has since been applied not only to the fast developing railroad network of Japan, but also to its roads and highways. Today in Japan, motor vehicles, trains, and subways run on the left-hand lanes.

9. For further details, see Kenneth Frampton, Botond Bognar, and Sandy Heck, *NIKKEN SEKKEI: Building Modern Japan 1900–1990* (New York, 1990).

10. For further details about Wright's utopian Broadacre City project, see Kenneth Frampton, *Modern Architecture: A Critical History* (London and New York, 1992), 186–87.

11. Antonin Raymond, *An Autobiography* (Tokyo and Rutland, Vt., 1973), 71.

12. Maekawa and Sakakura also studied and worked in Le Corbusier's Paris office in the 1930s.

13. Resistance to *wakonyosai* and to such eclectic and inconsistent mixing of technique and style came from a gradually emerging new generation of architects, who, later on, were to follow the budding movement of modernism and sought to derive architectural design or "style" from the modes of construction themselves.

14. In fact, the occupation of Japan was carried out by the Allied forces, as there were some small contingencies of armed forces of the United Kingdom, France, and Australia in Japan, but they were all under the command of American General Douglas MacArthur and were quite negligible compared to the vast numbers of American forces.

15. The War Damage Rehabilitation Plan envisaged satellite cities with populations of 100,000 within a 40 to 50 kilometer radius of downtown Tokyo (cities such as Yokosuka, Hiratsuka, Atsugi, Machida, Hachioji, Tachikawa, Kawagoe, Omiya, Kasukabe, and Chiba), as well as suburban cities with around 200,000 residents at places such as Mito, Utsunomiya, Maebashi, Takasaki, Kofu, Numazu, and Odawara. The idea was for these cities to accommodate a population of about 4 million, enabling the population in the ward area to be kept down to 3.5 million. The plan called for land use in the ward area to pick up and extend the prewar and wartime plans for a belt of vacant land encircling the city. This land use plan was adopted practically unchanged under the designation of green space areas in Article 3 of the Special City Planning Law. Although reduced in size from the original estimates, the green belt still amounted to 18,933 hectares or 33.9 percent of the ward area. In addition, several wide roads, including seven measuring 100 meters in width, were to make up a radial and ring road system as part of a network of arterial roads that had been planned and approved. Planning and approval were also extended to land readjustment areas amounting to 20,000 hectares, well above the 16,230 hectares that had been destroyed by fire. These plans were nevertheless only visionary dreams, with no possibility of ever being carried out. As more people returned to Tokyo and as others continued to gravitate to the city, the population in the wards grew from 3.44 million in 1946 to 3.82 million in 1947, summarily negating the fundamental assumptions of the reconstruction plan. Another handicap was the American General Headquarters' lukewarm reaction to the plan as unsuitable for a defeated country. Progress lagged behind schedule, and the land readjustment projects that were the primary purpose of the plan were reduced to about one-tenth their original size as a result.

The National Capital Region Development Plan of 1955 was intended to deal with the growth of the capital and the accompanying social changes, including the increasing concentration of population and industry in the capital region, the expansion of urbanized areas, and the growth of automobile traffic. The plan on which this legislation was based was the National Capital Region Plan established for the ward area of Tokyo by the Capital Building Commission, which dated from 1941. The approach adopted for the Tokyo region as a whole was influenced by the prewar Greater London Plan. All of the concepts and questions still being debated today—such as satellite-city green belts and the appropriate size for the region—were already perceptible, albeit in embryonic state, in the Conceptual Sketch of the Capital Region of 1955.

16. The 1923 Imperial Capital Reconstruction Plan for Tokyo City, the official name of the project, was drawn up by Shimpei Goto, a previous mayor of the city, who was appointed as home minister to head the reconstruction of the capital. In addition to a distinguished panel of experts on urban planning, Goto invited the American Charles Austin Beard (1874–1948), a political scientist and a renowned authority on urbanology and city administration, to advise him in the matters of reconstruction. This extensive plan had to be reduced several times due to the tremendous costs involved (4.08 billion Japanese yen, three times more than the entire annual national budget). Despite considerable achievements in

land readjustment and improvements in urban infrastructure, only a small part of the original plan (about one-eighth) was ultimately carried out.

17. Hiroshima had vast open land, while Nagoya had a history of more significant city planning than most Japanese cities.

18. Other cities where architects such as Eika Takayama and Moto Take were commissioned to devise reconstruction plans are Nagasaki, Maebashi, and Wakkanai.

19. Special treatment of Hiroshima, as the victim of the first atomic bomb as well as a symbol of peace, was approved by the Central Command of the occupying American forces, which meant the attribution of additional financial means for reconstruction plans.

20. This was particularly the case with regard to the quality and "city as artifact" image of its urban fabric and urban space. In classical urban planning and urban design ideologies, the city was regarded as an aesthetic "object," whose beauty had to be inscribed in the permanent material and formal built fabric. This too was an American notion, pioneered by the City Beautiful movement, which was initiated by the architect and city planner Daniel Burnham in nineteenth-century Chicago.

21. Maki (b. 1928) received his first Master's Degree from the Cranbrook Academy of Art in 1951, and his second from GSD of Harvard University in 1952, before working in the offices of Skidmore, Owings & Merrill and of Sert-Jackson Associates in Boston. He also taught at Harvard and at Washington University in St. Louis. Yoshinobu Ashihara (b. 1918) received his Master's Degree from GSD of Harvard University in 1953 and worked for Marcel Breuer in New York for a few years. Both Minoru Takeyama (b. 1934) and Yoshio Taniguchi (b. 1937) also received their Master's Degrees in architecture from Harvard's GSD in 1960.

22. Roland Barthes, *Empire of Signs* (New York, 1982), 108.

23. It should be added that urban conditions in Japan (density of the built fabric, lack of available space, traffic congestion, smaller-size homes and cars, for example) necessitate the modification of the original model in the cases of both fast-food restaurants and supermarkets; they are much more space effective (operate in smaller spaces) than their American counterparts.

24. The first such atrium building is said to be the Ford Foundation Building in New York (1968), which was designed by the American firm Kevin Roche & John Dinkeloo in 1963.

25. Moreover, while there is little or no tradition of large urban plazas in Japan, the evolution of an adroit or politically self-conscious citizenry has been delayed and weakened by the surviving remnants of the previous feudal society, which could be detected long after the fall of the Tokugawa shogunate in the mid-nineteenth century and, despite the process of democratization of the country, in some respects even today.

26. Henry D. Smith II, "Tokyo as an Idea: An Exploration of Japanese Urban Thought Until 1945," in *Journal of Japanese Studies* 4, no. 1 (Winter 1978): 45. Smith nevertheless correctly points out that "[w]hile the Japanese did in fact borrow such an intellectual form from China [i.e., the city conceived as a cosmic center with an ideal form] in the plans of Nara and Kyoto, they did not sustain it" (47).

27. Günter Nitschke, "From Ambiguity to Transparency: Unperspective, Perspective, and Aperspective Paradigm of Space," issue "Japan Today," *Louisiana Revy* 35, no. 3 (June 1995).

28. One of the latest large-scale events, the "Japan 2000" exhibition of recent Japanese architecture and design, took place in the Chicago Art Institute from

2 February to 3 May 1998, after which the exhibition traveled to San Francisco and Berlin, Germany.

29. Peter Cook, in an interview on the occasion of his appointment as a professor at Bartlett School of Architecture, London University; quoted in *Building Design* 5 (January 1990).

30. Kisho Kurokawa, "The Philosophy of Symbiosis: From Internationalism to Interculturalism," in *The Japan Architect* (February 1985); and Kisho Kurokawa, *Each One a Hero: The Philosophy of Symbiosis* (Tokyo and New York, 1997).

31. "Hidden" and "invisible" are references to Yoshinobu Ashihara, *The Hidden Order: Tokyo through the Twentieth Century* (Tokyo and New York, 1989).

32. Smith, "Toyko as an Idea," 47.

Part II

Drawing Cultural Boundaries, Forging the National

– *Four* –

PERSISTENT MYTHS OF AMERICANIZATION

German Reconstruction and the Renationalization of Postwar Cinema, 1945–1965

Heide Fehrenbach

Film histories consistently tell the story of West German cinema as an extension of World War II, in which the German economy and society were saturated and subdued by the products of American commercial firms bent on conquering defeated and debilitated markets. Military defeat is represented as the prelude to an ensuing commercial and cultural emasculation by Hollywood, which has been blamed for stunting the development of a native national cinema by monopolizing domestic screen time, by shutting West German films out of the international–and particularly European–market, and by colonizing the consciousness of West German citizens, transforming them into American-style consumers. Thus Hollywood's presence in the postwar–West German market has been characterized as both unimpeded and hegemonic, adversely affecting the economic recovery of a historically significant export industry as well as the cultural integrity of the new German nation. In certain incarnations, moreover, this narrative has suggested a corresponding psychological denationalization of the identity of German citizens.[1]

Although this interpretative constellation is based upon a number of unexamined, and I would argue faulty, assumptions, it does provide an impetus to rethink the conceptual basis of "Americanization" and to raise the issue of just what role *culture* plays in the cultivation of national sovereignty and a loyal citizenship.[2] The above sketch of the Americanization of West German cinema and audiences, although crude, reveals a number of strategies common to the literature. It casts the American presence as imperialist in a political, economic, and ideological sense and postulates an attendant American-style cultural leveling that threatens to undermine national integrity and disrupt the personal allegiances as well as gender, ethnic, and class relations assumed to underpin the modern sovereign nation-state. This interpretation, moreover, rests upon a still prevalent tendency to essentialize "the national" (whether American or German) when conceptualizing "Americanization" and to homogenize what more properly should be seen as hybrid. As a result, it inadvertently stresses consensus over contest, and consequently assumes–rather than demonstrates–the existence, exercise, and compatibility of political and economic goals that indisputably embody and express a unified "American" (rather than partisan) interest or agenda.

In assessing the cultural and commercial impact of the American occupation, one of the most basic and persistent mistakes of American and German scholars alike has been to assume an unproblematic identity of interests between official American occupation policy and Hollywood.[3] Despite Hollywood expectations that military defeat would finally crack the historically intractable German market and afford U.S. film companies unlimited control of distribution and exhibition outlets, this ultimately did not happen during the historical heyday of German film attendance in the decade and a half following the war. This essay seeks to explain why.

An examination of the postwar initiatives of the Hollywood majors in Germany, spearheaded by their trade association Motion Picture Export Association of America (MPEA), which was founded in 1946 as an export branch to handle the marketing of all U.S. motion pictures to Europe and Asia,[4] casts significant light on the complexities of Americanization. However, the postwar responses of protagonists on both sides of the Atlantic must be considered in relation to a longer history of commercial transfers and relations that emerged in the interwar period and gave birth to the alluring opposition of "national" versus internationalizing American cinema.

Hollywood and the Articulation of German National Cinema

A good case in point is the furor surrounding Erich Pommer's appointment in July 1946 as film production officer of the Motion Picture Branch of the American military government's Information Control Division (ICD). Pommer, who was assigned the task of restarting native film production in the American zone of Germany, drew heavy and sustained criticism from MPEA for his efforts to build a viable postwar German cinema, which worked against some of Hollywood's more extravagant commercial goals. MPEA's vitriolic response to Pommer's appointment (including a sustained attempt to orchestrate his recall to the United States) can be understood only in relation to both Pommer's professional past and previous American-German cinematic relations.

Pommer, a successful Weimar-era film producer and German-Jewish émigré who fled Germany in 1934, was credited with forging a notable national film industry in interwar Germany that was considered a worthy competitor to Hollywood. Pommer scored his first international hits in the early 1920s by insisting that German film compete on the world market on the basis of *difference* from Hollywood (giving rise to German expressionist film, for example, by encouraging artistic experimentation and improvisation with technical effects, camera work, editing, lighting, costuming, and acting at a time when Hollywood was developing rationalized production and management methods). By 1928, however, after returning from a two-year professional stint in California, Pommer abandoned this strategy in order to fashion a German product that would do good business abroad and at home. His ambition was to cultivate "entertainment value" by following Hollywood's example in developing simple stories with well-defined conflict and emotional immediacy. As a result, Pommer advocated and employed tried-and-true Hollywood techniques: product standardization, narrational economy, the cultivation of stars, and camera work and editing that situated the viewers in such a way that they identified with the action and actors on the screen. The point was to broaden the film's form of address–by manufacturing a universal appeal that would captivate both "demanding and less demanding" viewers and transcend the barriers of nationality, education, class, and sex–in order to reach the largest possible international audience and, just as importantly, to secure a larger loyal domestic viewership for German films.[5] Thus German film producers like Pommer increasingly acquired hands-on experience in Hollywood and employed American models and methods in order to articulate and institutionalize a German national cinema.

This point bears emphasizing: since World War I, the notion of national cinema in Germany was developed in sustained reference to Hollywood. Hollywood has served as a model, provocation, and standard of measurement for German cinema from the Weimar period to the present. As historian Thomas Saunders has noted, ongoing historical preoccupation with national identity itself "testifies to the tenacity of perceptions rooted in the 1920s–recognition of America's thematic and stylistic primacy but rebellion against its hegemonic pretensions."[6]

Germany's position as a film producer was unique among European countries, and a significant factor in this singularity was the timing of its cinematic debut on the international market. Unlike France and Britain, whose markets were quickly dominated by their wartime ally after 1914, German markets were closed to imports from the United States. As a result, German cinema developed independently from Hollywood influence through the early 1920s due to war and, later, postwar inflation and a radically devalued reichsmark. This "cinematic self-sufficiency" allowed German producers some initial breathing space to develop an indigenous alternative to Hollywood films. Thus German film achieved European prominence at the same time that Hollywood was securing global dominance. This timing, along with Germany's *Continental* commercial and cultural presence, determined the pattern of international competition and cooperation between the two vying film-producing markets, and ultimately stimulated discussion and debate regarding the *national* characteristics of German film culture and audiences.[7]

Hollywood's entry into the German market in 1922–23 posed a dilemma for the fledgling German industry. The popular appeal of American films like Charlie Chaplin's *The Kid* sparked German debates about whether the native industry should pursue a national or international motion picture identity. A consensus was never reached on this issue, in part because of increased American investment in German film ventures. By the second half of the decade, German film executives sought to forge profitable working relationships with Hollywood by attracting investment and by studying American business practices in order to sharpen their competitive edge vis-à-vis both European and domestic rivals. Thus, despite later allegations of American cultural and economic hegemony, German-American cooperation served the interests of *both* nationally based film industries. Hollywood, for example, acknowledged the competitive profile of German cinema by using its economic power to recruit German notables like Pommer, Marlene Dietrich, and Peter Lorre as one component of an ambitious—and ultimately successful—business strategy to attract talent in order to internationalize their products and build markets abroad (in the process illustrating the cultural plasticity and "mongrel" nature of the American product). German film interests, on the other hand, generally "considered collaboration with American companies to be compatible with the preservation of a domestic industry" as well as their own individual capitalist enterprises.[8]

Nonetheless, by the late 1920s a tension developed as German film firms positioned themselves as ready protégés of Hollywood benefactors, only to chafe in oedipal distress at their continued junior status. Increased Hollywood investments and imports on the German market sparked an "identity crisis" for Weimar cinema, along with a rhetoric of national cultural protectionism by German filmmakers. Film professionals and critics sought ways to articulate differences between German and American cultures and audiences on the basis of "incompatibilities of national taste or mentalities." In reviewing a Hollywood film, one German film critic, for example, judged that its screenplay might suffice "to feed the hillbillies in Arizona, [but] not an educated audience" in Germany. Critics also studied the careers of German émigré artists in Hollywood, such as Lubitsch, Jannings, Murnau, and Pommer, treating them as lessons-in-miniature of the larger processes of cultural exchange and national definition. Thus, interwar German critics lauded compatriots' contributions to Hollywood, engaged in "hairsplitting over the Germanness" of their films, and attempted to gauge the "corrosive or beneficial influence of America" on German culture. By reflecting on German émigrés' Hollywood experiences—and on German interactions with Hollywood more generally—contemporaries crafted the content and contours of German national cinematic culture.[9]

This national dialogue on the nature of German film did not end with the Weimar Republic, but continued into the Third Reich and the postwar period as well. In the decade and a half after 1918, German filmmakers became adept at manufacturing films with mass appeal by cultivating German stars and film genres (like the operetta, *Heimatfilm*, war film, and historical biography) that continued to draw audiences after 1933.[10] By the early 1930s, moreover, the ascension of National Socialism and sound film, which drowned out the universal language of Hollywood silents, assured the survival of this national cinema and allowed Goebbels to put some of Hollywood's lessons to the test. Cinema under National Socialism profited from the earlier commercial, aesthetic, and technological cross-fertilization with Hollywood. Feature films produced during the Third Reich were never straightforward "ideological containers" for the Nazi worldview. Rather, they continued to be fashioned by film professionals with an eye for commercial and popular appeal, and resembled both pre-Hitler and Hollywood-style productions in their film-formal strategies and modes of address. As a result, they won a broad following both within Germany and, later, even more tellingly, in Nazi-occupied Europe.[11]

Although the creation of the Film Chamber instituted political control over production, the Nazi regime won the loyalty of many non-Jewish film professionals by creating a Reich-controlled Filmkreditbank in June 1933 to provide much needed financing to German producers and ensure their independence from Hollywood interests. Nonetheless, Nazi-era film remained beholden to Hollywood, and even imitated it outright in productions like *Glückskinder* (Lucky Kids), a remake of *It Happened One Night*,[12] in order to win popular domestic and international acclaim and convince its subjects that the "national renewal" of the Third Reich would not entail confinement to the cultural provinces. Thus, despite stringent censorship measures, Goebbels's advocacy of entertainment value over ideological instruction in feature films (as opposed to newsreels and documentaries) encouraged a Nazi-era film-viewing experience which suggested that political membership in the German *Volksgemeinschaft* (national community) was not incompatible with the cultivation of consumer freedoms and modern (gender and generational) identities.[13] Despite a rhetoric of cultural purity and an autarkic economy during the war years that shut the German market off from Hollywood imports, German cinema was a culturally "promiscuous" product, based on adaptation of American forms and open to cultural impulses from abroad.[14]

Finally, the concept of Americanization and the articulation of a German national cinema were twin offspring of the same peculiar historical climate of the interwar years. The shifts in the reception and meanings of American economic and cultural influence over the course of the two interwar decades should persuade us of two things: first, of the compatibility of American cultural influence with political regimes both democratic and nondemocratic; and second, of the futility of employing an undifferentiated language of Americanization that bypasses the ebbs and flows, receptions and resistances, and most of all, the shifting historical meanings of American culture in the German context.

American Occupation and the
Postwar Politics of Film

While American occupation officials in Germany maintained that American feature films would play a considerable role in reorienting Germans to democracy after the defeat of National Socialism, and urged and expected the cooperation of American film companies with this political goal, they were unwilling to allow the eight major Hollywood production companies free reign in the German market. During the years between 1945 and 1949, in fact, Hollywood and U.S. officials did not pursue a unified agenda and only rarely presented a united front. Although American officials saw a political purpose in keeping the German market open to the "free flow" of American cultural products, they were determined to block the wholesale American commercial domination of markets in the interests of fostering a stable German reconstruction.

Still, American military government officials were not prepared for Hollywood's distinct lack of cooperation with the democratization program. Well into 1948, Hollywood companies dragged their feet in providing feature films for American reeducation efforts in Germany; those they did send were old or of low quality. They were withholding their best films for a time when German box-office receipts would be convertible to hard currency (which was not the case throughout the occupation), and were determined to use their films as negotiating chips with American officials to gain real and lasting advantages in the German—and, more generally, European—markets.[15]

After World War II, MPEA's strategy of noncooperation with military government policy irritated American officials and initially did nothing to promote Hollywood interests in Germany—especially when one considers audience response. U.S. intelligence reports for 1946–48 indicate that German audiences exhibited little patience for mediocre American film and overwhelmingly preferred native products of any vintage to imports. ICD officials in Bavaria, for example, reported that after the screening of U.S. features like *Here Comes Mr. Jordan* and *Tom, Dick, and Harry* the local population "stayed away in droves" for three or four weeks. The problem extended beyond charges of mediocrity: German audiences expressed irritation with the "carefree escapism and incomprehensible humor" of Hollywood films and pined for films in their native language, with familiar themes and actors.[16] Interwar fascination with American culture faded once it became associated with the unilateral policies of military occupation and doctrinaire didacticism. Harkening back to prewar habits, Germans demanded freedom in the form of consumer choice and scorned the exclusive presence of Hollywood films in their theaters. Thus, mere availability (and by the early 1950s, even a plethora) of Hollywood films on the German market did not ensure avid mass consumption, much less an Americanization of viewing preferences and viewer psychology. Throughout the 1950s, West German films and German rereleases from the Weimar and Nazi periods surpassed imports in popularity.[17]

Ironically, from its inception ICD envisioned using American feature films to reach a broad social spectrum of farmers, youth, housewives, shopkeepers, and workers, which it identified as "distinctly different from the one covered by books or theaters." Yet, as Hollywood products failed to peddle the American agenda to this presumed lowbrow audience, American film officers faced the dilemma of how to sell the American message of democracy, individualism, and free enterprise to Germans who refused to buy the package in which these messages were delivered.[18]

In order to bolster reeducation efforts, to counter competing Soviet cultural initiatives, and, not incidentally, to encourage the development of a permissible German export to help fund the high costs of occupation, U.S. officials approved renewed German film production, appointing Erich Pommer to head the effort. In the interim, to keep German audiences attending movies and offset the inadequate supply of American films, U.S. officials increasingly allowed rereleases of German films to fill screen time.

Hollywood interests became increasingly impatient regarding the policies of the American military government's Information Control Division, and, in particular, the unanticipated delay in opening the German market to the free enterprise of foreign commercial interests like themselves. With the advent of German film production and increased official reliance on German rereleases in 1946–47, the major Hollywood producers opted for a more confrontational approach.[19] Through MPEA, they fought loud and hard against these developments by taking their case to the State and War Departments, launching smear campaigns against Pommer and the altered U.S. film policy in trade papers like *Variety* and influential dailies like the *New York Times,* and trying desperately to get Pommer recalled to the United States. Ultimately, however, Pommer retained official support, and the Hollywood majors were defeated in their goal of blocking native German production and obtaining unimpeded access to the German market.[20]

Thus, despite much political pressure and lobbying by Hollywood, the principle of building a viable West German film industry with a modest export profile that could both secure the influx of badly needed hard currency from abroad and offset the ideological threat issuing from renewed domestic film production in the Soviet zone was sustained. The emphasis on viability also meant that German applicants for U.S. film production licenses were vetted not only for political background and beliefs, but for professional competency as well. This ensured a strong continuity in personnel between Nazi and postwar film production and affected the look of German filmmaking style that would come to dominate in the first decades after 1945. This continuity also encouraged ongoing Hollywood criticism of American film policy and talk of an insufficiently democratized German cinema still infused by "Nazi poison," along with (hyperbolic) scenarios of a resurgent German competitor with global ambitions extending beyond Europe to Latin America.[21]

In terms of industry structure, the nascent West German cinema differed considerably from that of the late Weimar and Nazi periods, due to the triumph of the American principle of decartelization in all three Western zones of Germany. This resulted in the breakup of Universum Film (UFI), a central film holding company created under Nazi sponsorship in 1942, and the proliferation of small, economically vulnerable firms. Nonetheless, American policy to permit German rereleases in occupied Germany did stimulate the rise of large, powerful West German distribution companies that made big money on German reprises and by 1950 became involved in film production, thus reintroducing vertical organization of the domestic film industry on a limited scale.

During the occupation years, then, one can speak of a distinct (although incomplete and ultimately ephemeral) Americanization of the principles of film organization and film control: first, because the American principles of decartelization, open markets, and free competition were applied to all the Western zones against initial British resistance and protracted French (and Soviet) opposition; and second, because this early postwar settlement included an American-style brand of censorship, again imposed on all three Western zones, which was modeled after the Hayes Commission in the United States and based upon the principle of industry self-censorship. Designed to dismantle the state control of culture in favor of a film censorship based upon the putatively nonideological dictates of the market, it was thus aimed against "totalitarian" forms of cultural control and employed to counter earlier National Socialist practices and the current centralized state control of culture exercised in Eastern Germany under Soviet rule.

The form of West German film censorship that emerged in 1949 under American sponsorship actually blended American and German principles. It compromised the principle of exclusive industry self-control by permitting German churches, youth offices, and state cultural ministries to participate in a deliberation process that reviewed and rated every film scheduled for release in West Germany, regardless of national origin. Despite the inclusion of nonindustry representation, the film industry retained the majority of votes on the review board (eight of fifteen), which consequently was perceived and criticized by German clergy, state officials, youth workers, and teachers, among others, as an American imposition. This appraisal culminated in a concerted public campaign, beginning with the end of the occupation in 1949 and lasting until early 1952, to revamp the censorship process by strengthening the "public voice" and weakening industry interests. This campaign, moreover, was couched in a public rhetoric of national self-defense and difference that centered around concerns regarding the nature and function of postwar German culture.

National Cinema as Cultural Integrity: Defending against Americanization

What emerged with the end of military occupation was a protracted, multivoiced domestic debate about the desired nature of postfascist German identity and the role that cinema would play in the process. Strikingly, given the widely diverse agendas of participants in this debate, all argued for the need to develop and maintain a distinct national-cultural identity. Where they differed was in their visions of the content and purpose of cinematic culture.

After 1945, cultural integrity struck many Germans as a crucial prerequisite for regaining national health and sovereignty. Early in the occupation, local state and church leaders in particular indicated their nervousness, and often antagonism, concerning the free market orientation of American policy. The United States was condemned as the producer of Wild West and gangster films, and the propagator of an insidious, if insipid, secularized commercial culture that addressed itself directly to the viewer, bypassing the mediation of traditional cultural and religious elites. Offending products need not even issue from Hollywood; German filmmakers and their wares were attacked with equal vehemence if they seemed too cosmopolitan.

Given their strong desire to encourage "normalized" gender and family relations after the disruptions of war, these critics also denounced the anticipated social ramifications of unconstrained commercial cultural exchange. In response to the new cold war paradigm, they constructed the notion of a "moral nation" based upon a renewed patriarchal family as a counterweight to the "immoral" influences of American-style commercial culture, Soviet-style socialism, and the now defunct National Socialism. Caught between an unusable past and the larger international forces at work in the present, social conservatives in church and state deemed it a matter of national survival to maintain a separate cultural identity. This required that they find a way to control the unmediated influence of cultural products that touted the merits of secular materialism—whether consumerist or communist in nature. The issue at stake for German state and church leaders was who would exercise cultural sovereignty within Germany's borders; who would define the nature—hence the social and moral parameters—of the new German nation.

Denouncing the circulation of "trash and smut" in the media and demanding its regulation, influential Christian clergy garnered the support of state cultural ministries and, in 1951, launched a high-profile public campaign against the American principle of industry self-censorship through an attack on the West German film, *Die Sünderin* (The Sinful Woman). What is striking in this regard is that despite both the explicit and implicit anti-American thrust to much of their rhetoric, these critics decided to target a *domestic* product, and, more specifically, *this* domestic product. I have discussed this film and the campaign against it at length elsewhere;[22] here I will simply note that in thematizing unregulated female sexuality, female prostitution (with German men and occupation soldiers), and an unstable, deeply flawed German masculinity (ultimately dispatched by poisoning at the hands of the female lover), the film resonated with the anxieties and social experiences of the "crisis years" of the occupation and suggested the futility of postwar reconstruction based upon traditional social and sexual norms. Critics of the film, moreover, consistently treated it as a national narrative of social and sexual disorder. The dramatic actions of the protagonist, Marina, were read as a reflection of the wartime and postwar experiences of German women or, alternatively, condemned as a potential influence on the future behavior of German women and girls. Church and state leaders, then, advertised their fight as a moral campaign to defend the "Christian West" by reestablishing the "spiritual health" of the war-weakened German nation. To them, film was no "mere entertainment," but a psychologically potent "mass" medium and a powerful school for inappropriate socialization.

Employing public demonstrations and apocalyptic language, an alliance of clergy, teachers, and state cultural ministry officials warned that unregulated viewing would spell the moral and social death of the enfeebled nation, and lobbied for the end of the "dangerous pluralism of values ... in a democracy that knows no limits."[23] In 1951, they won the reintroduction of state influence over film censorship and film production (through the awarding of tax credits for films deemed "especially valuable" by state cultural ministries). The voice of the churches was also strengthened, both in the formal censorship process and through the creation of Christian film leagues, whose members were oath-bound to attend only those films approved by their clergy, and whose numbers (four million by 1954) far exceeded the combined total membership of all West German political parties. Thus church and state officials fought successfully to reclaim their historical roles as cultural mediators in order to forge a cultural "third way" between American and Soviet materialism, and establish the cultural limits of the new democratic order.

The Reassertion of National Cinema

The nascent West German film industry, too, took up a rhetoric of national defense and difference, although in doing so, they articulated their interests as much in opposition to the initiatives of native officials in church and state as against Hollywood.[24] In fact, the abolition of the American principle of industry self-control robbed German film producers of a majority voice on the film censorship board and hence of the power to approve or reject the screening of (individual) Hollywood products in West German cinemas, since all films–domestic and imported–had to pass the censorship process before they could be exhibited. Industry members complained, moreover, that native conservative interference in film matters inhibited the recovery of the German film industry by influencing the look and content of its products and adversely affecting the industry's ability to market their films abroad.

In this second postwar period, then, interwar industry discourses of cooperation and competition with Hollywood (which reached their pinnacle in the late 1920s) gave way to one of survival, which bemoaned material shortages, territorial division (and particularly the splintering of film production in Berlin, Munich, and Hamburg), and domestic conservative interference and censorship. Since the loss of the war resulted in the loss of forcibly held European markets, the West German film industry was also faced with the problem of amortizing its products and feared economic extinction. Although conservative leaders in state cultural ministries and the churches were more concerned with controlling the social and cultural effects of film than in resurrecting a viable national industry, with the end of the occupation, German filmmakers were extended financial support from the state and federal economics ministries, which hoped to jump-start local economies and foster products for export. To accomplish this, they enacted guarantee credit programs to fund film projects; after 1950, German film production companies overwhelmingly looked again to the state (as they had during the Third Reich) to bolster their industry and increase profitability. The emphasis on assessing scripts for their potential financial return encouraged bureaucratic meddling into story line and staffing.[25] As a result, the reintroduction of state influence, along with moral control by the churches, conspired to produce a narrowly national native film product that was singularly unattractive for export to non-German-speaking audiences.[26]

Ultimately, then, early West German cinema (like early Weimar cinema) established an identity on the basis of difference from Hollywood. This time around, however, it did not compete successfully on the international market. Rather, film producers targeted the home market by revamping domestic genres like the interwar *Heimatfilm,* which became the most popular German film genre of the 1950s through box office hits like *Schwarzwaldmädel* (Black Forest Girl, 1950) and *Grün ist die Heide* (The Heath Is Green, 1951). In this second postwar period, German officials and filmmakers abandoned the quest to cultivate German cinematic superiority abroad and retreated from the aspirations of the Nazi and Weimar periods to build a commercial German alternative to challenge Hollywood's international hegemony.

For the past forty years or so, postwar *Heimatfilme* have been widely ridiculed as a peculiarly German brand of kitsch: an anti-modern filmic fantasyland that featured close-knit communities, townsfolk in traditional dress, color shots of an untouched native countryside, and sentimental German *Volkslieder* that celebrated the enduring bonds—and frictionless fraternity—of communal life, when outside the walls of the cinema, urban landscapes were still littered with rubble and ruins, unemployment was rife, and destitution and social tensions ran high. Given this characterization, numerous postwar critics have accused the genre and its directors of encouraging a convenient amnesia regarding the Nazi past—a retreat, that is, to the reassuring embrace of a depoliticized eternal Mother *Heimat* (as opposed to the martial, masculinized German fatherland recently rent by defeat, occupation, and competing cold war ideologies). Moreover, some have detected in the genre troubling ideological remnants of *Blut und Boden:* Nazi imaginings of racial Germanness as an organic outgrowth of the native soil, which located the spiritual heart of the German nation in the cyclical patterns and values of the hearty peasant and his sturdy forms of familial and village life.

I question the interpretation of postwar *Heimatfilme* as purely recidivist, and would rather indicate some of the ways in which the genre played a significant, even constituent, role in the reconstruction of national cinematic culture in West Germany. (Indeed, by the 1960s, *Heimatfilm* was invoked as a derisive synonym for postwar German cinema and helped to spawn its "artistic" antidote, Young German Cinema.) Official intervention—in the form of censorship, subsidies, and tax breaks—did encourage the production of such inoffensive depictions of communal and familial relations. Nonetheless, it doesn't account for the extraordinarily popular success of the genre, which topped the list of box office smashes in West Germany through the late 1950s and gave Hollywood films a run for their money. This, one suspects, is a tribute to *Heimatfilm*'s mass appeal: its ability, during its heyday, to address audiences across class, gender, party-political, even generational lines.[27] I would like to suggest, then, that *Heimatfilm* represented a cultivated space for the articulation of national imagery and national narratives based upon social consensus and harmony.

By projecting an affirmative representation of the German nation, *Heimatfilm* signified a new cultural orientation. Through a public presentation of the beauty of the native countryside, the genre reassured West Germans that their "new state was not all that bad." Ever present folksongs played a similar role by referring viewers back to an older oral tradition, passed from generation to generation according to a cyclical calendar of local celebration. By employing the trope of *Heimat*,[28] these films suggested that Germanness was rooted in a historic cultural heritage and grounded in the affective ties of matrimony, family, and community. In part, then, they provided a reassuring antidote to both Americanization and official American postwar appraisals of Germans' collective sociopathology and guilt. *Heimatfilme* also, however, employed musical conventions and popular stars from the Nazi period. Through sentimental content and modern form, the genre encouraged audiences to indulge in fantasy or nostalgia about a happier communal or individual past by simultaneously affirming cultural traditions forged across a hazy *longue durée* and recalling the personal pleasures of film spectatorship during the Third Reich.

Although they drew on film forms, stars, and notions of community marketed under Hitler, *Heimatfilm* of the early 1950s were not merely backward-looking, nor did they mark a simple reversion to either Nazi ideology or Nazi filmmaking tradition. Rather, by recasting gender and generational dynamics, their narratives oriented their audiences to the future by thematizing, if obliquely, the contemporary transition to a new political era: first, by taming or destroying the criminal past, embodied in the form of an aging, unacceptable masculinity and psychologized through the inability to master memories and adjust to the present; and second, by constructing new models of moral masculinity and femininity that reformulated what it meant to be German after 1945.

The phenomenal commercial success of *Heimatfilme* through the 1950s was therefore an outgrowth of a particular time and form of address. Like Hollywood, they provoked and played upon viewers' desires, addressing German audiences as potential consumers, for example, by rewarding the "authentic" German girl in *Schwarzwald-mädel* with a shiny red Ford–a true fantasy object in 1950. Yet *Heimatfilme* differentiated themselves from Hollywood films on the basis of their national appeal: if they dealt only indirectly with the recent national past, they overtly acknowledged postwar emotions of nostalgia, loss, and personal pain. They spoke to their audiences as Germans, exhibiting sensitivity to the magnitude of viewers' historical communal and domestic traumas, and projecting a vision of the future in which Germans could regain both their prosperity and their pride. By promising personal and national redemption, *Heimatfilme* offered postwar Germans something that Hollywood films could not.[29] As a result, between 1945 and 1960, at least, Hollywood controlled neither the West German market nor the consciousness of most German consumers, who continued to prefer home-grown products.[30]

Cultivating Consumer Taste, Revamping German Identity

Postwar responses to American culture, understood as it was as the effluence of a distinct political and ideological system, were conditioned by assessments of one's own native national past. One's relationship to American culture was complicated by historical considerations and was implicated in postwar efforts at communal and personal redemption and redefinition. Yet it would be a mistake to view signs of a positive embrace of American culture among vanquished populations as solely the result of self-serving attempts to unencumber oneself from an inconvenient political or professional past by proving one's openness to new democratic forms–a kind of cynical public exercise in auto-reeducation. It *was* that, but not merely that.

Viewing preferences in West Germany also varied according to educational and social status: while three-fifths of the lowest educational level preferred German films, only one-third of highly educated Germans expressed the same preference. After 1948 and currency reform, the newly "pauperized" educated classes (who until recently had preferred theater) increasingly switched to cinema and constituted a large proportion of the audience for quality American films such as *Gone with the Wind, The Best Years of Our Lives,* or *Father of the Bride.*[31] Yet I am reluctant to classify them as willing subjects for cultural Americanization, for they avidly consumed a full range of "quality" films (including French, Italian, and British in particular) without regard to national origin and exhibited preference for no particular national product. After Hitler, in fact, cultural cosmopolitanism became the mark of the enlightened "new" German, who sought to shed the chauvinism of a shameful past by exhibiting an openness to other national cultures in order to advertise a new political orientation and identity.

The 1950s witnessed the emergence of vocal groups of critical consumers, mostly educators and university students, who formed German film clubs–based upon French models and begun in the French zone in the late 1940s–along with municipal film festivals (at Mannheim and Oberhausen) that sought to screen domestic classics, documentaries, and *Kulturfilme* together with foreign feature films in order to acquaint German audiences with quality products of all national cinema. This small but significant group of self-cultivated filmgoers (which reached a peak national membership of 150,000 by the mid-1950s) assumed that the medium could make a decisive contribution to the cultural renewal of the new, democratic Germany and that an artistically reinvigorated German cinema would assist in forging an acceptable cultural identity for postwar West Germans.[32]

This was possible, however, only if the German public could be trained to demand a better domestic product. The barrier on the road to international cultural respectability was not, according to these film enthusiasts, the much heralded flawed German collective character. Rather, the problem was consumer taste, which many an intellectual found sadly lacking in the postwar German public. Condemnation was leveled in part against a native film industry that spent a dozen years pandering to the National Socialist state, along with its insipid postwar products of which the *Heimatfilm* was taken to be symptomatic. Nonetheless, in good elite fashion, these critics more broadly disparaged the mediocrity of mass culture, and suggested that Germany's cultural woes were rooted in the broader trends of the industrial West, whose publics lacked the means to distinguish quality products from trash. In contemplating cultural developments, then, they rejected the narrative of Germany's historical difference: Germans departed from other Western societies only insofar as they were limited to consuming ideologically tainted native products during the war, and thus were out of touch with the latest international products. What they—and German filmmakers—needed, they argued, was sustained contact with, and instruction from, the best examples of contemporary foreign film production, regardless of the politics of the country of origin.[33]

The clubs' public visibility and cultivation of government favor worried German film industry representatives, who found the clubs particularly troubling because they originated during the occupation under foreign (French and British) sponsorship, and regularly screened international products to their memberships. In the first postwar decade, club members enthusiastically consumed images forbidden during the late years of the Third Reich. Industry members resented the equation of foreign origin with quality and suspected that their commercial interests would be compromised by the activities of the film clubs. Sensitive to a weakened position on the world market, German film professionals feared the loss of their home market as well.

By the mid-1950s, a younger generation of film club members— mostly university students and aspiring young filmmakers—split from the national club movement, seeking more political engagement and ideological analysis. Their goal was to work toward a national cultural renewal through a revaluation of cinema: from commodity to culture, from economics to art. While they continued to employ the language of consumer "taste" and cinematic "quality" in their elitist response against mediocre "mass" culture, they increasingly narrowed their focus to attacks against *native* products and producers, tracing continuities—in style, ideology, and personnel—between contemporary and National Socialist film production and film-viewing habits. Due to a focus on national filmmaking and the national past, their response against American film was mostly implicit. Nonetheless, it is indicative that they advocated national cinematic renewal through the systematic study and emulation of films produced in Europe, *not* in Hollywood. Initially (in the early to mid-1950s), these youthful critics were particularly enamored of French and Italian feature films and British documentaries; within a few years, however, they increasingly turned to an appreciation of Polish, Czech, and Soviet films to counter the disappointing mass entertainment issuing from Hollywood and West German studios. Their critique was political and ideological, since in voicing a rejection of "Nazi filmmaking fathers and style"–which they assumed had continued undisturbed into the present–they also questioned whether postwar West German film had been sufficiently democratized. Moreover, they invoked an acceptable national culture by resurrecting the work of Weimar filmmaking "grandfathers," particularly those whose oeuvre represented intellectually engaged leftist or aesthetic alternatives to Nazi, West German, and Hollywood films. They sought, then, a national cultural redefinition based upon meaningful ideological and formal difference from the commercialized present *and* past.[34]

By the early 1960s–with the marked decline of postwar film attendance and a commercial cinema in crisis–ambitious young film critics (like Enno Patalas) and budding young filmmakers (like Alexander Kluge, Ulrich Schamoni, and Edgar Reitz) won financial support from the West German state based upon a redefinition of national cinema as *Kultur,* and a recognition that it, like opera or theater, should be protected from market forces. The recognized birth of an internationally marketable West German cinema began at the 1962 Oberhausen Film Festival, which was founded in the early 1950s as a forum for the exhibition of independent short films by West German industry outsiders and other filmmakers from Western and Eastern Europe. Thus, an internationally recognized West German cinema emerged by circumventing the requirements of commercial cinema (e.g., a dependable market and adequate profits) through state sponsorship and, somewhat later, coproduction arrangements with television. As film historian Thomas Elsaesser has argued, "[T]he scheme implied a notion of film as an art work and act of self-expression whose value lay in the fact that it existed at all, and only secondarily in its possibilities of circulating as commodity."[35] Bonn funded and fostered national cinema for international cultural prestige, rather than profits, and–in a continuing cold war climate–for the political capital that would derive from it.

Film Sponsorship, Spectatorship, and the Mutating Meanings of American Culture

Bonn's sponsorship of Young German Film as high *Kultur* marked a departure from federal sponsorship of film as mass commercial culture over a decade earlier. Beginning in the early 1950s, officials earmarked federal funds to subsidize an annual film festival in the Western sectors of Berlin.[36] Like the Oberhausen festival, the Berlin event exhibited an international array of products. But the similarity stopped there. This was no art festival, aimed at cultivating public appreciation for neglected film genres or experimental films. The majority of films screened in Berlin were commercial fare, readily accessible at one's local theater. Bonn officials were not in Berlin to encourage cultural diversity, nor were they primarily interested in bolstering Berlin's ailing film industry, segregated as it was from the West German mainland and the international market. Rather, their ambitions were overwhelmingly political.

Following the lead of American cultural officers, Bonn officials sculpted the Berlin Film Festival as a cultural accompaniment to their pro-Western, anti-communist politics. Berlin became an important symbol of West Germany's democratic renewal. The festival was embraced by local politicians as a way to revive the former capital's interwar reputation as an important European cultural center. Yet the Bonn government also fostered this image for more narrowly national purposes, expecting a thriving colony in the East to lend a certain legitimacy to its claim to represent the best interests of *all* Germans—not just those residing in the West.

Over the course of the 1950s, various West German ministries played out their version of cold war politics to an international audience, eager to score a public relations coup by enticing East Berliners to film showings that excluded the products of socialist countries. Promoted as the "Western cultural showcase in the East," Berlin was not just a symbol, but the site where political and ideological differences acquired a palpable presence in the form of physical and linguistic barriers, protected military compounds and airfields, and even the distinct national uniforms of foreign occupiers. The Soviet blockade and ensuing airlift had further dramatized the East-West split, and Western media coverage firmly established Berlin as a necessary, democratic outpost in a no man's land of Soviet-sponsored totalitarianism. Berlin became the epicenter of the cold war topography. Its film festival was no mere commercial or cultural event, but a celebration—and public enactment—of Western values. Bonn officials carefully cultivated their stage in the East with an eye toward promoting the sovereignty of *their* Germany in a way that flaunted their new, Western political orientation.

The festival did succeed in attracting international films and stars such as Gary Cooper, Bob Hope, Jeanne Moreau, William Holden, Yves Montand, Yvonne DeCarlo, Sophia Loren, and Gina Lollobrigida, as well as German heartthrobs like Hans Albers, Curd Jürgens, Hildegard Knef, Horst Buchholz, and Hardy Krüger. Officials attempted to "democratize" the festival with open-air events (such as autograph afternoons and Disney screenings) at the RIAS Park and Waldbühne, and film screenings at border theaters to attract the East Berlin crowd. Moreover, through 1955, when a jury was introduced, all prizes awarded were determined by public vote, allowing federal and festival officials to declare it a genuine *Volksfest*. The decision to market the festival with international star power and public participation generated enthusiastic response from both West and East Berliners.[37]

Yet federal officials also engaged in ideological showmanship, awarding a German "Oscar" (Bundesfilmpreis) to the best domestic production, with awards regularly going to feature films with anti-communist or pro-NATO slants.[38] Through 1955, they were even more heavy-handed in arranging special screenings (which no doubt drew much smaller audiences than Disney films), such as the politically tendentious exhibit of "Films behind the Iron Curtain" sponsored by the federal Ministry of Greater German Matters. Throughout the decade, moreover, West German officials adamantly refused to allow Soviet entries into their "free world" festival, despite the entreaties of festival organizers, who had an increasingly difficult time securing a sufficient number of good films for screening year after year. Since the festival received federal funds, invitations were issued only with the permission of Bonn ministries and were required to conform to federal government policy and follow official etiquette.[39]

West German officials were responding to more than the dictates of cold war cultural policy in their efforts to control Eastern bloc participation. A subtext to the debate was the issue of West German sovereignty—including Bonn's claim as legitimate heir of the old German Reich. Bonn officials were not merely battling the cultural forces of communism in Berlin; they needed to prove the justice of their political claims on this cultural "front."

The festival succeeded in attracting hordes of East German visitors by reducing ticket prices and increasing star presence at border screenings. Yet, ironically, festival officials were less adept at keeping Western visitors from heading east. Members of the Berlin Senate and federal ministries chafed at reports of visiting notables crossing the border to tour state-run DEFA film studios in East Berlin. Their best solution for stemming the eastward tide was to "keep them busy" with a full festival program "so they won't get bored."[40]

The Berlin festival became as much a display of West German economic vitality as a Western cultural showcase. By the end of the 1950s, it resembled the high-profile glitter fests at Cannes and Venice and offered a schedule packed with trade shows, receptions, and industry association meetings. West German film companies optimistically set up export offices as well, hoping for an entry to the world market. And the ailing Berlin film industry profited from the publicity; after a flurry of contracts for sound synchronization and dubbing, Berlin film workers were producing a steady one-third of West German output by the end of the decade.[41]

Conceived as a cultural accompaniment to cold war politics, the Berlinale became a tribute to Western capitalism, American-style commercialism, and the popular allure of cinema.[42] The Berlin festival peddled propaganda through spectacle. What was being sold was not merely an image of material abundance, leisure, individual fulfillment, and cultural superiority, but a political system as well.

* * *

The Bonn government's celebration of American-style culture at the Berlin Film Festival in the 1950s differed considerably from the typical response of West German elites, which was characterized by marked antagonism to the commercial culture issuing from Hollywood. But Berlin's political situation as a West German outpost in the ideologically inhospitable East was also unique. Amid the rubble and reconstruction of early postwar Berlin, "mass" commercial culture—in both its American and West European variants—emblematized the wealth and wonders of the "free" Western world. Moreover, it supplied a visible promise of consumer vitality for Germany's postwar future. Both symbolically and materially, it served to delimit Berlin's Western sectors from the communist provinces in Eastern Europe.

In Berlin, the populations being plied with commercial culture were, in a sense, peripheral; they were not part of the West German mainland. On home turf, state officials tended to see things differently. There they joined forces with religious leaders to define a German cultural nation in opposition to American commercial culture. In West Germany proper, American culture was not hailed as an alluring helpmate for national reconstruction and Western integration, but excoriated as a force of social and sexual disintegration—a response that was shaped by the specific historical conditions that accompanied German defeat and occupation after World War II.

Germany's defeat in 1945 and the international censure of Nazi crimes against humanity initiated an unprecedented period of national self-redefinition. The struggle for cultural integrity resumed with a vengeance with military occupation and the sudden reintroduction of American economic and cultural forms after a half-decade of isolation due to Hitler's autarkic policies. Packaged first as part of a foreign program of political reeducation, the cinema itself—and particularly its American incarnation—came to represent a broad social and cultural threat precisely because Germany's nature and future were unstable and in flux.

Traditional elites strenuously attempted to construct a national identity based upon the family, Christian (Democratic) values, and notions of a German moral community to deflect American- and Soviet-style materialism. In the process, they enlisted the aid of the West German film industry, which again looked to the state to provide the economic assurances and protection it had enjoyed under Hitler. In exchange for limited state guarantees—and to build a domestic market for a national cinematic culture distinct from the American internationalizing variety—the industry churned out genres with interwar antecedents like the *Heimatfilm*, and experienced a brief golden age on the domestic market throughout the 1950s.

Tellingly, the heyday of *Heimatfilme*—and cinema-going in general—ended with the decade. By the late 1950s, young Germans, who would constitute the overwhelming majority of film-viewers in the coming decades, began to identify it with their parents and the National Socialist past. It appeared cramped, outmoded, and thoroughly unacceptable compared to the more "modern" impulses issuing from the United States. Accordingly, the cross-generational and transgender appeal of the genre was spent by the 1960s.

American culture therefore played a central role in a second wave of postwar redefinition. In the wake of the *Wirtschaftswunder* (economic miracle), consumer choice (and a preference for foreign imports) spawned youth cultures that expressed solidarity on the basis of generation rather than nationality, and thus implicitly criticized received forms of German identity. Nonetheless, if American culture assisted members of the postwar generation in forging social identities distinct from those of their elders, its consumption also highlighted the economic and social cleavages in the Federal Republic. Cultural consumption, after all, was influenced by factors like class, social status, educational level, and sex, and, as a result, became important for both indicating and expressing one's social position, self-image, aspirations, and fantasies.

Hollywood heroes of the 1950s, like Elvis Presley, James Dean, and Marlon Brando, became important models for rebellious young men from working- and middle-class milieus and romantic fantasy figures for young women seeking release from the social and cultural restrictions of the parental home. Highly educated middle- to upper-class youth may have enjoyed Hollywood films and American rock 'n' roll as individual consumers, but their group identities were based instead on cultural consumption and physical styles that advertised the fact that they—unlike their social "inferiors" decked out in leather jackets and jeans—enjoyed elevated European tastes. Their cultural preference was consciously "nicht Amerikanisch." In opposition to the machismo of the *Halbstarken*, or young punks, who ran wild in the streets upon seeing Bill Haley's *Rock around the Clock*, these reluctant Germans exhibited their cosmopolitan openness by listening to cool jazz in dark coffeehouses, studying and discussing cinematic "art," and adopting the personal style of French existentialists. As self-conscious intellectuals, they spurned the stereotypical "philistine addiction to order" and stiff conventionality of adult middle-class German respectability, but did so in a way to differentiate themselves from the consumer masses.[43]

Student film club members who denounced "Papa's" (postwar) cinema appear to have shared this profile. They advocated a more intellectually demanding and aesthetically sophisticated alternative to American cinema, based on a "cerebral" or European style of filmmaking. The clubs and smaller municipal festivals—at Oberhausen, for example—initially fostered artistic solidarity with French filmmakers, but Germans with leftist sympathies gradually expanded their definition of European culture to include the cinematic currents from Eastern Europe as well. Young independent German filmmakers employed the lessons they learned from studying other national products primarily against their own native "culture industry," which like Hollywood was suffering from declining audiences in the late 1950s.

The relationship of these young German filmmakers to American mass culture was, however, complex and deeply ambivalent.[44] Nurtured on American films in the late 1940s and 1950s, they nonetheless expressed an elitist distaste for the crudeness and standardization of American cultural conventions, often grounding their criticisms in Adorno and Horkheimer's theories. Yet, following the trend set in André Bazin's *Cahiers du Cinema*, they were equally fascinated by "unique" American myths and genres (especially the Western) and the putatively highly individual visions of American "auteurs" like Howard Hawks and John Ford.

Ultimately, of course, the intellectually demanding products of Young German Cinema failed to capture the general West German audience, and viewers had to be sought elsewhere—at international festivals and through television broadcasting. Over the past thirty years, moreover, American cinema has come to dominate the programs of German commercial cinema, in part because of the striking juvenilization of movie audiences.

It is ironic, given the fact that the Oberhauseners grounded their revolt firmly within the politics of generation, that their films never achieved a broad-based following among their peers, who, after all, continued as the most avid filmgoers in a period of declining attendance. Their project of confronting and countering the cultural legacies of the national past found little resonance among a generation that increasingly turned away from questions of national identity to focus on the formulation of alternative social identities, firmly grounded in class and gender and articulated through individualized consumption. Cultural consumption is not merely a form of self-indulgence but an avenue for self-definition. In postwar Germany, it was embraced as a way to chart a new identity. The varied responses to cinematic consumption and American culture in the postwar period suggest the range of ways postwar Germans differentiated themselves from one another on the basis of class, generation, and educational level, and simultaneously positioned themselves, both explicitly and implicitly, in relation to their national past and their cultural heritage.

Notes

1. See, for example, Klaus Kreimeier, *Kino und Filmindustrie in der BRD: Ideologie-produktion und Klassenwirklichkeit nach 1945* (Kronberg, 1973); Michael Dost, Florian Hopf, and Alexander Kluge, *Filmwirtschaft in der Bundesrepublik Deutschland und in Europa: Götterdämmerung in Raten* (Munich, 1973); Brewster Chamberlain, *Kultur auf Trümmern: Berliner Berichte der amerikanischen Information Control Section Juli–Dezember 1945* (Stuttgart, 1979); Thomas Elsaesser, *New German Cinema: A History* (New Brunswick, N.J., 1989); Ian Jarvie, *Hollywood's Overseas Campaign: The North Atlantic Movie Trade, 1920–50* (New York, 1992); H. G. Pflaum and H. H. Prinzler, *Film in der Bundesrepublik Deutschland* (Munich, 1979); Peter Pleyer, *Deutsche Nachkriegsfilm, 1946–48* (Münster, 1965).

2. On this last point, see Victoria de Grazia's suggestive comments for fascist Italy in "Nationalizing Women: The Competition between Fascist and Commercial Cultural Models in Mussolini's Italy," in *The Sex of Things: Gender and Consumption in Historical Perspective,* ed. Victoria de Grazia (Berkeley, 1996), 337–58.

3. By "Hollywood" I mean the big eight production companies: Columbia Pictures, Metro-Goldwyn-Mayer, Paramount, RKO, Twentieth Century Fox, United Artists, Universal, and Warner Brothers.

4. MPEA was founded in 1946 to handle the marketing of all U.S. motion pictures to Europe and Asia. Its enduring goal was the commercial penetration and domination of open, unregulated markets abroad.

5. Ursula Hardt, "Kunst für Waschfrau Minna Schulze: Die Produktions-Konzepte des Erich Pommer"; Thomas Elsaesser, "Kunst und Krise: Die Ufa in den 20er Jahren"; Axel Schildt, "Auf Expansionskurs: Aus der Inflation in die Krise"; Schildt, "Hugenberg ante portas: Rationalisierung mit nationalem Besen"; and Hermann Kappelhoff, "Lebendiger Rhythmus der Welt: Die Erich-Pommer

Produktion der Ufa," all in Hans-Michael Bock and Michael Töteberg, *Das UFA-Buch: Kunst und Krisen, Stars und Regisseure, Wirtschaft und Politik*, 90–93, 96–105, 170–73, 190–95, and 208–13 (Frankfurt, 1992). Also Ursula Hardt, *From Caligari to California: Erich Pommer's Life in the International Film Wars* (Providence, R.I., 1996).

6. Thomas Saunders, *Hollywood in Berlin: American Cinema and Weimar Germany* (Berkeley, 1994), 10.

7. Ibid., 4–5.

8. Ibid., 59.

9. Ibid., 130 and 216–17.

10. By 1933, German film producers already had recaptured a good chunk of the domestic market. Hollywood's share of the German market declined from 44.5 percent in 1926 to 21 percent in 1933, while the German share rose during this same period from 39.2 percent to 65 percent. Kristin Thompson, *Exporting Entertainment: America in the World Market, 1907–1934* (London, 1985), 125, 220.

11. Eric Rentschler, "German Feature Films, 1933–1945," *Monatshefte* 82, no. 3 (1990): 257–66. See also Rentschler, *The Ministry of Illusion: Nazi Cinema and Its Afterlife* (Cambridge, Mass., 1996); and Linda Schulte-Sasse, *Entertaining the Third Reich: Illusions of Wholeness in Nazi Cinema* (Durham, N.C., 1996).

12. On this film, see Rentschler, *Ministry of Illusion*, 99–122.

13. For an elaboration of this point, see Heide Fehrenbach, *Cinema in Democratizing Germany: Reconstructing National Identity after Hitler* (Chapel Hill, N.C., 1995), 41–50.

14. For example, German film star Marika Rökk modeled herself on her Hollywood idol, Eleanor Powell. Cinzia Romani, *Tainted Goddesses: Female Film Stars of the Third Reich*, trans. R. Connolly (New York, 1992), 163. Also Andrea Winkler, "Starkult auf germanisch: Goebbels und Hitler hielten sich an die Rezepte Hollywoods," *Medium* 18 (July–September 1988): 27–30.

15. Thomas Guback, *The International Film Industry: Western Europe and America since 1945* (Bloomington, 1969), 128–29; Robert Joseph, "Our Film Program in Germany: How Far Was It a Success?" *Hollywood Quarterly* 2, no. 2 (January 1947): 122–30; and Erich Pommer Collection, University of Southern California (EP-USC), box B, #8-9, U.S. Information Services, "U.S. Feature Films approved for exhibition in U.S. Area of Control as of 30 September 1948" and "Annex L: Synchronization in the U.S.-operated Studios as of 30 June 1949."

16. Office of the Military Government for Germany, U.S. (OMGUS), ISD-MPB #260, confidential report from Robert Schmid, ODIC, Intelligence Branch, to FTM Branch, 1946, deposited in the National Archives (NARA), College Park, Maryland.

17. For a survey of the opinions of German filmgoers in the early 1950s, see NARA, RG 306: USIA, Research Reports on German Public Opinion, Box 6, File HICOG 197: "The Impact of American Commercial Films in West Germany," 14 June 1954; and Box 8, File HICOG 223: "The Relative Influence of USIS, Informal and American Commercial Media in West Germany," 27 December 1955. Also Ludwig Thome, "Der Film und sein Publikum: Der deutsche Filmbesucher," *Internationale Film Revue* 1, no. 4 (1951/52); and Helga Haftendorn, "Zusammensetzung und Verhalten des Filmtheaterpublikums in der Mittelstadt," in *Filmstudien: Beiträge des Filmseminars im Institut für Publizistik an der Universität Münster*, ed. Walter Hagemann (Emsdetten, 1957) 3: 13–25.

18. Michael Hoenisch, "Film as an Instrument of the U.S. Reeducation Program in Germany after 1945 and the Example of 'Todesmühlen,'" *Englisch-Amerikanische Studien* 1/2 (1982): 196–201.

19. Joseph, "Our Film Program in Germany," 122–23; also Karl-Heinz Pütz, "Business or Propaganda? American Films and Germany, 1942–1946," *Englisch-Amerikanische Studien* 2/3 (1983): 394–415.

20. OMGUS, MPB-ISD #277 and 287. Also EP-USC, Box B, #6.

21. OMGUS, MPB-ISD #287. Also EP-USC, Box B, #6.

22. Fehrenbach, *Cinema in Democratizing Germany,* 92–147.

23. Bavarian Cardinal Faulhaber, quoted in "Bischöfe fordern Jugendschutz-Gesetz," *Münchner Merkur,* 24 March 1950.

24. As early as 1948, German director Helmut Käutner held a press conference condemning the censorous interference of German state and Christian officials in film production, and in particular the informal if very public campaign initiated against his filmic parody of Adam and Eve, *Der Apfel ist ab.* Comparing the tactics used against his film to those of the *Nazizeit,* he questioned whether democracy could be successfully introduced in a country where such attempts at public intimidation were tolerated. Into the 1950s, filmmakers continued to assert their democratic rights to freedom of expression but did so in less impassioned and provocative rhetoric. With the introduction of film credits, they blamed state and federal officials for postwar cinematic mediocrity due to their meddling with story lines and production decisions. NARA, OMGUS, MPB-ISD #281. Also, Thiel, "Filmförderung oder Schnulzenkartell?" 46.

25. Robert Liebig, "Filmbürgschaften aus Frankfurt," and Reinhold E. Thiel, "Filmförderung oder Schnulzenkartell?" both in Herbert Stettner, *Kino in der Stadt* (Frankfurt, 1984), 40–43, 44–46. Also Jürgen Berger, "Bürgen heißt zahlen–und manchmal auch zensieren: Die Filmbürgschaften des Bundes, 1950–1955," in *Zwischen Gestern und Morgen: Westdeutscher Nachkriegsfilm, 1946–62,* ed. Hilmar Hoffmann and Walter Schobert (Frankfurt, 1989), 80–97.

26. It also produced a West German commercial film industry with an inferiority complex, unwilling to participate in the Berlin Film Festival even when specifically invited to showcase its films in the early 1950s, for fear that the international forum would disadvantage its wares. Landesarchiv Berlin, Papers of the Senator für Wissenschaft und Kunst, Rep. 14 (hereafter LAB), File: International Festspiele Berlin (IFB), 1951.

27. While anecdotal evidence suggests that older moviegoers were especially drawn to the genre, film industry statistics published in 1961 indicate its substantial popularity among younger cohorts as well. The percentage of Germans polled who listed *Heimatfilm* as their favorite film genre were: 50 percent for ages 55–65; 46 percent for ages 45–54; 36 percent for ages 35–44; 33 percent for ages 25–34; and 26 percent for ages 16–24. See table 12 in Willi Höfig, *Der deutsche Heimatfilm* (Stuttgart, 1973), 452.

28. For a discussion of the historical development of the notion of *Heimat,* see Celia Applegate, *A Nation of Provincials: The German Idea of Heimat* (Berkeley, 1990); and Alon Confino, "The Nation as Local Metaphor: Heimat, National Memory, and the German Empire, 1871–1918," *History and Memory* 5, no. 1 (1993): 42–86. The quote is from Projektgruppe deutscher Heimatfilm, *Der deutsche Heimatfilm–Bildwelten und Weltbilder: Bilder, Texte, Analysen zu 70 Jahren deutscher Filmgeschichte* (Tübingen, 1989), 82.

29. For an extended discussion of the points in the previous two paragraphs, along with an analysis of individual films, see Fehrenbach, *Cinema in Democratizing Germany,* 148–68.

30. Seventy percent of Germans polled preferred native films in 1950; by 1953 this number had risen to 78 percent. NARA, RG 306: USIA, Research Reports on

German Public Opinion, Box 6, File HICOG 197: "The Impact of American Commercial Films in West Germany," 14 June 1954; and Box 8, File HICOG 223: "The Relative Influence of USIS, Informal and American Commercial Media in West Germany," 27 December 1955.

31. NARA, RG 306: USIA, Research Reports on German Public Opinion, Box 6, File HICOG 197: "The Impact of American Commercial Films in West Germany," 14 June 1954; and Box 8, File HICOG 223: "The Relative Influence of USIS, Informal and American Commercial Media in West Germany," 27 December 1955.

32. Although organized on a national scale by 1949, film clubs were an elite, rather than mass, movement. According to the most optimistic estimates, in the mid-1950s they reached a peak membership of 150,000, which was dispersed among 180 adult clubs, 144 youth clubs, and 12 university clubs located in over two hundred German cities. Nevertheless, the national club movement achieved an influence exceeding its numbers, in part due to the composition of its leadership, which was dominated by secondary school teachers, municipal cultural officers, and university professors who recruited young adults into the clubs. In addition, they successfully solicited the support of state and federal funds. See Anna Paech, "Schule der Zuschauer: Zur Geschichte der deutschen Film Club-Bewegung," in *Zwischen Gestern und Morgen: Westdeutscher Nachkriegsfilm, 1946–62,* ed. H. Hoffmann and W. Schobert, 226–45; Johannes Eckardt, "Die Film-Club-Bewegung im Bundesgebiet," *Schwäbische Zeitung,* 24 April 1954; and Fehrenbach, *Cinema in Democratizing Germany,* 169–210.

33. From newspaper clippings in the "Film Club" files located at the Deutsches Institut für Filmkunde, Frankfurt and the Landesbildstelle Berlin.

34. Enno Patalas, "Von Caligari bis Canaris: Autorität und Revolte im deutschen Film," *film 56* 2 (February 1956): 56–66; Patalas, "Filmclubs in Plüschfauteuil," *Filmkritik* 11 (November 1957): 161–62. The film journals *film 56* and *Filmkritik* served as the mouthpiece for youthful critics.

35. The quote is from Elsaesser, *New German Cinema,* 3. Also Jan Dawson, "A Labyrinth of Subsidies: The Origins of New German Cinema," *Sight and Sound* 50, no. 2 (Spring 1981): 102–7; Ronald Holloway, *O Is for Oberhausen: Weg zum Nachbarn* (Oberhausen, 1979); Alexander Kluge, "What do the Oberhauseners want?" reprinted in Eric Rentschler, ed., *West German Filmmakers on Film: Visions and Voices* (New York, 1988), 10–12; Krischen Koch, *Die Bedeutung des "Oberhauseners Manifestes" für die Filmentwicklung in der Bundesrepublik Deutschland* (Frankfurt, 1985).

36. For an expanded discussion of the Berlinale, see Fehrenbach, *Cinema in Democratizing Germany,* 234–53; Wolfgang Jacobsen, *Berlinale: Internationale Filmfestspiele Berlin* (Berlin, 1990); Felix Henseleit, ed., *Die Internationalen Filmfestspiele Berlin von 1951–1974* (Berlin, 1975); Axel Marquardt, ed., *Internationale Filmfestspiele Berlin, 1951–1984: Filme, Namen, Zahlen* (Berlin, 1985).

37. LAB, IFB files for 1952, 1955, 1957 and "Sitzungen" file for 1957–62; also newspaper clippings in the Berlin Film Festival file at the Landesbildstelle Berlin.

38. Elsaesser, *New German Cinema,* 20.

39. By 1959, Bonn relented and a number of East European states were invited, but "only those with which we have diplomatic relations," commanded an Interior Ministry memo. The first Soviet feature film was screened at the Berlinale in 1974, after Willy Brandt had initiated his *Ostpolitik.* LAB, IFB files for 1957, 1959, 1960 and "Sitzungen" file for 1957–62; LAB Filmfestspiele/Festwochen, 1956–58. Also Will Wehling, "Was wird aus der Berlinale?" *Die Welt,* 16 February 1957; and

Ludwig Thome, "'Berlinale' ohne Sowjets: Politisch belastete Filmfestspiele/ Ungelöste Probleme," *Hannoversche Presse,* 21 June 1957.

40. LAB, IFB file, 1953 and "Sitzungen" for 1957–62.

41. LAB, Filmfestspiele/Festwoche, 1956–58.

42. Faced with a budget crunch in 1956, West German federal officials were nonetheless shrewd enough to beef up the budget for advertising and travel subsidies for movie stars attending the festival to ensure popular interest in the event. LAB, Filmfestspiele/Festwoche, 1956–58.

43. Kaspar Maase, *Bravo Amerika* (Hamburg, 1992), chapters 5–7, especially 177–91. For a discussion of female response and of the shifting official reception of American music in both Germanys, see Uta G. Poiger, "Rock 'n' Roll, Female Sexuality and the Cold War Battle over German Identities," *Journal of Modern History* 68, no. 3 (September 1996): 577–616; and her contribution to this volume.

44. See, for example, Eric Rentschler, "How American Is It? The U.S. as Image and Imaginary in German Film," *German Quarterly* (Fall 1984): 603–19.

– *Five* –

NO MORE SONG AND DANCE

French Radio Broadcast Quotas,
Chansons, and Cultural Exceptions

James Petterson

"Whenever I hear the word culture, I bring out my checkbook." So spoke the mad American movie producer in French cinematographer Jean-Luc Godard's aptly entitled 1963 movie *Le Mépris* (Contempt).[1] In this same year, the French sociologist Pierre Bourdieu began research on the sociological variant of Godard's contempt: the formation of class distinctions based on musical taste and reception. This research led Bourdieu, in his 1979 work *Distinction: A Social Critique of the Judgment of Taste,* to develop the notion of "cultural capital," whereby one's knowledge and ability to manipulate cultural notions establishes one's social position.[2] I suggest, however, that the meaning of "cultural capital" is nowhere more ambiguous than in France, above all in the context of the 1 January 1996 implementation of the Pelchat Amendment (after French deputy Michel Pelchat) requiring most of France's 1,300 FM radio stations to broadcast a minimum of 40 percent music of "French expression." In this instance, cultural capital evokes not only abstract power relations, but the checkbook economics underlying the word and world of culture.

The present study addresses the tangible assets of the two enterprises that produce and distribute French music and song: the recording and broadcasting industries. With respect to these enterprises, I read the convergence of two so apparently divergent terms as "capital" and "culture" within the framework of the debate over the means of producing and the means of disseminating music in France. Cultural capital, defined as the use of culture as a means of establishing class distinctions, allows us to understand the debate surrounding the French radio broadcast quotas in terms of a parallel reading of culture *with* capital (where "capital" is defined as the tangible assets of given productive and reproductive enterprises). In terms of radio broadcast quotas, however, cultural capital (in Bourdieu's sense, a form of cultural capital facilitating and promoting class distinctions) cloaks the capital of culture. In other words, the imposition of broadcast quotas implies the legislative disguise of the monetary interests of those enterprises whose assets are defined as cultural. Yet, perhaps because of other concerns (the strikes in Paris and the terrorist bombings of 1995, or the 9 January 1996 death of François Mitterrand) the Pelchat Amendment was implemented with very little fanfare.[3]

Following an overview of this amendment's formulation in December 1993, two years prior to its becoming law, I examine how, in this context, the term "cultural capital" conflates aesthetic and economic forces, and how it is primarily based on a definition of French song that reduces the musical content of a work to its Francophone linguistic content. In other words, this amendment is linguistically reductionist: it asserts that the French language content of a song is the defining element of a song's French cultural distinctness. Yet, this reductionism is not grounded solely in what the media, specifically in the United States, consider a very French valorization of the poetry of the French written word. I subsequently present the various agendas behind this amendment, as they relate to two very distinct interpretations of Francophone *chanson*–what French backers of the Pelchat Amendment have named "song of French expression." All questions of language and culture aside, linguistically based nationalist conceits vie in importance with such central economic questions as authorship and copyright royalties: French concerns for cultural hegemony closely intersect with concerns for the profit margins of several of France's major communications industries.

Scarcely a week after the conclusion of the Uruguay round of the General Agreement on Tariffs and Trade (GATT) talks, in December 1993, the French National Assembly gave initial approval to Michel Pelchat's suggested quotas. This was not without protest from both sides of the political aisle: from those who proposed stronger quotas, and from those who resented this regression to what in France is called *dirigisme*, a throwback to governmental control of the private sector, typical of the post–World War II leadership of Charles de

Gaulle. One of the initial fervent supporters of a higher quota for the broadcast of French music was assemblyman Adrien Gouteyron, who, in early December 1993, suggested that "song is the expression of the soul of the people."[4] Gouteyron coupled French song and French national identity. He also linked "song" and "the soul of the people" in a way that evokes nineteenth-century romantic clichés regarding art as the incarnation of national spirit. He avoided suggesting that French song is also bound to a multibillion French franc national music industry. This suggests that, though the monetary aspect of this debate over broadcast quotas and French song is central, there are higher stakes.

Gouteyron spoke as a conservative when he draped himself and French song in the French flag. Yet his statement also struck a cord among leftist policymakers. In 1993, for instance, Socialist French president François Mitterrand politicized the economic issue in terms of French cultural hegemony: "It would be disastrous to help in generalizing a unique cultural model. Will the laws of money in alliance with technological forces succeed where totalitarian regimes failed?"[5] Mitterrand's remarks equate present-day foreign economic forces with the political and social totalitarianism of the past. He criticized the generalization of the "unique cultural model" propagated by U.S. and Japanese economic interests, and echoed Gouteyron's strategy of equating French culture and song with this founding myth of French national identity: the French spirit of resistance and revolution in the face of any form of oppression.[6] Both the left and the right suggested that declaring the French movie industry a "cultural exception" and imposing French song quotas on the French broadcasting industry were a way of preserving French culture. France was cast in the role of resisting external pressures toward homogenization and economic globalization; in so doing, it was also cast in the role of a positive example for other European nations.[7]

Thus, just as the right and the left suggested that cultural exceptions were a positive approach to the preservation of French and European culture, so they denied the apparent nationalist overtones of the Pelchat Amendment. On 23 December 1993, the office of then communications minister Alain Carignon released a centrist communiqué suggesting that the amendment merely serves "to defend French and Francophone music.... It is not meant to be nationalistic."[8] Indeed, it would be a mistake to assume that the Pelchat Amendment is simply the outward manifestation of increased activity and power on the part of right-wing politicians in France. My point is that the notion of "cultural capital" blurs the distinction between culture and capital, and between the politics of the right and of the left. To blithely attribute the protectionism of the Pelchat Amendment to the rise of right-wing politicians is to further play into the politicization of the economic interests underlying this amendment, whose stakes are greater precisely because they are irreducible to an extreme rightist or leftist political perspective. Indeed, it was Jack Lang, Mitterrand's Socialist minister of culture and minister of communications, who, in August of 1991, proposed the need for what he understatedly called "a minimum level of Francophone music."[9]

France's major effort during the 1993 GATT talks was to protect the French movie industry from being considered a service subject to free trade. It was notably the United States that sought to subject the movie industry to this definition, and the term "cultural exceptions" was a means of protecting France's billion-dollar motion picture industry from "the Brussels Commission and some of the twelve member-states inclined to embrace the free trade postulates of the American negotiators."[10] It was following the partially successful use of this strategy of cultural exceptions for the French movie industry that it was imported into the National Assembly's consideration of quotas, and into the barely concealed battle between the French recording and broadcasting industries. The word "imported" underscores the irony of using the strategy embodied in the notion of cultural exceptions–a strategy that was meant to protect French industries from *external* economic forces–to wage an *internal* economic battle between two major French national industries.

The origins of the Pelchat Amendment help explain the conflict between the French recording and broadcasting industries. In part, the amendment was conceived within the context of intended modifications to the French Telecommunications Law that was passed in 1986, the same year that the Uruguay round of the GATT talks began. The amendment was also intended to standardize a preexisting quota system. Prior to the Pelchat Amendment, broadcast quotas existed in the form of individual and informal agreements between French radio stations and the French government. In accordance with this arrangement, the quotas ranged from as little as 7 percent to as much as 70 percent. On 24 November 1993, Michel Pelchat first opined, in the conservative French newspaper *Le Figaro*, that it seemed "indispensable that a quota of 40 percent of French songs be applied both to radio stations that aim a general or a specific audience."[11] A week later, on 30 November 1993, he proposed that the French Audiovisual Council (Conseil Supérieur de l'Audiovisuel [CSA]) "require a minimum diffusion of French language songs of all radio stations."[12] In referring to a "minimum diffusion," Pelchat (a member of the conservative coalition UDF–PR (Union for French

Democracy – Republican Party) revived Jack Lang's 1991 call for "a minimum level of Francophone music." What is specific to Pelchat's amendment, however, is its intent to generalize the application of a quota standard to all French FM radio stations, whether they target a specific or a general market.

Though Pelchat's initial proposal was rejected by the French Commission for Cultural Affairs, he reintroduced it shortly thereafter with the blessing of Communications Minister Alain Carignon. This time, he explicitly linked the French defense strategy of "cultural exceptions" to his own amendment, thus linking it to the larger question of the capital of culture. On 3 December 1993, Pelchat spelled out this link during an interview with *Le Monde*:

> During the GATT talks we have been fighting, rightly so, for audiovisual *cultural exceptions*. But if, at a national level, the movie industry has revenues of 6 billion francs, we should recognize that the music industry has revenues of 30 billion francs. Don't you think the Americans would laugh if they saw that our National Assembly rejected an amendment that would ensure a quota of 40 percent French songs on our radio stations?[13]

Pelchat underscored the economic motivation for his amendment: the question of market shares and continuing subsidies to the French recording industry. In so doing, he established the alliance, denounced by François Mitterrand as disastrously totalitarian, between "money" and "technological forces." While endorsing resistance to the generalization of a supposed "unique cultural model," Pelchat simultaneously affirmed that France had to be just as competitive (on the same terms) as the other leaders of the audiovisual markets, one of these leaders being, as Pelchat suggested, the United States.

In France considerations of economic motivation such as Michel Pelchat's are rapidly transposed into a cultural framework. For example, in his 1987 work entitled *Élan Culturel*, published one year after the beginning of the Uruguay round of the GATT, Jacques Renard presents data indicating that in 1985, a year after the introduction of the compact disc player into the French market, over one million units sold. Renard's response is to suggest that France "needs to win the gamble of new technologies,"[14] thus acknowledging that the stakes are not so much about this or that song, but about the means of producing and the means of disseminating these songs. Renard nevertheless shifts from economic data to a cultural interpretation of what he calls the "invasion" of foreign technology, thereby blinding himself and his audience to the underlying objective economic factors he had initially presented. With a typically military cliché and alarmist tone, he warns:

What does this invasion mean at the cultural level? It means that if our country does not react, the music produced by tomorrow's French composers will be dictated by sounds invented in Japan. It will be as if, in the nineteenth century, Hector Berlioz had composed … the *Symphonie Fantastique* while thinking of the tonal structure and somber hues of a German orchestra, whereas, to this day, the works of Berlioz are the symbol of the French orchestral and instrumental tradition.[15]

Such hypotheses come very close to a more sinister form of cultural elitism that views cultural preservation in terms of the eradication of all that is "other" or foreign to the culture in question. Just as François Mitterrand sought to establish a causal link between the "technological forces" of the United States and Japan and the threat of vaguely Soviet or National Socialist "totalitarian regimes," so too is Jacques Renard's analysis framed in terms of the fear of the annihilation of French culture by Japanese, German, and U.S. cultural and economic influences.[16]

Jacques Renard's culturally xenophobic rhetoric aside, what most dates his commentary is the concern for material products (compact disks and compact disk players). The debate surrounding the Pelchat Amendment concerns products that are altogether less tangible. For instance, on 8 December 1993, a week after Michel Pelchat had officially requested the 40 percent quota, this debate was redefined in the following point-blank opening question published in *Le Monde*: "Does the audio-visual industry produce a national heritage [*patrimoine*] or does it simply provide a service?"[17] This question demonstrates that the term "cultural exceptions," popularized by France's lawyers at the GATT talks, was not a term born of the *social critique of the judgment of taste*, but the result of a purely legal maneuver to protect a given French industry regardless of whether this industry's product is material or spiritual. The terms "material" and "spiritual" underscore that what is being manipulated is the confrontational language of *them or us*, since this debate focused on whether the output of the audiovisual industry in France was to be considered "cultural works," "audiovisual products," or "audiovisual services." As Serge Regourd noted in 1995: "This reduction of works to simple *services* was not new: in 1974 the Court of the European Community decided that televised programs belonged to the juridical category of services; they thus entered into the field that applied the rule of the free circulation of merchandise, services, capital and individuals."[18] Though Regourd spells out the history of this debate, he sides with the view that redefining cultural works as services is not only ill conceived but unjust.

In his 1997 article "Hollywood à l'offensive: Cultures à vendre," Jack Ralite goes further by denying the underlying capital of cultural products: "Faced with the steamroller of the merchandising of culture, of which the large American groups are the principal beneficiaries, the Old Continent can and must react, in another manner than most of its large audiovisual groups and their respective governments have—governments that content themselves, all too often, with aping American practices."[19] The false distinction between culture and the business of entertainment and communications was belied further by President François Mitterrand's appointment of Jack Lang as both the minister of culture and the minister of communications, and by his endorsement, in October 1993, of the notion of French cultural exceptions: "[C]reations of the spirit are not merchandise, the services of culture are not mere commerce."[20] Mitterrand underscored the spiritual nature of material cultural products, thus concealing the economic function of the material or capital involved.

The term "cultural exceptions" was an effective linguistic means of protecting the French movie industry from the requirement that all service industries be opened up to the laws of free trade. More precisely, this maneuver occurred within the framework of Article 14 of the General Agreement on Trade in Services of the GATT that allows for certain "exceptions" and "nationally specific" situations. Not surprisingly, France and the other members of the GATT talks agreed to disagree on the question of telecommunications products and services. The French politicians' job was to give meaning to the empty signifier named "cultural exceptions" by motivating the French people to the point of establishing a national interest that would be covered under the exceptions included under Article 14, thus allowing the French market to "except" its cultural capital from U.S.- and Japanese-led globalization.[21]

Following the end of the Uruguay round of the GATT talks, in mid-December 1993, the Pelchat Amendment was reintroduced before the French National Assembly by the representative for the Commission for Cultural Affairs, none other than Adrien Gouteyron. Subsequently, on 22 December 1993, this amendment was adopted by the Senate and, on the next day, by the National Assembly. Five weeks later, on 1 February 1994, the amendment was voted into law, with the following final wording: "As of 1 January 1996, all French radio stations must broadcast a minimum of 40 percent of songs of French expression during prime time. One-half of these songs should come from new talent or new productions."[22] This last sentence is key, since it requires French radio stations to include recordings from artists whose only merits are that they are relatively new and/or unknown, that they sing in French, and that they do not yet have a hit.[23] In France, given the present state of the music industry, this assures that virtually every music product will find its way onto the airwaves, thereby guaranteeing a royalty payment from the broadcasting industry to the recording industry.

The Pelchat Amendment did not arise as a means of saving high culture from low culture for the simple reason that the amended law encourages the French recording industry to perpetuate the reproduction of the same (profitable) music, even as it deems this same music to be of irremediably foreign expression. The music remains the same; it is only the language that needs to be changed from a foreign language (read Anglophone) to the French language. The endorsement of cultural difference and hegemony and the rejection of a cultural model that is seen as totalizing or globalizing represents, in fact, the rhetorical process through which to better enforce a homogeneous economic model internal to France. Behind the notion that "cultural exceptions" are a means of protecting France's "national heritage" is the far more sobering governmental and legislative commonplace that music (specifically pop music and rock 'n' roll) means big business and, consequently, big governmental policy decisions. The clear economic importance of the battle between French broadcasting and recording industries, exemplified by the Pelchat Amendment, can also be seen in a similar 1973 law in Canada which stipulates that at least 65 percent of all airtime on Francophone radio stations be devoted to French-language vocal music (FVM). As in the Canadian case, the Pelchat Amendment includes provisions guaranteeing the subsidy of so-called "new talent," thereby subsidizing the producers of the product that would fulfill the requisite demand for music of French expression. Thus, as in Canada, by imposing the 40 percent quota of music of "French expression" on music played during prime time on French radio stations, the French government sided with the recording industry by guaranteeing continued royalties for the French recording industry, even as the privatization of French radio becomes a *fait accompli*. The amendment guarantees continued governmental control over the direction of income flow, at a time when the Telecommunications Law of 1986 provided for the continued privatization of French radio, and permitted further station mergers.[24] More pointedly, this amendment ensures that the French broadcasting industry does not gain the upper hand, and that it does not squeeze the French recording industry out of the business by relying almost solely on products of foreign origin.

As I have already suggested, the stakes of this amendment and the reasons for this economic battle go beyond material products. In the words of Simon Frith, in his 1987 article "Copyright and the Music

Business": "For the music industry the age of manufacture is over. Companies (and company profits) are no longer organized around making *things* but depend on the creation of *rights.*"[25] This supersedes analyses such as Jacques Renard's by proposing that the assets of the music industry lie largely in "rights," and that the broadcasting industry generates a very large "basket" of such rights.[26] Thus, with this transition from the age of the manufacture of material products to the age of the "gathering of rights," the recording industry's dependence on the broadcasting industry is on the rise. In an age in which rights are the new product of choice, the recording industry depends on the broadcasting industry for producing both demand and, as a derivative, the recording industry's most profitable product: copyright royalties.

The textual bias of the Pelchat Amendment can be understood by considering this question of rights, and by looking at the primary lobbies backing this amendment. Implementation of this amendment was crucial for one organization in particular, the French Society of Authors, Composers, and Editors of Music, whose acronym, SACEM, appears on virtually every French recording product. This society lobbied heavily, for the commonsense reason that passage of the Pelchat Amendment guaranteed royalties on 40 percent of everything played, every day, on French radio. SACEM's lobbying activities have not been limited to the 1980s and 1990s. In 1969, some twenty-five years prior to the Pelchat Amendment, the previous incarnation of SACEM—the Union of Authors and Composers—complained to the government that over 50 percent of songs broadcast on French radio were not of "French expression."[27] Jacques Attali, President Mitterrand's former special councilor, notes in his 1977 work *Noise: The Political Economy of Music* that the role of writers and their desire to copyright their material go back to the 1920s. As of 1937, "radio stations had to pay for representation and reproduction rights" to the authors of songs.[28] The proprietary battle surrounding French cultural production is thus clearly inscribed in the history of the French economy.[29] Thus, the Pelchat Amendment crystallized a sixty-year-old struggle between the recording and broadcasting industries. The notion of cultural exceptions, initially used to protect the French motion picture industry from U.S. dominance, was subsequently used to cloak a struggle internal to France: the battle between those who furnish demand—the broadcasting industry—and the suppliers to this demand—the recording industry.[30]

My second point bears on this economic history and on the clearly ongoing redefinition of copyright law within the French music industry. One of the specific characteristics of the music being legislated by the Pelchat Amendment is its connection to the French language, considered as both a French cultural icon and as an item that can be copyrighted. In other words, the Pelchat Amendment underscores the connection between music and song in general and, specifically, song of French expression. The linguistic reductionism of this amendment not only benefits the recording industry and SACEM, but also conveniently perpetuates the myth of the culturally exceptional nature of French song or *chanson*. The major moments of the myth of French *chanson* are well worth tracing. In the early 1960s, France experienced the rise of rock 'n' roll in the form of what was called *la vague yéyé*, (the "*yéyé* wave"). This did not spell the end of what was and still is called French song (*la chanson française*). Rather, it was seen as the occasion for a battle between what was deemed the linguistically meaningless (hence culturally and spiritually worthless) "drivel" of the "*yéyé* wave," and what was portrayed as the grand poetry of French *chansonniers*.[31] As opposed to the Anglo-Saxon "I love you, yeah, yeah, yeah ..." music of the early 1960s, these *chansonniers* were, then and now, portrayed and perceived as the protectors of France's clearly nonnegotiable spiritual product: the French language. Yet, the music of the *chansonniers* from the 1950s and early 1960s (such singers as Georges Brassens, Charles Aznavour, and Yves Montand) was characterized by a cultural homogeneity that deprived French song of the vitality contained in regionally diverse aspects of French culture. As such, French song lacked the explosive energies born of the musical and cultural fusion that exemplified youth music in other countries in the late 1950s and early 1960s, and that is also expressed in today's youth music.

The relative absence of an equally explosive youth music scene in France during the late 1950s and early 1960s is explained by the strength of French *chanson* during this same period. The homogeneity of *la chanson française* acted as a barrier to the heterogeneity of French youth and obstructed the development of alternative forms of French youth music, which might have been capable of dislodging the *chanson*, this active symbol of monoculturalism. Thus, in the 1950s, French song persisted in its homogeneity at a time when rock 'n' roll was perceived as a transcultural, transclass, polysemic, and dialogical message in other industrially advanced nations. Yet the monoculturalism of French *chanson* also served as a catalyst, encouraging French youth to turn to non-Francophone forms of music.[32]

Paul Yonnet's study of French culture and society, *Jeux, modes et masses: La société française et le moderne, 1945–1985,* remains one of the more perceptive readings of the social implications of French song for the period from the late 1950s to the early 1960s. Yonnet suggests an important avenue for future research on youth music and youth culture in France by proposing a more radical but plausible hypothesis. He points out that the relative weakness of the rock 'n' roll experience in France, in the context of the continued importance of French song, can be attributed not only to the postwar French cultural state produced under Charles de Gaulle, but also to a reaction to France's loss of its colonies, which provoked a period of introspection for French culture, a nostalgic turn toward pre-Vichy notions of social and cultural identity and purity. France created a kind of modern-day cultural Jacobinism to defend an ideal notion of culture from any form of external oppression. The novelist André Malraux, Charles de Gaulle's minister of culture, underscored this cultural Jacobinism in 1963 during a speech before the French National Assembly, when he hyperbolically suggested that France, the French people, and French culture were "responsible for man's destiny."[33] More recently, Jack Ralite suggested that the notion of "cultural exceptions" represented a "new and constructive position" from which to defend the "freedom of artistic and civic expression [*expression citoyenne*]; a freedom that constitutes one of the authentic rights of man, and which is in the process of disappearing."[34]

Whereas such *chansonniers* as Edith Piaf and Maurice Chevalier were lauded as singers of the French resistance and of the revolutionary spirit of the French during World War II,[35] the French singers of the 1950s and 1960s were equally acclaimed as French poets. Their songs are still published as poems in such well-known poetry series as Pierre Seghers's "Poètes d'aujourd'hui," they are recited as poetry by French school children, they are used as literature topics for the high school diploma examinations, and they are even the topics for doctoral dissertations in departments of literature.[36] The traditional association of French *chanson* with the intellect, with the textual, with resistance, and with France's revolutionary spirit is common not only to the *chansons* of the 1950s and 1960s, but also to our present debate. For example, in his 1973 work on and anthology of French songs, *La Chanson française de contestation des barricades de la Commune à celles de mai 1968*, Serge Dillaz suggests that French *chanson* "touches every social level, at every time, and in every place."[37] Dillaz's definition of French *chanson* evokes a collective myth applicable to all people, at all times, in all places. Indeed, for Dillaz French song is "one of the noblest traditions of popular French poetry," that expresses France's revolutionary spirit aimed at both foreign and national tyrants.[38] He also devalues the radio broadcasters of *chansons* by attributing to them the pejorative diminutive title *commerçants de la chansonnette* (sing-song peddlers).[39] The scandal of the broadcast song (specifically of the *yéyé* generation) is that "it systematically sac-rifices the text for the sake of music."[40] Indeed, for Dillaz the condi-tion *sine qua non* for the renewed success of French song rests in "a return to its textual aspect and to a careful melody no longer imbued in the false revolutionary stance of electrified guitars and staged con-vulsions."[41] This said, Dillaz recognizes the hypocrisy of political commercial circles that relate the text of their songs—made for mass consumption and drained of any political content—to a revolutionary tradition. In so doing, however, Dillaz must admit that a return to the "textual aspect" of song does not necessarily guarantee the authen-ticity of a song's "revolutionary stance."[42]

Dillaz's call for a return to the textual is precisely the judgment being applied to both the music that is penalized by and the music that benefits from the Pelchat Amendment. This law penalizes artists who may be living and working in France, but who write and sing in a lan-guage other than French. Such artists are often from France's ex-colonies (for example, the Algerian singer Khaled or the Senegalese singer Youssou N'Dour). Artists producing contemporary instrumental music, including such musical genres as ambient music and techno-pop, are also penalized. In this case, the Pelchat Amendment em-braces Jacques Renard's reactionary call to arms to protect French musical production and composition from foreign technology. By proposing a quota law that is inclusive only of music considered "song of French expression," the Pelchat Amendment effectively penalizes, through exclusion, all contemporary youth music that is without text (be it of French or any other origin) and that relies on complex, advanced technologies for its composition and perfor-mance—technology that, in the case of France, is very often of foreign origin. By contrast, a genre that has benefited from the Pelchat Amendment has been French rap (including such groups as MC SOLAAR, NTM, or Alliance Ethnik). Not surprisingly, Francoph-one rap has been touted as a poetic form and Francophone rappers as modern-day troubadours keenly aware of the subtleties of the words of the French language and of their poetic and humorous affinities. Indeed, not only is the linguistic prowess of French rappers compared to that of the singers of the 1950s and 1960s, but also they are inducted into the entire tradition of French poetry.[43]

It is commonplace to suggest that the study of French youth music culture is in no way as advanced in France as it is in the United States, Germany, or Italy. The clearest reason for this lag is due more to a certain reticence on the part of French intellectuals than to some fundamental inability to grasp French youth culture. The reluctance to seriously study the so-called "*yéyé* wave" of the 1960s, or the

Johnny Halliday phenomenon of the 1970s (the immense success of this singer rests, in great part, on songs translated from the English into French, but set to the same rock beat as the Anglo-Saxon original), or the early French youth reception of Seattle Sound in the late 1980s, or today's active French ambient and techno scenes does not stem simply from some inability to recognize the legitimacy of these experiences. Rather, it stems from the fact that in France culture remains, in the words of Pierre Bourdieu, the "present incarnation of the sacred."[44] I hope to have demonstrated, however, that it is in the material interest of certain French industries that culture be forced to "remain" sacred. Intellectual reluctance before popular culture thus stems from an inability, fostered by economic interests, to completely part with the high-culture bias toward linguistic structure and content in music. This bias is all the more devilishly difficult to relinquish since today it is linked ever more firmly to culture *and* to capital.

Notes

1. The humor of the line Godard attributes to the mad American movie producer becomes more macabre when read as a comment on the Nazi era: "Whenever I hear the word culture I bring out my gun." As we will see, Godard is not alone in drawing the parallel between the National Socialist conquest of Europe and the United States' monopoly over the international film industry.
2. Pierre Bourdieu, *Distinction: A Social Critique of the Judgment of Taste,* trans. Richard Nice (Cambridge, 1984), 11–96.
3. It was not until 10 January 1996, in fact, that the French daily newspaper *Le Monde* took note of this *fait accompli.*
4. Howard LaFranchi, "New Quota Law for French Music Draws Praise on Parisian Streets," *Christian Science Monitor,* 24 December 1993, 1.
5. Armand Mattelart, "Les nouveaux scénarios de la communication mondiale," *Le Monde Diplomatique,* no. 8 (1995): 24. Unless otherwise noted, all translations from the French are my own.
6. The Mitterrand era is marked by criticism of the socioeconomic systems of both the United States and Japan. A further analysis would require a rereading of the French data here presented in light of a more detailed study of the French reaction to Japan's successes in the field of media technologies.
7. Whereas the term "globalization" has tended toward the value-neutral, even value-positive in the United States, in France "globalization" and "*mondialisation*" remain value-negative.
8. LaFranchi, "New Quota Law for French Music," 1.
9. Ariane Chemin, "Le *Quota de chansons françaises* voulu par M. Pelchat (UDF-PR) sème le trouble dans les radios," *Le Monde,* 2 December 1993, 15.
10. Serge Regourd, "L'Audiovisuel réduit à une simple marchandise," *Le Monde Diplomatique,* no. 1 (1995): 11.

11. Cited in Chemin, "Le *quota de chansons françaises*," 15.

12. Alain Rollat, "La Réforme de l'audiovisuel divise la majorité," *Le Monde*, 2 December 1993, 15.

13. Alain Rollat, "Le oui, mais ... de Michel Pelchat (UDF-PR)," *Le Monde*, 3 December 1993. 24.

14. Jacques Renard, *L'Elan culturel: La France en mouvement* (Paris, 1987), 98.

15. Ibid., 98–99.

16. See my note 3.

17. "Jacques Toubon prépare des mesures en faveur de la production audiovisuelle," *Le Monde*, 8 December 1993, 24.

18. Regourd, "L'Audiovisuel réduit à une simple marchandise," 11.

19. Ibid., 32.

20. Lucie Tamaris, *Le Monde Diplomatique,* no. 4 (1995): 27.

21. Legally, this official disagreement between France and the United States means that the French audiovisual sector will eventually be integrated into the service sector and become subject to the rules of free trade. See Jack Ralite, "Hollywood à l'offensive: Cultures à vendre," *Le Monde Diplomatique*, no. 2 (1997): 32.

22. Michel Colonna D'Istria, "L'Obligation pour les radios de diffuser 40% de chansons françaises est renvoyée à 1996," *Le Monde*, 24 December 1993, 19.

23. In order to enforce this amendment, the CSA hired a polling company to monitor everything aired on the twenty most popular radio stations, and to occasionally monitor smaller stations.

24. Ariane Chemin, "Le Paysage radiophonique va être remodelé," *Le Monde*, 11 December 1993, 15.

25. Simon Frith, "Copyright and the Music Business," *Popular Music* 7 (1988): 57.

26. Though a bit pastoral, "basket" is indeed the technical term used to designate the aggregate of rights that derive from a given product, hence the anthropological image of the recording industry as a modern-day "gatherer."

27. Serge Dillaz, *La Chanson française de contestation: Des barricades de la Commune à celles de mai 1968* (Paris, 1973), 116.

28. Jacques Attali, *Noise: The Political Economy of Music,* trans. Brian Massumi, with a foreword by Fredric Jameson and an afterword by Susan McClary (Minneapolis, 1985), 99.

29. Jack Ralite denies the issue of copyright and proposes a writers' summit, similar to the 1992 Rio summit on environmental protection, during which "artists, writers, lawyers, researchers, producers could work together to groom the notion of the rights of the author, on a moral basis, and not on the basis of copyright." Ralite, "Hollywood à l'offensive," 32.

30. Attali, *Noise*, 96–102.

31. See Peter Hawkins, "How Do You Write about *Chanson*?" *French Cultural Studies*, vol. 4 (1993): 69–79.

32. See Paul Yonnet, *Jeux, modes et masses: La société française et le moderne, 1945–1985* (Paris, 1985).

33. With reference to this perhaps surprising mention of Jacobinism, consider this recent commentary in *Le Monde Diplomatique:* "La France est l'archétype de l'Etat-nation, jacobine de surcroît." (France is the archetype of the nation-state; it is also Jacobin.) Edgard Pisani "'Tous ensemble' contre la mondialisation," *Le Monde Diplomatique*, no. 1 (1996): 32. This Jacobin metaphor cannot be dismissed. Consider, for instance, that the French Ministry of Culture has called for the establishment and subsidy of clubs and *cafés-musiques* throughout France for the purpose of discussing the role of and promoting French song.

34. Ralite, "Hollywood à l'offensive," 32.

35. Dillaz, *La Chanson française de contestation,* 86–96.

36. See Hawkins, who refers to Lucienne Cantaloube-Ferrieu's book version of her doctoral dissertation: *Chanson et poésie des années 30 aux annés 60: Trenet, Brassens, Ferré–ou, Les "enfants naturels" du surréalisme* (Paris, 1981).

37. Dillaz, *La Chanson française de contestation,* 13.

38. Ibid., 95.

39. Ibid., 113.

40. Ibid., 119.

41. Ibid., 122.

42. Ibid., 134–35.

43. "Les Réseaux FM protèstent contre les quotas de chansons francophones," *Le Monde,* 10 January 1996, 27. There is a rather savory irony in naming Francophone rappers "troubadours," given the decidedly non-Francophone nature of the original troubadour's *Langue d'Oc.*

44. Bourdieu, *Distinction,* xiii.

Part III

Transnational Stylings: American Music and the Politics of Identity

Six

AMERICAN MUSIC, COLD WAR LIBERALISM, AND GERMAN IDENTITIES

Uta G. Poiger

When East German authorities built the Berlin Wall in August 1961, they sought to halt more than the drain of workers that was debilitating their economy. Just as importantly, they hoped to stop the influx of West European and especially American cultural products into East Germany. Within a week of the building of the Wall, the East German press reported that state-run youth clubs had turned boys in blue jeans (referred to as "Texas pants") into respectable young men who wore suits and who danced with girls in fashionable dresses. Newspapers were full of stories about East German, and especially East Berlin, adolescents who, finally protected from the cultural imperialism of the United States and West Germany, were converting to the socialist cause.[1] Meanwhile, in West Berlin adolescents continued to dance to American music in three government-sponsored dance cafés. The West Berlin government had started these so-called "jazz cafés" in 1960 in an effort to provide modern, clean entertainment for adolescents aged sixteen to twenty-five. For the first time, these cafés integrated American music on a large scale into state-sponsored programs.[2]

Both these events point to the differences, and similarities, in the conceptions of Germanness that East and West German authorities had developed by the early 1960s. It is these (re)constructions of

German national identities on the two sides of the iron curtain that I briefly want to discuss in this essay by comparing reactions to American-influenced youth cultures in the two states in the decade before the Wall.[3] In the 1950s and 1960s, East German authorities were more or less consistently hostile toward American imports. In West Germany, on the other hand, what I call an emerging cold war liberal consensus made consumption, including the consumption of American popular culture, increasingly part of a new, liberal West German identity.[4]

American imports such as jazz and later rock 'n' roll were extremely popular with German adolescents, and, as a result, they constituted some of the most controversial aspects of consumer culture in the two states. Reactions to jazz and rock 'n' roll were shaped by two factors in particular: gender and race. Commentators in both states feared that American imports led adolescents to transgress proper gender roles: they made young men either weak or overly aggressive and young women sexually expressive. Moreover, commentators were concerned about alleged racial transgressions that jazz and rock 'n' roll produced.[5] This essay will explore the changing understandings of gender, race, and consumption that were part of the diverging, yet always connected, trajectories of the two German states.

Fears about American influences have had a long tradition in Germany. Since the 1920s many Germans had equated America with modernity—an association that raised both hopes and fears. During the Weimar Republic, for example, Germans were not just fascinated with American management and production methods; in big cities like Berlin, American popular culture, especially music and movies, also made a splash.[6] With the arrival of American jazz in the early 1920s, Germans had to come to terms with a music that they saw as black and that came to define one aspect of modernity. As many young people embraced jazz and the musicians who brought it to Germany, conservatives and fascists leveled anti-black and anti-semitic attacks: jazz was a music created by "niggers," linked to "primitive sexuality," and marketed by Jews. Together with lascivious women, jazz allegedly endangered Germany's young men.[7]

During the Third Reich, the National Socialists sought to root out all cultural products perceived as non-Aryan, and jazz was one of their prime targets. In the 1940s the Nazis viciously prosecuted "swing youths," groups of young women and men who listened to jazz together and wore distinctive clothes. Yet even the National Socialists, caught between their racial utopia and the need to accommodate a population under the conditions of war, never banned jazz completely from the airwaves.[8]

After 1945, with the Allied occupation and the opening of its market, West Germany experienced an unprecedented influx of American products, from nylon stockings to popular music. The impact of these imports was by no means restricted to West Germany; especially via Berlin, it reached well beyond the iron curtain. Until the construction of the Wall in 1961, a constant stream of people flowed back and forth between East and West Berlin. Large numbers of East Berliners and East Germans came to shop and to enjoy themselves in West Berlin. Sometimes whole East Berlin school classes would cross into the Western sectors to watch movies. Many East Berlin boys and girls frequented West Berlin music halls, and young people from all over the German Democratic Republic (GDR) would go to West Berlin to buy jeans, leather jackets, or records, in spite of prohibitive exchange rates. At home some of them would tune into Western radio stations, including the American Forces Network (AFN) and Radio Luxembourg, to listen to the latest American hits. Thus, whenever American music and fashions hit West Germany and West Berlin, their impact was felt in both Germanys.

East German Hostilities

When the Wall went up, East German officials continued to walk a tightrope they had been on for years. Since the early 1950s, they had described allegedly "decadent" and "degenerate" imports like boogie-woogie and jazz as part of an "American cultural barbarism," which they saw at the root of American and West German imperialism.[9] Historically, Europeans also had often used the concept "degeneracy" to label, for example, Jews or Sinti and Roma (Gypsies) as inferior. In connected attacks they had employed "degeneracy" to criticize cultural styles or behavior, such as "wild" dancing, that they perceived as racial transgressions. Moreover, both degeneracy and decadence had connoted deviations from respectable womanhood and manhood. These patterns persisted in cold war East Germany. One cultural official spoke of boogie-woogie as a channel through which the American entertainment industry propagated "the degenerate ideology of monopoly capitalism with its lack of culture," another official was worried about the "public display of sexual drives" among jazz fans who danced, and a music critic announced that some rhythms in jazz led to "degenerate" dancing.[10]

Such concerns became more pronounced when rock 'n' roll music and dancing arrived in Germany in 1956 via American movies and numerous press reports about rock 'n' roll concerts. In December 1956 a cartoon in the East Berlin daily *Berliner Zeitung* showed a small, emaciated Elvis Presley performing under larger-than-life female legs in front of a crowd of girls much bigger than he was. The cartoon implied that female Presley fans were sexual aggressors who emasculated men: the girls were throwing off bras and garter belts and licking their lips in obvious sexual excitement. Their hairstyles marked some of these young women as possibly black (short curly dark hair) and others as white (blonde ponytails), but in portraying all of them with stereotypical "negroid" features (wide noses, thick lips) the cartoon labeled their behavior as typically black. The accompanying article also put this reversal of gender roles into a racial context: it claimed that young women were the main consumers of rock 'n' roll (described as American nonculture) and asserted that rock 'n' roll appealed to primitive humans. In such a depiction, allusions to gender upheaval and to alleged racial transgressions reinforced one another to portray rock 'n' roll as dangerous.[11] East German authorities frequently reacted with open repression. In 1957 one Culture Ministry official gave explicit orders to prevent the spread of rock 'n' roll since the music and dancing represented a "degeneration" inherent in the American way of life.[12] Other measures ranged from prohibitions of American music and so-called "open" dancing to arrests for shouting "Ulbricht, pfui, pfui, pfui–Elvis, yes, yes, yes."[13]

The fact that many of the products of American culture were rooted in the culture of African-Americans, whom communists recognized as an oppressed group, did not dissuade East German authorities from attacks on American music and dances, especially jazz, boogie and rock 'n' roll. Race played a complicated role in these attacks. It would seem that the racialism and racism apparent in East German charges of "decadence," "degeneracy," and "primitivism" against American popular culture were clearly at odds with East Germany's public stance against racism in the United States. After all, East German papers in the mid-1950s reported extensively on efforts to integrate schools and public accommodations in the American South. However, East German visions of racial equality relied on ideals of male restraint and female respectability, including female sexual passivity, across races. This insistence on specific norms of male and female respectability found one of its most powerful articulations in official rejections of jazz as a music associated with gangsters and prostitutes. With such condemnations of jazz, which they saw as a black music, East German officials reasserted racial hierarchies in the realm of culture. Attacks on rock 'n' roll reinforced this. Even though highlighting American racism was one way to fight the cold war against the United States and West Germany, East German authorities could not relinquish their own association between female sexual passivity, "civilization," and "whiteness."

However, throughout the 1950s, jazz fans and music critics argued that some forms of jazz were a protest music for African-Americans; as such, jazz could be part of developing a new, "clean" German dance music. In 1956 even the state youth organization Free German Youth (FDJ) publicly promoted this notion.[14] Well aware of such arguments, East German authorities in 1961 tried to avoid any public debates over jazz and American music. They suggested that jazz fans pursue their interests in "authentic" folk music in existing, carefully supervised dance and music groups.[15]

Still, in the aftermath of the Wall, the East German press and youth officials focused heavily on transforming the boys and girls who had frequented bars and dance halls in West Berlin and who had consumed, among other things, rock 'n' roll. The official attention to the more conservative fashions of suits and dresses that the transformed youths allegedly wore shows how important proper gender roles were to the socialist conversions. An internal report, however, revealed that these former *Grenzgänger* (transgressors of the border) were young men and women hostile toward the state, who continued to cause riots and "striptease scenes" in some East Berlin youth clubs. Clearly, these young people had transgressed more than the borders between the sectors of Berlin.[16]

Thus the space for maneuver remained limited. When East Berlin jazz fans tried to found a jazz club at Humboldt University in the fall of 1961, authorities were highly alarmed. As part of their agenda, the jazz fans tried to abolish the "60:40 rule" that restricted how much music imported from the West could be played at concerts and on the radio. (Only 40 percent of the music could be licensed in the West, including West Germany, Western Europe, and the United States.) Officials of the FDJ Central Committee claimed that such jazz associations were founded by West German agents and urged local FDJ functionaries to be aware "of the political background of a strengthened jazz movement." Present-day jazz, these officials said, was shaped by commercialism and imperialist ideas and was thus part of the "decadent trends of bourgeois ideology." As throughout the 1950s, East German authorities viewed adolescent consumption of American-influenced popular culture as a potential political threat.[17]

West German Hostilities

Until the second half of the 1950s, hostility also dominated commentaries on American popular culture in West Germany. West Germans found themselves fighting on several fronts: against their fascist past, against the present cold war enemy, and against the specter of an American-style consumer culture.[18] For example, in the early 1950s, West German authorities attacked American dances like the boogie as part of their youth protection efforts. The supposed "primitivism" of faster-paced dances, like the boogie, threatened the proper gender roles so necessary to postwar West German identity. In West German discussions of dancing, concerns about premarital sex, especially by women, intersected with misgivings about working-class culture *and* with a hostility toward black culture. Contemporaries cast working-class girls who hung out in the streets and who danced to boogie-woogie as potential sexual delinquents. A connected attack was to point to the emasculating and feminizing effect of "sultry negro songs" for boys. As education manuals warned, boys, too, had to restrain themselves in order to reach full manhood.[19]

Such West German fears were exacerbated by the arrival of rock 'n' roll and by youth riots in the mid-1950s. West Germans connected what they saw as adolescent misbehavior to American influences. In 1956, for example, the West German youth magazine *Bravo* reported about male rioters who had roamed the streets in Britain after showings of the Bill Haley movie *Rock around the Clock. Bravo* claimed that Bill Haley's music was rooted in the "ritual music of Africa's Negroes." Further, the magazine maintained that the influence of rock 'n' roll had turned "cool Englishmen" into "white Negroes" who rioted. *Bravo* thus labeled rioting a typically black behavior and warned against rock 'n' roll in racist terms; it also urged its German audience not to behave like the British. When it became clear that rock 'n' roll had many admirers in Germany and that German adolescents, too, took to the streets after showings of *Rock around the Clock,* another West German commentator worried about what he called "wild barbarians in ecstasy."[20]

Like their East German counterparts, some West German commentators were particularly worried about Elvis Presley, who, they implied, lacked respectability. As in the United States, gender ambiguity was one of Presley's outstanding characteristics for German promoters as well as opponents.[21] The music industry and negative press commentary worked together to feminize him. In 1956, RCA decided to market Presley in Germany with the slogan "He sings like Marilyn Monroe walks, but at home he is a model son." Both West and East German papers picked up on the press releases from RCA, sometimes playing with the slogan to underline Presley's gender ambiguity, while dropping the reference to Presley's exemplary private life. An article in an East Berlin paper, for example, announced that Presley was trying to compensate for his bad voice by "wildly swinging his hips like Marilyn Monroe."[22] The close association with Monroe, who like the French actresses Marina Vlady and Brigitte Bardot had become a symbol of female sensuality in Germany, in fact made Presley into a rebel quite different from such predecessors as Marlon Brando, who represented male aggression. When describing Presley's concert performances in the United States, *Der Spiegel* doubted that Presley's moving hips were an allusion to male sexual behavior and instead described his gestures as those of a "talented female striptease dancer."[23] That description had also been used by American papers, and, along with the American expression "Elvis, the Pelvis," was taken up by many Germans.

West German commentators again harnessed alleged racial characteristics to criticize rock 'n' roll, but in Presley's case they used them to support the notion of *female* aggression and male weakness. Some West German reports on Presley drew a clear connection between his gender and racial ambiguities: Presley's way of moving put not just his male gender but also his racial origins in doubt. Newspapers in the West suspected that Presley must have black blood in his ancestry to be able to move and sing in this extraordinary fashion.[24] In another attack, one West German paper directly referred to Presley's thick lips as an attribute of the ideal man in the United States—a country described as run by women (*Frauenstaat Amerika*).[25] Such statements used references to racial stereotypes, like thick lips, to underline the notion that in the United States gender norms were reversed.

Gender and racial ambiguities on Presley's part elicited and required gender and racial transgressions on the part of his female fans. At first, West German writers associated rock 'n' roll with male overaggressiveness and blackness, but increasingly commentators worried about female aggressivity. They reported that in the United States Presley's female fans attacked policemen and exhibited active sexual desire toward this feminized man with what they described as stereotypically black features. West German commentators thus conflated male weakness with blackness and linked both to female desire. These associations of blackness with both male overaggression and male weakness reaffirmed Western stereotypes of black men.[26]

When it became clear that Presley and rock 'n' roll found many fans in Germany as well as in the United States, some West German educators, particularly disturbed by young German female fans, derided women in pants and tight sweaters who were among the rock 'n' roll fans hanging out in the streets.[27] And in 1957 the state-sponsored West German movie rating board demanded that scenes allegedly showing the "aggressive flirting" of girls be cut from another rock 'n' roll movie, because the film would otherwise foster a "materialist understanding of life" among adolescents.[28] Rock 'n' roll was so disturbing precisely because it seemed to undermine the ideal nuclear family with its restrained male breadwinner protectors and asexual female caretakers. The various reactions to rock 'n' roll reveal West German fears that American cultural influences led to transgressions of gender and indeed also of racial norms—with potentially dire political consequences.

Cold War Liberalism

After the mid-1950s, however, West German authorities began to transform such ideas about American popular culture, consumption, and rebellious youths. By the end of the 1950s, West German cold war liberals increasingly outnumbered the religiously inspired conservatives who saw consumption as a terrible and indeed political threat. The cultural vision associated with the conservatives is that of the *christliches Abendland*; the rejection of American music was part of efforts to promote this "Christian West." This vision, which dominated West German cultural politics in the first half of the 1950s, was increasingly pushed aside by a different, cold war liberal understanding of culture and consumption.

Cold war liberals, a loose conglomeration of intellectuals and politicians who began to transform the cultural conservatism of the first half of the 1950s, included politician Ludwig Erhard and sociologists like Helmut Schelsky, F. H. Tenbruck, Viggo Graf Blücher, and Curt Bondy. For them, adolescent rebelliousness was a nonpolitical, psychological phenomenon. Seen in these terms, both male aggression and female sexual expressiveness became less threatening, and the parameters of acceptable adolescent behavior were widened.[29]

In making this argument, West German cold war liberals were influenced by American social scientists and, in particular, David Riesman's *The Lonely Crowd* (Riesman had in turn been influenced by the Frankfurt School). Translated into German in 1956, *The Lonely Crowd* became influential at the exact time that youth riots, which West Germans connected to adolescents' consumption of American popular culture, happened all over Germany. In his book, Riesman described postwar American society as characterized by economic abundance, bureaucratization, permissiveness, and a population of outer-directed personalities. In contrast to the inner-directed personalities of earlier bourgeois societies, who had internalized guidelines of behavior, these outer-directed personalities were yearning for approval from their peers. While Riesman did not focus on youth per se, his studies of the effect of consumer culture in America at once explained, affirmed, and, within limits, critiqued a transformation West Germans saw their own country undergoing. Moreover, Riesman's analysis, though critical of a consumption-oriented society, ultimately confirmed its basic stability. This attitude proved to be attractive in the context of the West German situation. In 1956 Schelsky, in his introduction to the German edition of *The Lonely Crowd*, and sociologist F. H. Tenbruck, in a lengthy review, stressed that Germans should not be shocked at the American conditions Riesman described. Neither Riesman nor they saw the development of a society consisting of outer-directed personality types as a necessarily bad development.[30]

West German sociologists took up Riesman's conclusion that increased automation and leisure time leveled class distinctions.[31] Schelsky and the architect of the West German miracle, Ludwig Erhard, developed these themes further. In 1957 both published books that became blueprints for changing society and politics in West Germany: Erhard's *Wohlstand für alle* (Prosperity for All), and Schelsky's *Die skeptische Generation* (The Skeptical Generation).[32] Both authors embraced the consumer society that had emerged in West Germany by the mid-1950s.

West German cold war liberals made cultural consumption compatible with a new German identity that they located beyond fascism and totalitarianism, indeed beyond all ideologies. To postulate an end of ideologies was likely their most powerful move. Schelsky, for example, favorably called the West German youth "skeptical" because they had moved beyond the world of ideologies.[33] In the late 1950s West European and American intellectuals, among them Daniel Bell, were likewise propagating "the end of ideology" in the West.

For Schelsky and other West German cold war liberals, a lot was at stake. They sought to disconnect themselves from Weimar and Nazism by erasing differences between West Germany and other Western societies and by fully integrating themselves into the fight against communism.[34] Schelsky now proclaimed German youths to be "nonpolitical democratic" and put them at the center of a liberal system, thus abandoning the fight for a third, German way between consumerism in the West and socialism in the East.[35] At the same

time, Schelsky also whitewashed his own generation from its association with Nazism. He maintained that the parents of the postwar
youth–and Schelsky himself belonged to this parent generation–had
turned themselves into a skeptical generation.

Schelsky's assessments rested on rendering the German youth
culture of the 1950s into a "private" matter. Rebellious youth behavior like listening to jazz or rock 'n' roll became a mere "nonpolitical"
expression of style.[36] In his final chapter Schelsky explicitly talked
about the recent youth riots and about what many Germans saw as
adolescent misbehavior. As his three examples of unruly adolescent
behavior, Schelsky referred to the "ecstatic devotion to the lively
music of jazz sessions," to certain "acrobatic dissolved" forms of
dancing, and to the "individual rage" of adolescent rioters. Thus he
explicitly connected rebellious behavior to American influences; yet,
he did not refer to these as challenges to traditional gender roles and
rejected accounts of this youth behavior as a turn to primitivism.
Schelsky's rhetoric helped to diffuse the issues of gender and race as
central components of the youth cultures.[37]

Considering the hype that the youth rebellion was receiving in
West Germany during these very years, it is clear that Schelsky's
interpretation continued to be contested. Both Erhard and Schelsky
contended with critics of consumer culture. Schelsky himself echoed
some of the concerns of cultural conservatives, worrying that German adolescents could succumb to vulgar materialism with consumerism as their life goal, or, worse, turn into criminals. And in
1963, in his first speech as chancellor to the West German parliament, Erhard responded to critics who bemoaned West Germany's
growing materialism by urging his fellow West Germans not to lose
track of Christian values.[38]

West German cold war liberals like Schelsky and Erhard retained
a fair amount of hostility toward cultural styles associated with unre-
spectable lower-class behavior and specifically with American popular culture. While avoiding open prohibition, liberals continued to
portray styles like rock 'n' roll negatively and actively promoted
alternatives. Yet these hostilities were not incompatible with their
efforts to render youth cultures nonpolitical and to celebrate a consumption-oriented West German society. In the second half of the
1950s, for example, the West Berlin government, run by the Social
Democrats, promoted ballroom dancing, especially in working-class
neighborhoods. Subsidized lessons included instruction about correct behavior toward the opposite sex.[39] At the same time the rhetoric against rock 'n' roll turned more mild. Liberal critiques of rock
'n' roll relied on psychological explanations to account for the

attraction of rock across classes and saw the institution of proper gender roles as a solution to the youth rebellion. Psychologist Curt Bondy and his team, in a study of juvenile delinquency funded by the West German Ministry of the Interior, rejected the notion that rock 'n' roll was responsible for the recent youth riots; rather, they suggested that the two forms of behavior fulfilled the same needs for psychological and physical release. At the same time, Bondy's analysis mostly ignored the female consumers of rock 'n' roll, who were clearly present in his sources. Instead, women became the solution to the problem: the study concluded that most boys gave up rioting as soon as they had steady girlfriends. This assessment was echoed in the West German press. West German cold war liberals rarely reacted to challenges of gender norms with outright prohibitions of cultural products. Rather, they portrayed both riots and rock 'n' roll as mere cultural styles whose threats could be resolved "privately."[40] Young men had to release "normal" aggressions, while restrained young women could provide them stability as girlfriends.

The reframing of the youth rebellion as nonpolitical was facilitated by efforts on the part of state officials, the press, and the entertainment industry to alter the practices adolescents engaged in. As rock 'n' roll caught on, a new West German female emerged: the "teenager." In Germany this American term had first been used to describe American female Presley fans, but from 1957 onward "teenagers" increasingly became a label for young German women of all classes. For many of these young women, the term "teenager" carried a much more modern image of femininity, one that included greater openness in sexual matters. It also had implications for female adolescent consumption: the image of the teenager ran counter to the traditional ideal image of the woman who exerted self-restraint in matters of consumption and sexuality. Initially viewed critically, the "teenager" was quickly turned into marketing tool.[41]

As rock 'n' roll spread, its black origins were increasingly effaced from discourses on German youth cultures. At the same time, the fashion industry and the magazine *Bravo* worked to transform the styles that had posed challenges to gender norms. Deracialization and a clear separation of gender roles went hand in hand. Elvis's induction into the army in 1958 resolved his gender ambiguity: *Bravo* celebrated his new respectable appearance with short hair and no sideburns, and other commentators soon referred to him as a "tame" (yet now properly masculine) member of the "occupying forces" in West Germany. One paper urged parents not to worry if their daughters displayed his picture on their walls.[42] At the same time, reviews of *King Creole,* released in 1958 in Germany, never even mentioned that large parts of the movie were set in a black nightclub.[43] In West German renditions of Presley's success story, his rise from truck driver to millionaire took center stage, while references to the black origins of his music all but disappeared. Thus Presley was "whitened" and masculinized as his story became compatible with the West German "economic miracle mentality" (*Wirtschafts-wundermentalität*). While eliminating race from such discussions signified the greater acceptability of rock 'n' roll, it also diminished the acceptance of black culture in West Germany.

An increasing focus on a heterosocial realm with clearly defined gender roles for adolescents appeared to be successful in taming the radicalism of the youth rebellion. The effects were contradictory. On the one hand, public visibility became an option for women of all classes. On the other, female behavior that had transgressed racial and gender lines was tamed: women were allowed to become visible primarily as potential girlfriends and wives of men. Conversely, women were seen as taming men: in press commentaries and psychological research reports, male rioters were portrayed as harmless once they had girlfriends. And in popular usage the term "teenager" underwent a significant shift in meaning: by 1960 it could include both young men and young women, and it now connoted generational difference rather than conflict.

Such a shift was certainly fostered by the systematic marketing of Peter Kraus and Conny Froboess as ideal teenagers. Initially, Kraus (who happened to be an Austrian citizen) was sold as the "German Elvis." Racial ambiguity was not part of his image, and nobody referred to his thick lips (which he did have). Although Kraus, too, encountered "hysterical teenagers," he was mostly portrayed as a nice German boy, much "more likable in voice and behavior" than the American original.[44] When he was joined by a female mate, Conny, his domestication was almost complete. Conny and Peter made movies together and were celebrated as West German rock 'n' roll stars. The West German fashion industry used their popularity to market teenage fashions and claimed to direct the "not so complaisant" wishes of adolescents into "pleasant forms."[45] "Conny sweaters" for young women and "Peter Kraus pulls" (vests) intended for young men stressed different cuts for women and men and thus tried to reinstate a larger measure of gender difference.

In the promotion of Conny Froboess and Peter Kraus, traditional gender roles were partially resurrected. Thus Froboess had to be protected from association with too much "sexiness." Froboess's manager/father invoked the differences between young male rebels and teenagers and criticized Kraus when he allegedly turned too "sexy":

"That is something for *Halbstarke* (male rioters) and not for teen-agers.... If teenager music declines into sex, then [it will do so] without me."[46] On the one hand, the duo was part of a heterosocial teenage world where young men and women together challenged older standards of respectable dancing or clothing, while, on the other hand, they tried to steer away from open challenges to sexual mores.

Newer styles of rock 'n' roll dancing also stressed gender differences, developing from a "wild" style, in which men *and* women threw their partners into the air, to a "tamed" version in which the male partner hardly moved at all. In 1960 *Bravo* published directions for dancing rock 'n' roll as part of a series on ballroom dancing. The man depicted in the photograph, German singer Rex Gildo, wore a dark suit and guided a young woman, Conny Fro-boess, who was dressed in a petticoat skirt. Gildo was clearly avoiding any excessive movements. This style of rock 'n' roll dancing could be safely adopted at the private house parties that became the fashion among middle-class youth. It effectively symbolized the ideal female teenager as the acolyte of the controlled and controlling man, avoided allusions to black culture, and made rock 'n' roll compatible with a bourgeois gender system.[47]

While the subversive gender, racial, and class implications of rock 'n' roll consumption lessened, the greater acceptance of rock 'n' roll and sexuality as modes of "private" expression constituted a widening of options for West German adolescents, especially young women. The West German attempts to tame rock 'n' roll had only limited success. Many young Germans perceived the German rock 'n' roll songs as weak imitations and preferred the American original songs and dance styles. And fashion makers were hardly able or even willing to prevent girls from wearing Peter Kraus pulls along with James Dean jackets. Moreover, even with their tamed German version of rock 'n' roll, Froboess and Kraus introduced American words like "baby," "sexy," and "love" into the German vocabulary.[48]

State officials apparently did not see the efforts of the entertainment industry as sufficient and made their own attempts to channel adolescent consumption. A 1960 report on the "situation" of the West Berlin youth located the founding of jazz cafés by state agencies in the liberal ideas of Schelsky and Riesman, who had confirmed the basic stability of consumption-oriented societies. The report used Schelsky's and Riesman's terminology and spoke of a "skeptical generation" growing up in an "outer-directed" consumer society. In this context, the report claimed, state youth agencies had to fulfill their prime task in the realm of leisure and consumption: to teach adolescents "how to evaluate critically the offerings of the consumer and entertainment industries and how to use them in a meaningful manner." In this vision, state youth officials, as agents of the expanding welfare state, were to educate adolescents to be sensible consumers.[49]

As part of reframing the youth rebellion as nonpolitical, West German state officials still tried to alter the practices adolescents engaged in. The dance clubs that the West Berlin government supported were attempts to fulfill this goal. The first dance café, called Jazz-Saloon, opened at the end of April 1960, and was modeled on a similar institution in the West German city of Mannheim. The West Berlin minister of youth affairs Ella Kay herself served nonalcoholic drinks and beer in the club. Officials offered what they called jazz, which by the late 1950s carried connotations of both youthfulness and proper restraint and was largely devoid of connotations with black culture. The West Berlin officials thus clearly tried to avoid the controversies surrounding rock 'n' roll.

West German promoters of jazz had for the most part convinced the West German public by the late 1950s that jazz was an art music and not responsible for male aggression and female sexual expressiveness. At the same time, references to the fact that most American jazz musicians were African-Americans or Jews were largely missing from West German commentaries on jazz. The West Berlin dance cafés did not focus on jazz styles such as bebop or cool that were highly admired by German jazz fans, but by using the term "jazz" in the names of the clubs and in their musical offerings, West Berlin officials sought to portray the dance cafés as at once modern, open, and respectable. As one social worker concluded, these clubs educated young people not with "the sledge-hammer, but with the jazz trumpet."[50]

West Berlin officials were satisfied that the clubs fulfilled their educational mission. Pictures in the press revealed a "respectable" audience: young women in skirts and sweaters and young men in suits. (This shows clear similarities to the emphasis East German officials put on the changed clothing styles of East German adolescents after the building of the Wall). One West Berlin commentator reported that pants for young women and jeans for young men, which had been the fashions for female and male rock 'n' roll fans and rioters, were not "desirable" in the new club.[51] Reinscribing gender differences through the clothing styles of adolescents was central also to cold war liberal attempts to resolve any threats posed by rebellious adolescents.

With the state-sponsored dance cafés, West Berlin officials fostered a "private" solution to overly rebellious behavior—a solution that liberal psychologists and sociologists, and even the entertainment industry, had also proposed: heterosexual relations among adolescents. Like other cold war liberals, these officials saw adolescent rebelliousness as part of the normal life stages for adolescents of all classes, and, departing from conservative ideology, they did not view it as a result of working-class culture. The dance cafés thus were part of West German efforts to diffuse the 1950s youth rebellion, while providing adolescents with an inexpensive opportunity to listen to "hot" (if not too hot) American music in a safe environment. In West Germany, definitions of acceptable adolescent behavior had clearly widened.[52] The West German press and state officials increasingly accepted the assessments that adolescent rebelliousness was a psychological phenomenon, yet they also employed "bourgeois" notions of gender difference and respectability to tame the 1950s rebels. By the mid-1960s the notion of a youth rebellion all but disappeared. (This was of course somewhat ironic, given the upheaval that members of the counterculture and the student rebellion would cause just a few years later.)[53]

It was an "achievement" of West German cold war liberals in the late 1950s and early 1960s to push the issues of popular culture consumption and sexuality into arenas defined as nonpolitical. The redefinition of consumption was an important aspect of the West German "end of ideologies" paradigm, with which West German cold war liberals sought to integrate themselves into the alliance of Western societies on the one hand, and to divorce themselves from the Weimar and Nazi past on the other.

As West German authorities "depoliticized" consumption, it increasingly became a cold war weapon. For example, West German officials made efforts to draw East Germans into the movie theaters on the Kurfürstendamm in the center of West Berlin. Here East Germans were also exposed to West Berlin shop windows, and, as one West Berlin official put it, they "came to see the West with new eyes."[54] The jazz dance cafés, accordingly, fulfilled a dual function: they drew young people off the streets, and they displayed the openness of West German society—in pointed contrast to the ongoing repression of American cultural influences in East Germany. It would still be a few more years until West Berlin officials integrated rock 'n' roll into state-run youth programs, but in 1962 a review of an East German dictionary mocked the entry that described rock 'n' roll as a political threat.[55] For the West German authorities of the 1960s, leisure and pleasure were not what would destroy the West; in fact, enjoyed in good measure they would actually be a key weapon against the East, exposing its economic inferiority and lack of democratic choice. West Germans successfully countered East German attacks that had mobilized the ambivalence and even hostility toward

America that existed on both sides of the Wall. In this climate, consumption in fact remained politicized, if on a different terrain.[56]

This exploration of East and West German encounters with American popular culture shows how closely intertwined hostilities toward black culture and the rejection of female sexual expressiveness were in East and West German culturally conservative visions. Indeed, reactions to American popular culture afford us with a look at post–World War II German racialist concepts that were not merely leftovers from fascist times. Even as West Germany underwent a liberal transformation and as East Germany reasserted Stalinism, gender conservatism continued to set limits on tolerance toward cultural differences in both states and thus helped to maintain racial and ethnic hierarchies.

In the 1950s (and beyond) authorities in both German states made their citizens' *cultural* consumption central to their *political* reconstruction efforts. Whereas East German authorities remained hostile toward American popular culture, West Germans began to draw on American styles and American ideas. Yet the debates over American cultural influences were not simply about Germany becoming more American. Rather, in the East and West German conflicts over American influences we can see how each state tried to lay claim to a German identity in the aftermath of National Socialism and in the face of the cold war. These debates were one site where the two states crystallized as separate entities, all the while making consumption into an important cold war weapon. This dynamic, which developed in the second half of the 1950s, would have continued significance until the end of the cold war.

Notes

1. See "Am Tag darauf ohne Texashose," *Neues Deutschland,* 22 August 1961; "Heiße Rhythmen waren erster Schritt," *National-Zeitung,* 27 August 1961; "Bericht über Jugendklubs," 11 November 1962, Landesarchiv Berlin Außenstelle Breite Straße (LAB [STA]) Rep. 121 Nr. 62.

2. Senator für Jugend und Sport, "Bericht über die Situation der Berliner Jugend," *Der Rundbrief* 10, no. 11/12 (1960): 1–24, especially 5–10; "Totenkopf bürgerlich," *Revue,* no. 19 (1962).

3. Reconstruction has been mostly used to describe West Germany after 1945, but it is a useful concept for both Germanys.

4. Investigations of American influences on postwar Germany are numerous. See especially Volker R. Berghahn, *The Americanization of West German Industry, 1945–1973* (New York, 1986); Anselm Doering-Manteuffel, "Dimensionen von

Amerikanisierung in der deutschen Gesellschaft," *Archiv für Sozialgeschichte* 35 (1995): 1–34; Michael Ermarth, ed., *America and the Shaping of German Society 1945–1955* (Providence, R.I., 1993); Heinz-Hermann Krüger, ed., *"Die Elvis-Tolle, die hatte ich mir unauffällig wachsen lassen": Lebensgeschichte und jugendliche Alltagskultur in den fünfziger Jahren* (Opladen, 1985); Konrad Jarausch and Hannes Siegrist, eds., *Amerikanisierung und Sowjetisierung in Deutschland* (Frankfurt a.M., 1997); Alf Lüdtke, Inge Marßolek, and Adelheid von Saldern, eds., *Amerikanisierung: Traum und Alptraum im Deutschland des 20. Jahrhunderts* (Stuttgart, 1996); Kaspar Maase, *Bravo Amerika: Erkundungen zur Jugendkultur der Bundesrepublik in den fünfziger Jahren* (Hamburg, 1992); Reiner Pommerin, *The American Impact on Postwar Germany* (Providence, R.I., 1995); Michael Rauhut, *Beat in der Grauzone: DDR-Rock 1964 bis 1972 – Politik und Alltag* (Berlin, 1993); Timothy Ryback, *Rock around the Bloc: A History of Rock Music in Eastern Europe and the Soviet Union* (New York, 1990); Dorothee Wierling, "Jugend als innerer Feind: Konflikte in der Erziehungsdiktatur der sechziger Jahre," in *Sozialgeschichte der DDR*, ed. Hartmut Kälble, Jürgen Kocka, and Hartmut Zwahr (Stuttgart, 1994): 404–25. For a more extensive treatment of many issues covered in this article, see Uta G. Poiger, "Rock 'n' Roll, Female Sexuality and the Cold War Battle over German Identities," *Journal of Modern History* 68 (September 1996): 577–616.

5. On the role of gender in West German reconstruction, see, for example, Erica Carter, *How German Is She? Postwar West German Reconstruction and the Consuming Woman* (Ann Arbor, 1997); Heide Fehrenbach, *Cinema in Democratizing Germany: Reconstructing National Identity after Hitler* (Chapel Hill, N.C., 1995); Elizabeth Heineman, "The Hour of the Woman: Memories of Germany's 'Crisis Years' and West German National Identity," *American Historical Review* 101 (April 1996): 354–95; Maria Höhn, "Frau im Haus und Girl im *Spiegel*: Discourse on Women in the Interregnum Period of 1945–1949 and the Question of German Identity," *Central European History* 26 (1993): 57–90; Robert G. Moeller, *Protecting Motherhood: Women and the Family in the Politics of West Germany* (Berkeley, 1993). For East Germany, see Ina Merkel,… *und Du, Frau an der Werkbank: Die DDR in den 50er Jahren* (Berlin, 1990); Barbara Einhorn, *Cinderella Goes to Market: Citizenship, Gender, and Women's Movements in East Central Europe* (New York, 1993); Ute Gerhard, "Die staatlich institutionalisierte 'Lösung' der Frauenfrage: Zur Geschichte der Geschlechterverhältnisse in der DDR," in *Sozialgeschichte der DDR*; Atina Grossmann, *Reforming Sex: The German Movement for Birth Control and Abortion Reform 1920–1950* (New York, 1995); Donna Harsch, "Society, the State, and Abortion in East Germany, 1950–1972," *American Historical Review* 102 (1997): 53–84.

6. For Germans' fascination with America in the 1920s, see especially Frank Costigliola, *Awkward Dominion: American Political, Economic, and Cultural Relations with Europe, 1919–1933* (Ithaca, N.Y., 1984); Mary Nolan, *Visions of Modernity: American Business and the Modernization of Germany* (New York, 1994); Thomas J. Saunders, *Hollywood in Berlin: American Cinema and Weimar Germany* (Berkeley and Los Angeles, 1994).

7. Quotes from Michael H. Kater, "The Jazz Experience in Weimar Germany," *German History* 6, no. 2 (1988): 145–58, 154.

8. On "swing youths," see Michael Kater, *Different Drummers: Jazz in the Culture of Nazi Germany* (New York, 1992). Studies of American popular culture in the Third Reich have pointed to its function as a source of resistance as well as of Nazi manipulation. See Kater, *Different Drummers*; Detlev J. K. Peukert, *Inside Nazi Germany: Conformity, Opposition and Racism in Everyday Life* (New Haven,

Conn., 1987); Hans Dieter Schäfer, "Amerikanismus im Dritten Reich," in *Nationalsozialismus und Modernisierung,* ed. Michael Prinz and Rainer Zitelmann (Darmstadt, 1991), 199–215.

9. See HA Jugendhilfe und Jugenderziehung, "Entwurf: Präambel 'Verordnung zum Schutze der Kinder und der Jugendlichen,'" Berlin, 18 February 1952, LAB (STA) Rep. 120 Nr. 2614.

10. Hermann Meyer, *Musik im Zeitgeschehen* (Berlin, 1952), quoted in Michael Rauhut, *Beat in der Grauzone: DDR-Rock, 1964–1972–Politik und Alltag* (Berlin, 1993), 19–21; Ludwig Richard Müller, "Dekadenz und lebensfroher Neubeginn," *Musik und Gesellschaft* 5 (April 1955): 114–17; Reginald Rudorf, "Die Tanzmusik muß neue Wege gehen," *Musik und Gesellschaft* 4, part 1 (February 1954): 51–56, part 2 (March 1954): 92–95. For an example of the use of decadence in racial terms, see Kater, "The Jazz Experience in Weimar Germany," 153. See also Sandra Siegel, "Literature and Degeneration: The Representation of 'Decadence,'" in *Degeneration: The Dark Side of Progress,* ed. J. Edward Chamberlin and Sander L. Gilman (New York, 1985), 199–219.

11. "Appell an den Urmenschen," *Berliner Zeitung,* 13 December 1956.

12. Dr. Uszukoreit to state concert agency (Deutsche Konzert- und Gastspieldirektion), 21 August 1957, BArch P DR1 Nr. 243.

13. See "Zuchthaus für Presley-Fans," *Depesche* (3 November 1959).

14. Reginald Rudorf, "Für eine frohe, ausdrucksvolle Tanzmusik," *Musik und Gesell-schaft* 2 (August 1952): 247–52; Reginald Rudorf, "Die Tanzmusik muß neue Wege gehen," *Musik und Gesellschaft* 4, part 1 (February 1954): 51–56, part 2 (March 1954): 92–95; *An Euch alle, die Ihr jung seid! Material der 12. Tagung des Zen-tralrats der Freien Deutschen Jugend vom 3. und 4. Februar 1956* (Berlin, n.d.), 26.

15. See Abt. Agit.-Prop., "Einige Bemerkungen zu Frage des Jazz," Berlin, 29 No-vember 1961, and "Unser Standpunkt zum Jazz," Berlin, 7 December 1961, both Jugendarchiv beim Institut für Zeitgeschichtliche Jugendforschung Berlin (JA-IzJ) AB547.

16. "Bericht über Jugendklubs," 11 November 1962, LAB (STA) Rep. 121 Nr. 62.

17. See Abt. Agit.-Prop., "Einige Bemerkungen zu Frage des Jazz," and "Unser Stand-punkt zum Jazz," both JA-IzJ AB547. See also Rauhut, *Beat in der Grauzone,* 118.

18. See also Fehrenbach, *Cinema in Democratizing Germany.*

19. See A. Gügler, *Euer Sohn in der Entwicklungskrise* (Stuttgart, 1952), 32–48, re-printed in Kuhnert and Ackermann, "Jenseits von Lust und Liebe?" 50; Hans Engelbach, "Entwurf eines Gesetzes zum Schutze der Jugend in der Öffent-lichkeit," n.d. [1949] LAB (Landesarchiv Berlin Kalckreuthstraße) Rep. 13 Acc. 1046 Nr. 18.

20. "Die ganze Welt rockt und rollt," *Bravo,* 30 September 1956. "Außer Rand und Band," *Beratungsdienst Jugend und Film* 1 (November 1956): BVII.

21. On Elvis's challenge to respectable manhood, see Steven Smiles, *Gender Chame-leons: Androgyny in Rock 'n' Roll* (New York, 1985), 14–16.

22. Werner Micke, "Philosophie des Stumpfsinns," *Junge Welt,* 5 February 1957, quoted in Rauhut, *Beat,* 31; "Elvis, the Pelvis"; Ker Robertson, "Elvis Presley, Idol von Millionen von Backfischen und bestürzendes Symptom unserer Zeit," *Depesche* (18 January 1957); "Gold aus heißer Kehle," *Beratungsdienst Jugend und Film,* vol. 3 (February 1958): BI–BII.

23. "Elvis, the Pelvis." This comparison was also made in the United States. For a quote from the *New York Daily Mirror,* see Smiles, *Gender Chameleon,* 16.

24. Manfred George in *Tagesspiegel,* 7 February 1957.

25. "'Rock and Roll': Öffentliches Ärgernis," *Badische Neue Nachrichten,* 22 August 1956.

26. See "Elvis, the Pelvis."
27. "Außer Rand und Band 2. Teil," *Beratungsdienst Jugend und Film* 2 (January 1957).
28. Arbeitsausschuß der FSK, "Jugendprotokoll: Außer Rand und Band, II. Teil," Landesbildstelle Berlin, Pressearchiv.
29. A consensus is emerging among scholars of West Germany that the years after 1956 saw important social and political transformations. See Anselm Doering-Manteuffel, "Deutsche Zeitgeschichte nach 1945: Entwicklung und Problemlagen der historischen Forschung zur Nachkriegszeit," *Vierteljahrshefte für Zeitgeschichte* 41 (January 1993): 1–29; and idem, "Dimensionen von Amerikanisierung"; Paul Erker, "Zeitgeschichte als Sozialgeschichte," *Geschichte und Gesellschaft* 19 (1993): 202–38. The question whether West Germany indeed developed into a liberal system has been the subject of much concern. Konrad H. Jarausch and Larry Eugene Jones, "German Liberalism Reconsidered," in *In Search of a Liberal Germany: Studies in the History of German Liberalism from 1789 to the Present*, ed. Jarausch and Jones (New York, 1990), 1–23, 20, have asserted that liberalism has shaped West Germany's political landscape. See also Theo Schiller, "Parteienentwicklung: Die Einebnung des politischen Milieus," in *Die fünfziger Jahre: Beiträge zu Politik und Kultur*, ed. Dieter Bänsch (Tübingen, 1985), 37–51; Erica Carter, "Alice in the Consumer Wonderland: West German Case Studies in Gender and Consumer Culture," in *Gender and Generation*, ed. Angela McRobbie and Mica Nava (London, 1984), 185–214. On cold war liberalism in the United States, see Robert J. Corber, *In the Name of National Security: Hitchcock, Homophobia, and the Political Construction of Gender in Postwar America* (Durham, N.C., 1993). On the vision of the Christian West, see especially Fehrenbach, *Cinema in Democratizing Germany*.
30. David Riesman, *Die Einsame Masse*, with an introduction by H. Schelsky (Darmstadt, 1956). *The Lonely Crowd* had hardly been noticed in West Germany when it was first published in the United States in 1950. Schelsky's introduction to Riesman, *Die Einsame Masse*; Helmut Schelsky, "Im Spiegel des Amerikaners," *Wort und Wahrheit* 11 (1956): 363–74; F. H. Tenbruck, "David Riesman: Kritik und Würdigung," *Jahrbuch für Amerikastudien* 2 (1957): 213–30.
31. Viggo Graf Blücher, *Freizeit in der industriellen Gesellschaft: Dargestellt an der jüngeren Generation* (Stuttgart, 1956), 11–13, 118–24; Blücher, "Jugend auf dem Weg zur Selbstbestimmung," *deutsche jugend* 4, no. 6 (June 1956): 260–65. Helmut Schelsky had introduced the concept of a "leveled middle-class society" in his *Wandlungen der deutschen Familie in der Gegenwart* (Stuttgart, 1954), but had seen it mainly as a result of war and postwar conditions. In 1956 Blücher and he began to relate it increasingly to the rise of a consumption-oriented society. See Hans Braun, "Helmut Schelskys Konzept der 'nivellierten Mittelstandsgesellschaft' und die Bundesrepublik der 50er Jahre," *Archiv für Sozialgeschichte* 29 (1985): 199–223; Robert G. Moeller, *Protecting Motherhood*; Moeller, "'The Homosexual Man Is a 'Man,' the Homosexual Woman Is a 'Woman': Sex, Society, and the Law in Postwar West Germany," *Journal of the History of Sexuality* 4 (1994): 59–92.
32. Ludwig Erhard, *Wohlstand für alle* (Düsseldorf, 1957). Schelsky, in *Die skeptische Generation: Eine Soziologie der deutschen Jugend* (Cologne, 1957), claimed to analyze the West German adolescent from 1945 to 1955. He indeed drew occasionally on empirical research from this period, but in the context of this study his work is more interesting as a blueprint for West German society. Moeller, *Protecting Motherhood*, 191, has correctly called Schelsky "a sociologist for all seasons." Schelsky had assumed his first university position during the Third Reich. In the first half of the 1950s he made a name for himself with his sociology of the family,

which promoted the role of a female homemaker and a male breadwinner, and a treatise against Kinsey. Also he had served on an advisory board to conservative family minister Wuermeling. On Schelsky, see also M. Rainer Lepsius, "Die Entwicklung der Soziologie nach dem zweiten Weltkrieg 1945 bis 1967," in *Deutsche Soziologie seit 1945: Entwicklungsrichtungen und Praxisbezug,* ed. Günter Lüschen (Opladen, 1979), 25–70, 38–39.

33. Schelsky, *Die skeptische Generation,* 84–95; Blücher, *Freizeit in der industriellen Gesellschaft,* 118–24; Erhard's speech at the April 1960 Christian Democratic convention, "Wirtschaftpolitik als Teil der Gesellschaftspolitik," reprinted in *Ludwig Erhard: Gedanken aus fünf Jahrzehnten,* ed. Karl Hohmann (Düsseldorf, 1988), 607–23.

34. This concept of totalitarianism was a feature of German (and Western) postwar thought and politics.

35. Schelsky, *Die skeptische Generation,* 493.

36. Ibid., 488.

37. Ibid., 494–97.

38. Ibid., 88–90; Erhard, "Politik der Mitte und der Verständigung," speech to the West German Bundestag, 18 October 1963, reprinted in *Ludwig Erhard,* 814–46.

39. Interview with Susanne Quandt, who attended one of these courses in 1958 (my files). All interviews were conducted by the author and the names of the interviewees changed.

40. Curt Bondy et al., *Jugendliche stören die Ordnung: Bericht und Stellungnahme zu den Halbstarkenkrawallen* (Munich, 1957), 71–72, 86–89, 92. Bondy and his team even rejected the notion that attacks on policemen could be politically motivated. See also Klaus Eyferth, "Es reicht nicht zu Revolutionen," *Die Welt,* 8 November 1958; "Totenkopf bügerlich," *Revue,* no. 19 (1962).

41. See "Das Phänomen Elvis Presley," *Telegraf,* 11 October 1956; "Das Phänomen Elvis Presley," *Spandauer Volksblatt,* 12 October 1956; "Teenager," *Blickpunkt,* nos. 48/49 (1956): 21; "Elvis, the Pelvis." See also the West German dictionary *Der große Herder,* vol. 8 (1956), quoted in Maase, *Bravo Amerika,* 162. By 1958 the term had become common currency in Germany. See the teenager books directed specifically at girls: Eric Godal, *Teenagers,* ed. Rolf Itaaliander (Hamburg, 1958), and G. Hilgendorf, *Das Teenagerbuch* (Munich, 1958), both cited in Maase, "Der (Teenager)-Spleen," *Blickpunkt* (February 1960): 17. See also Doris Foitzik, ed., *Vom Trümmerkind zum Teenager: Kindheit und Jugend in der Nachkriegszeit* (Bremen, 1992); Maase, *Bravo Amerika,* 161–75.

42. *Bravo,* no. 12 (1958), quoted in Maase, *Bravo Amerika,* 168. "I Like Elvis," *Abend,* 10 October 1958.

43. See, for example, reviews of *King Creole* in *Telegraf, Kurier, Die Welt,* all 1 November 1958.

44. "Vom Spieltrieb besessen," *Telegraf,* 11 July 1957. Rainer Erd, in "Musikalische Praxis und sozialer Protest: Überlegungen zur Funktion von Rock and Roll, Jazz und Oper," *German Politics and Society,* no. 18 (Fall 1989): 18–35, sees Kraus, in contrast to Presley, as whitened in the German context.

45. Interview with teenager fashion producer, quoted in Helmut Lamprecht, *Teenager und Manager* (1960; reprint, Munich, 1965), 39.

46. Quoted in ibid., 107. See also Maase, *Bravo Amerika,* 169.

47. See "Erlaubt ist, was gefällt," *Bravo,* no. 6 (1960); interview with Renate Ebert (my files).

48. Maase, *Bravo Amerika,* 164. He has correctly warned against seeing the teenage culture as devoid of all challenges to dominant norms. See also oral history with

Klaus Woldeck, quoted in ibid., 169; and interviews with Susanne Quandt and Dietmar Iser (my files).

49. Senator für Jugend und Sport, "Bericht über die Situation der Berliner Jugend," *Der Rundbrief* 10, no. 11/12 (1960): 1–24, especially 5–10.

50. Herbert Rudershausen, "Jugendpflege in der Bar," *Der Rundbrief* 10, no. 9/10 (1960).

51. See "Pressekonferenz des Berliner Jugendclub e.V. am 28. April 1960 anläßlich der Eröffnung des 'Jazz-Saloons,'" LAB Rep. 13 Acc. 2285 Nr. 464; "Ein ganzes Haus für Jugend und Jazz," *Kurier*, 30 April 1960; Horst Sass, "'Jugend-Jazz-Saloon' überfüllt," *Die Welt*, 2 May 1960; *Kurier*, 24 May 1960; "Berliner Geschichten," *IBZ*, 18 June 1960; "Das haben sie nicht in Paris gelernt," *Blickpunkt*, no. 97/98 (July 1960); Reiner Breitfeldt, "Es sind keine 'müden Senatsschuppen,'" *Blickpunkt*, no. 104 (1961).

52. Rudershausen, "Jugendpflege in der Bar." See also *Abgeordnetenhaus von Berlin: Stenographische Berichte*, 61st session, 4 May 1961, 123–24.

53. See Viggo Blücher, *Die Generation der Unbefangenen: Zur Soziologie der jungen Menschen heute* (Düsseldorf, 1966).

54. See "Bericht über Erfahrungen und Ergebnisse der Massnahmen zur Förderung des Gesamtberliner Kulturlebens," 18 November 1958; Senator für Volksbildung to the Bundesminister für gesamtdeutsche Fragen, Berlin, 8 December 1958; Dr. Antoine to the Bundesminister für gesamtdeutsche Fragen, 12 March 1959; all in LAB Rep. 7 Acc. 2186 Nr. 53.

55. "'Krieg' mit Rock 'n' Roll," *Abend*, 16 September 1962.

56. Erhard, like American politicians, stressed the intimate connection between consumption and democracy. See Carter, "Alice in the Consumer Wonderland," 192; for similar arguments in the United States, see Elaine Tyler May, *Homeward Bound: American Families in the Cold War* (New York, 1988).

– Seven –

JUKEBOX BOYS

Postwar Italian Music and the Culture of Covering

Franco Minganti

Transitions in the Late 1950s

This essay attempts a reconaissance of the American impact on post-war Italian music and youth culture. After World War II, Italy became a newly mass-mediated society, where the word "media" specifically referred to the entertainment media (and to electric appliances as well). The essay emphasizes practices that were, and always are, border dialogues of sorts between the United States and Italy, and it pays particular attention to various forms of Italian "covering." In rock culture, "to cover" means to perform or record a song originally written, played, and recorded by a different artist, but the term is used somewhat more broadly here to include other cultural artifacts. These forms of communication between Italy and the United States are characterized by syncretism—that is, the combination of Italian and

---

This essay is indebted to two former works of mine, some portions of which have been revised: see Franco Minganti, "Rock 'n' Roll & Beat. L'Italia e la musica giovanile americana 1958–1964," in *Nemici per la pelle. Sogno americano e mito sovietico nell'Italia contemporanea*, ed. P. P. D'Attorre (Milan, 1991), 429–51; "Rock 'n' Roll in Italy: Was It True Americanization?" in *Cultural Transmissions and Receptions: American Mass Culture in Europe*, ed. R. Kroes, R. Rydell, and D. Bosscher (Amsterdam, 1993), 139–51.

American cultural products—and by mediation, which often results in curious effects of creolization. The latter is an apt metaphor for the transformations that languages and cultures undergo when, far from their original heritage, they turn into new, recombinant formations "among groups of diverse geographical and cultural origins."[1] It is in the world's peripheries, some have argued, that the practices of cultural semantics may liberate the often reductive results of "pidgin" imitation into more harmonious patterns of fusion, freeing them to interact in cultural arenas, while interrogating, often facetiously, the rules and effects of the transformation.

Elaborating on such insights, I will provide the reader with materials that refute the faulty notion of a one-way colonization of Italy by American music, which is still a widely circulating assumption. It is interesting to note, for example, how imitation music and covers reveal more about those who imitate and cover—and about the selection and translation processes—than about the (musical) "hegemonizers." Italy seems to make room for "America" in a context of meaning and significance that becomes typically Italian.

This study deals with the crucial transformations of the late 1950s through the early 1960s, an era when a social group termed *i giovani* (the youth) was invented and marketed in Italy. Domenico Modugno's national and international hit "Nel blu dipinto di blu" (also known as "Volare") in 1958 marked the beginning of this period; Beatlemania and the invitation of the first foreign singers to the Festival di Sanremo in 1964 symbolically sealed it.[2] These were years of "turbulent transitions."[3] In Italy as well as in other European countries, significant changes in taste and patterns of consumption took place, which tended to be associated—often obsessively—with "objects and environments either imported from America or styled on American models (e.g. film, popular music, streamlined artefacts, hair styles and clothes)."[4]

The disorienting transition from traditional to modern mass society was mediated by the market and a new consumerist ethos. As Italy became more urban, pervasive foreign influences extended first into literature, theatre, and the cinema, and then into various aspects of everyday life. Of course, this process of *sprovincializzazione* (cultural deparochialization) entailed a renegotiation of roles and identities. Some experienced these changes as an erosion of fundamental Italian values and attitudes, and a leveling down of moral and aesthetic standards. Others saw them primarily as an expression of healthy evolution and of a joie de vivre. Italy would never be the same, as American Rosemary Clooney had aptly foreseen in her 1954 "Mambo Italiano," which begins with an almost anthropological account of fundamental change in Italy: "A girl went down to Napoli / because she missed the scenery, the native dances and the charming songs / but, wait a minute ... something's wrong." Clooney's song opens with mandolins and torch effects in the tradition of Italian *paisan* songs.[5] But then it turns quickly into a wild, wacky mambo, where the very term "Italian mambo" seems like a contradiction. According to the lyrics, Italian *paisanos*, Siciliani and Calabresi, "do the mambo like crazy," give up tarantella and mozzarella, accept the recipes to a new mestizo cuisine ("try an enchilada with the fishy baccalà"), and adopt a new, "modern" lifestyle in the form of foreign-influenced dancing ("but take some other advice paisano / learn how to mambo / if you're gonna be a square / you ain't gonna go nowhere"). At the same time they try hard to preserve the mythic passion of latino dancing, a lingua franca for sexual innuendo ("it's so delicious everybody can capisce / how to mambo, mambo italiano").

In the boom years of the Italian economic miracle, adolescents (*i giovani*) were a new group of consumers, whose identities were shaped at the crossroads of short-circuited styles, music, and icons. In the early twentieth century, when Italian Futurists and International Modernists alike had employed the metaphor of youth as "machinic" and "energetic," youth had become an anthropological category; youth was considered both antagonistic to the status quo and necessary for renewal. Moreover, youth came to encompass speed, beauty, and an ineffable touch of grace.

The 1950s were crucial for redefining the status of youth in Italy, particularly in the social climate of pervasive cultural eclecticism. Italian adolescents developed a distinct lifestyle and became a distinct social group. They mixed American, British, and French imports with a revolutionary outcome: their attributes included chewing gum, blue jeans, boogie-woogie, women out alone at night, outrageous male and female fashions (if tailored at home), smoking, the wearing of existentialist black, the night as the new frontier of encounters and entertainment, jazz, the French *chanson*, and the scooter (a diminished, feminized motorbike).[6] Such elements, as enhanced by the industry that catered to them, helped establish youth as a world apart, a world of its own, almost a class in itself. Youths tended to slip out from under the control of traditional institutions, with their own meeting points and sites of empowerment (jukebox bars), their own time (the night), their own uniforms (jeans and highly stylized fashions). At a time when most Italians would speak only regional dialects, they also developed distinct jargons with frequent inclusions of so-called *forestierismi*, words and expressions from foreign languages. In spite of criticisms by cultural conservatives, these adolescent styles did not represent a passive integration into alien–namely American–music and fashion. Rather, adolescents used these styles to mark their difference from previous generations of Italians and from Italian tradition.[7]

One Step Back: Musical Americanization

The complex, almost mythic scenario of "Americanization" is, possibly, one of "coerseduction": this neologism, coined by P. J. Ravault, sees both coercion and seduction at work. It thus introduces an ambiguous assessment of American influences as having both damaging and subversive, progressive potential. It reveals that issues of translation are at stake, which involve language and culture and entail processes of adaptation and mediation.

Who translates? For whom? What is translated? How much of the original message or product filters through? Simple questions like these must be raised whenever something "American" or "Americanized" is analyzed. In Italy, as elsewhere, "America" and "Americanness" represent specific histories, conceptualizations, and commonplace identifications–of which modernization is only the most obvious. As Umberto Eco once put it, at least two major conceptualizations exist for the phrase "American model": models of products (objects or behaviors to be copied and reproduced) and productive models (that is, theoretical formulations, abstract structures, sites of simulation).[8]

The influence of modern American popular music in Italy, including pop and rock, has its own history. The Fascists had proscriptions against jazz and all American swing music, which they rejected as "barbaric negroid anti-music" (*barbara antimusica negroide*) or as degenerate "Afro-demo(cratic)-Pluto(cratic)-Jewish-Mason-epyleptoid music" (*musica afro-demo-pluto-giudo-masso-epilettoide*). Such pronouncements went hand in hand with the public encouragement to play American swing music for entertainment or propaganda purposes. The Fascists also continued to import Hollywood and Walt Disney productions. Mussolini himself was known to own a conspicuous jazz record collection, and jazz music filtered through the ban in radio orchestra programs.[9] Programmers and disc jockeys filed the music as "dance music" and changed or translated the names of the interpreters and lyrics and titles of songs. Louis Armstrong became Luigi Braccioforte, Benny Goodman was Beniamino Buonomo, Hoagy Carmichael turned into Carmelito, Duke Ellington became Del Duca, Coleman Hawkins was Coléma, The Hot Club de France Quintet turned into The Five Rhythm Devils (*I cinque diavoli del ritmo*) and the Italian group named Three Niggers of Broadway became Three Italians in America (*Tre Italiani in America*). The "St. Louis Blues" turned into "Le tristezze di San Luigi," or "Louisiana Rhythm" (Il ritmo della Louisiana), "Jeepers Creepers" was translated as "Ah, Giulietta!," "Sonny Boy" became "Sleep My Adored Child" (Dormi bimbo mio adorato), "In the Mood" was "Tristezze!" or "With Style" (Con stile), "Stomping at the Savoy" was translated as "Savoiardi," while the chorus of "Pennsylvania Six-Five Thousand" became "Aunt Francesca, it's Cicci speaking here" (Zia Francesca, sono Cicci, Oh, Oh, Oh!).[10] In spite of these efforts at face-value Italianization, fans of American music were often scorned as "negrophiliacs," supporters of the Anglo-American "demoplutocracy," and *esterofili anti-autarchici. Esterofilia* literally means "sympathy for foreign cultures and their artifacts": it expressed a distinctive Fascist phobia when used in association with nationalistic discourse and autocratic and autarkic proclamations.[11]

In the early 1930s a feud developed between promoters of "authentic," melodic Italian songs (*canzone all'italiana*) and proponents of modern compositions with a strong rhythmic feel. This tension often produced campy cross-fertilizations. For example, the sentimental pattern of "two hearts, one love nest" (*due cuori e una capanna*) came to "rhyme" with rhythmic exoticism. Images of Italian colonialism in Africa mixed with dance fads like the tango, and African lakes began to look oddly like Argentinian pampas. In the 1940s a new phenomenon arose when young swing singers emerged. Natalino Otto, who had been a crooner and a drummer on the Genoa-New York liners, was one of them; he was boycotted as *esterofilo* by EIAR, Italy's national broadcast radio, but his records sold pretty well anyway. Another swing singer was Alberto Rabagliati, who first visited the U.S. billed as the next Rodolfo Valentino and became famous for his swing signature refrain "when he sings, Rabagliati swings like this" (*quando canta Rabagliati fa così*). The Trio Lescano, modeled on the Andrew Sisters, swing-sang mixing a Central European accent and a stylized American pronounciation.

Ambiguity and occasional hostility toward foreign music continued into the 1950s, when Italian television began to broadcast French *chansonniers* and other foreign crooners from Milan, Italy's "modern," industrial capital. Furious listeners would call in, asking for those "barbarous screams in foreign languages" to be stopped, and requesting Neapolitan melodies instead.[12] Unfortunately, Neapolitan repertoires did not fare too well under pressures from young singers soon to be addicted to rock 'n' roll and twist. According to one incensed critic, these singers "abused melodies with nasal voices and wild drums."[13] To this day *esterofilia* is still a commonplace accusation for entertainment media imports like music, movies, and even cultural fads.

Esterofilia? or, the Practice of Covering

Rock first came to Italy as one dance fad among others. However, the music and image of rock immediately triggered a comprehensive speculation about its meanings and the articulation of similar practices in the Italian context. In 1956, a *Cinema Nuovo* review article brought together the movie *Rock around the Clock*, just released in Italy as *Senza tregua il rock 'n' roll* (Breathlessly, Rock 'n' Roll); the first official rock 'n' roll floor exhibition in Italy in Rome; the fads, practices, and typical characters of the nightclub scene all over Italy; and the presence of *tabarins* (the world of luscious dance halls fictionalized as "French" by Italians) in Italian cinema, as contrasted to American nightclubs.[14] This combination reads as an agenda for contrastive cultural analysis: we must be able to recognize signs in a foreign language before we can possibly understand them.

In the late 1950s and early 1960s, firsthand information on the U.S. music scene was hard to come by in Italy: music magazines had correspondents in London and Paris, sometimes Amsterdam, but not in New York. Thus, when it came to American topics, Italians had to rely on second- or thirdhand information full of clumsy distortions and shallow hype. Confusion was furthered by the vague category of "foreign music in English," which combined American, British, and international-style rock/pop into one genre—and by the incomprehension of rock lyrics. Even radio stations would hardly ever identify who the performers were, let alone say where they came from. The result was a relatively low profile for American imports.

The culture of "covering" is a significant element in the canon of popular music; indeed, the practice of producing Italian-language versions of American and other foreign songs became a major feature of the Italian rock industry in the 1950s and 1960s. Hundreds of cover bands were born who spread the new sounds across the Italian peninsula, via live concerts, gigs, rock festivals, and music contests.

American music in Italy was empowered by the image of a mythic America, musically young and lively, energetic, barbaric, fast and restless, if also fad-ridden. But it is important to ask what components of American music really filtered into the *versioni italiane*, as the local record industry proudly labeled the 45 rpm records, the latest technological leap of the music industry.[15] Was Italy really colonized by

American music, or did Italian covers and new songs help to counter American (musical) hegemony? An early, paradoxical example was Renato Carosone's "Tu vuo' fa l'americano" (You Pretend to Be an American, 1957), a hit sung in the Neapolitan vernacular–thus by-passing the national language–to American-like rhythmic patterns. The song mocked Italian youths passing for Americans but made its parody of rock 'n' roll in perfect rock rhythm.

Hardly ever would a *versione italiana* match the American original–and the same was true of the dub-all Italian film industry. Covers were more adaptations than translations, but due to commercial promotion Italians believed that the covers and originals were equivalent. Lyrics were often revised and rewritten, but refrains and key words remained, making the song recognizable. As a result, Italian covers would often outsell their American originals. What was transmitted, then, was an "aesthetics of sensuousness,"[16] a secondary system of meaning that implied physical and symbolic deciphering, and evoked the utopia of a distant America.[17]

Italian covers often produced implausibilities and involuntary parody. According to Umberto Fiori, "[W]hat should have been revolutionary music inherited all the poverty of the traditional popular song (*vecchia canzonetta*), including the lame rhyming verses, but with the added problem of trying to fit itself to Anglo-Saxon scansion patterns."[18] Some would cheer the fact that not all the foolishness of American rock passed into Italian culture; they would emphasize the autonomy of the musical message and be optimistic about creative misreadings.[19] However, the failure of translation meant that what might have contributed to a better understanding of the whole phenomenon of rock and of American culture was quarantined in Italian recording studios, manipulated and substantially censored, if not deleted.

Side Effects

It is important to consider the material outcome of covering, in order to touch on some of the realities of creolization. Fiori explains that when Italian musicians seemed to be distancing themselves from the new foreign music, they were in fact appropriating it, playing "in inverted commas": "As in a cabaret number, rock was displayed rather than played … and in the process of composition an external viewpoint was inserted by means of direct or indirect, musical or verbal comment."[20] In other words, singers acted as if they were commenting on a musical or social phenomenon while participating in it. For example, "Rock around the Clock" was turned into a song *about* "Rock around the Clock": "The clock is real crazy / it boogies while ticking" (*l'orologio è proprio matto / batte il tempo a bughi bughi*). It almost seems that after the efforts to bypass Fascist cultural censorship, Italian musicians continued the practices of purposeful mistranslation, parody, and irony; the Italian strain of rock was dominated by non-sensical hues.[21] It was as if, "forced by circumstances, [Italian rock] based itself on parody ... recognizing the objective situation of alienation and trying to activate it and give it an energy of its own."[22] In talking about rock in France in 1956, Boris Vian had shown that rock adaptations seemed to succeed to the extent to which they were burlesque. Maybe in Italy, as in France, this was a necessary *reframing*, a marker of relation to a somehow irreducible "other" culture, a sort of exorcism.[23]

In Italian covers and new songs conflicts were removed, decontextualized, and reframed as generational bouts or beach games of innocent, nonpoliticized youths. On their way to Italy, American "coffin songs" (like "Leader of the Pack," "Tell Laura I Love Her," "Teen Angel")–a subgenre that combined the themes of juvenile delinquency and of "live-fast-and-die-young" ethics, as epitomized by Marlon Brando and James Dean–became melodramatic cries against automobile casualties in the Italian boom years of motorization, when highways and scooters became part of Italian life.[24] Protest was sweetened–Bob Dylan and Barry McGuire heavily romanticized–and generational malaise was turned into a generic jeremiad. In both the Rokes' "Don't Blame It on Us" (Ma che colpa abbiamo noi), a cover version of Bob Lind's "Cheryl's Going Home," and Nomadi's "How Can You Possibly Judge?" (Come potete giudicar), two big hits of the era, pacifism bordered on "victimism." In other songs, rebellion was nothing more than a vindication of styles such as long hair. This mood was intertwined with adolescent sexual skirmishing: "If I Had a Hammer," Trini Lopez's "surfing" rendition of the political anthem "The Hammer Song," was soon turned into "Datemi un martello" (Give Me a Hammer), which became a cry of jealousy by a teenage girl (Rita Pavone) against her antagonist ("I'd hammer the ones I hate / that made-up brat"). With this particular case in mind, the transformation of American lyrics into their Italian cover versions could be seen as a sign of progressive desublimation, since some of these American songs were themselves already softened covers for more "authentic" folk and protest songs.

In the Italian soundscape of the era, sexuality was hardly ever a shocking issue.[25] The explicit sexual menace of rock 'n' roll–gyrating pelvises and all–was softened, even though Italian Catholics protested

vigorously also against the Italian productions. Male Italian performers (Giorgio Gaber, Enzo Iannacci, Adriano Celentano, Peppino Di Capri) were anything but menacing; their nonsensical lines
and attitudes were generally turned into benevolent and reassuring
folly. In 1958, along with Giorgio Gaber ("Ciao ... ti dirò"), Adriano
Celentano was the first to record rock 'n' roll in Italy. Elvis Presley
and Little Richard covers were his forte: his debut album contained
"Rip It Up," "Tutti Frutti," "Jailhouse Rock," and "Blueberry Hill."
Celentano came from Milan, Italy's "avant-garde city, able to fulfill
youths' desire for action."[26] In 1960 *I due corsari* (The Two Pirates:
Gaber and Iannacci) and Celentano were the madcaps (*gli svitati*),
the crazy-but-nice "beach boys" who asked for sympathy mainly
from girls' parents. They posed no threat to anyone, neither physically nor sexually—not even symbolically, even though Celentano's
body was oddly double-jointed and out of control, and he would
sport his nickname "Springy" (*il molleggiato*) for life. After all, his
"grotesque body" was perfectly in line with popular culture; Federico
Fellini aptly cast him "as himself" in *La dolce vita* (The Sweet Life,
1960). By contrast, some female singers (Mina, Brunetta, Ornella
Vanoni, Iula De Palma, Patty Pravo) proved far more provocative
and transgressive, in both sexual and social terms. They redefined
gender relations in their songs, provided Italian girls with communal
fantasies that were at once sexually charged but not sexually explicit,
and above all defied Catholic normalcy by openly engaging in "il-
licit" relations and even giving birth to babies out wedlock.

When it came to the construction of teenage sexuality and gender,
Italian television chose to celebrate the image of a musical "fairy
tale." In particular, the new shows it introduced especially for its
teenage audience featured the good boy and the lovely girl—rock and
yé-yé aesthetics, but with sound traditional ethics. The teen figures
who dominated in Italy in the early 1960s, Gianni Morandi and Rita
Pavone, were symbolically born the same day on the same television
show and were immediately adopted as Italian mothers' darlings.
Morandi would soon have all Italy follow his military service in
anguish (a déjà vu of Presley's service in the American army), while
Pavone was an androgynous kid menace (*gianburrasca*), sometimes as
virginal as Gigliola Cinquetti, and quite different from the dangerous
Lolitas that French and British starlet-singers often impersonated.

Love songs, with their free-floating sentimentality not tied to a
particular time or place, erased the differences between Americans
and Italians, telling an Italian audience that Americans loved just
like Italians did. Within this genre, an interesting phenomenon soon
developed that we could sum up here as "Little America in Big

Italy": the Italianization of American performers. Italian record and television producers looked for the slightest detail in American singers' biographies that justified their Italianness. Connie Francis, Frankie Laine, Paul Anka, and Neil Sedaka were turned into Southern Italian villagers and *cumpá* who, like Clooney's Calabresi, "[did] mambo like crazy." These alleged expatriates recorded hits "in their mother tongue," as the hype pumped; "Sings for the first time in Italian" was stamped on the record jackets. They also recorded fake Italian folklore like "Chitarra romana" or "Mamma." In 1960 Elvis himself appropriated "O' sole mio" as "It's Now or Never," inflating the Italian national ego with moving pride—and perhaps a sense of satisfaction since the song appeared to Italians as a homage to their country, the "land of music," in the wake of Domenico Modugno's success with "Volare" in the United States.

Some of the most significant changes that occurred as part of this musical creolization took place in the material grain of the sound, its rhythm, and its cultural potential. As a pop icon, rock 'n' roll in Italy was a ready-made artifact, an *objet trouvée* with no lines of development out of indigenous roots. Therefore, it was hard for Italians to perceive the differences between the rebellious, nonconformist American rock songs and their tame adaptations by American crooners. They could not easily tell the differences between Little Richard and Pat Boone, or Elvis Presley and Perry Como. Most Italian covers copied those tame, "white" American rock 'n' roll arrangements that already sounded more rounded and commercially acceptable; the African-American heritage of rock 'n' roll could not be heard. For example, in "Il re dei pagliacci," Neil Sedaka's Italian cover of his own "The King of Clowns," the arrangement erased the unmistakable sound of black/white musical crossover by replacing the Teenage Idols, the doo-wop male background voices, with a sugary Italian-style female vocal group. Ethnic difference was largely sanitized in the Italian practices of covering.[27]

Syncretisms at Work

In this atmosphere of confrontation, mediation, and creolization, Anglophone rock became the symbolic alternative to the Festival di Sanremo—the sacred temple of Italian music—the triumph of melody, romance, and emptiness framed by violins and cataracts of flowers. By the end of the 1950s, the Italian record industry sensed growing business opportunities and appropriated the pop fringes of youth music. The media immediately coined the phrase "scream versus melody." Sensational headlines, readers' polls, and even a movie, *Urlo contro melodia nel Cantagiro* (Scream versus Melody at the Cantagiro, 1963), appeared, paving the way for formulas that softened the confrontation between "Americanized," modern music and Italian-style songs. The Festival di Sanremo first paired the new with the old, the Italian rookies with the Italian "senators" (Toni Dallara with Renato Rascel, Betty Curtis with Luciano Tajoli, Domenico Modugno with Claudio Villa), then it teamed foreign performers with Italian singers, and finally it even introduced pop/rock groups. The Festival still stuck to its foundation, that of being a *song* contest, but it was clear that the industry was trying to profit by courting different consumer groups, especially the new teenage public. This entailed compromises. International stars came to the Festival but paid homage to Italian heritage by singing in Italian. A similar compromise between tradition and innovation was institutionalized on singles; as with Elvis Presley's early records, with their A-side/B-side combination of one rock/blues song and one country and western number, young Italian singers would cut somewhat different sides: one romantic (and "Italian"), the other a dance fad tune or a modern, "rockier" song (likely a cover of an American original).

Movies, too, proved influential in this process of Italian-style creolization. *Go Johnny Go*, which had been produced by Alan Freed and directed by Paul Landres in 1959, was released in an Italian version with a new narrative frame that featured Celentano as the Italian "legitimator." Celentano introduced the story on the screen, translating the innocent American *giovanilismo* for an ignorant Italian public. A poster of the movie showed the silhouette of *Adriano il molleggiato* embracing his guitar: "Adriano Celentano presents the most famous American screamers (*urlatori*) ... Alan Freed, Jimmy Clanton, Sandy Stewart, Chuck Berry in *Dai Johnny dai!* ... featuring Eddie Cochran, The Flamingos, The Cadillacs, Jackie Wilson, Jo-Ann Campbell Harvey, and Ritchie Valens." Celentano also promoted himself as singer and authority; he performed two rock songs in a fake studio (among them "Bislacco, sfasato, distratto, suonato ... da te"–Weird, deranged, distracted, and played ... by you) and claimed that he was smarter than the film's protagonist, since unlike the American, he would not be trapped into marriage.

Using American juvenile rock movies as inspiration, the Italian film industry soon developed the low-budget formula of the so-called *musicarelli*, movies especially made for youth, with famous singers as protagonists and their hit songs as titles. They perfectly captured the combination of music, popular culture, and industry. Record companies and movie productions, along with advertising agencies, worked together to shape this interesting site of mediation, resulting in the triumph of an Italian melodramatic and tragicomic cultural subtext. Like the songs, these films sought to reassure Italian cultural consumers that there was nothing wrong with American music and behavior: conflict was either resolved or deferred, protest was defused into melodrama, difference was smoothed over. In fact, quoting America one way or another, these films told more about Italy than America. In those years of social integration and assimilation, Italy's mythic geography emerged (the modern North versus the traditional South), and the films presented this divide in its musicological variant (Sanremo versus Napoli, that is Festival della Canzone Italiana versus Festival della Canzone Napoletana); watered it down to a series of stock characters (*macchiette locali*) and regional, vernacular traditions; and spread all this aided by television advertising.

The films starred *urlatori* (screamers) and *yé-yé*/beat performers,[28] but also featured familiar names from Italian variety shows—that is, the very same performers who in the 1940s and 1950s had dominated comedy films (Macario, Peppino De Filippo, Nino Taranto, Gianni Agus, Gino Bramieri, Renato Pisu, and the double act of Franco Franchi and Ciccio Ingrassia)—and some well-known faces from television's *caroselli* (Giacomo Furia, Dolores Palumbo). The actors in these films were chosen through a precise regional sampling. Cast as the parents-relatives-tutors of the young singer-rookies, they guaranteed legitimacy of the story and continuity with the past. They were the old (*matusa*, slang for Methuselah) who were not exactly open-minded (in fact, the grandparents often proved more up-to-date than the parents), but who had golden hearts; against them it was legitimate to rebel, but only to an extent. In two movies, *Una lacrima sul viso* (Tears on Your Face, Ettore Maria Fizzarotti, 1964) and *Rita, la figlia americana* (Rita the American Girl, Piero Vivarelli, 1965), the theme was played out to perfection. In the first, Bobby Solo, an "Americanized" teen-singer, returns to Italy with the new sounds – and a fresh American name, Bobby Tonner, adapted from his original Tonnerelli surname; in the second, Rita Pavone, back from South America, is able to embrace Italy's modernized youth music. Their conflicts with the father-figure music professors (Nino Taranto and Totò) center around new musical forms that, by the end of the films, are completely accepted.

Such movies largely testified to a contamination of tradition (the God-nation-family complex) and legitimized the world of Italian entertainment by means of those stock characters who were at its very core, and again celebrated the comic, ironic nature of Italian youth music. There were no tragic views and no dramatic confrontations in the *musicarelli* versions of those boom years of reconstruction and (seeming) national solidarity. The sole exception was *La battaglia dei Mods* (The Battle of the Mods, Franco Montemurro, 1966), a curious mix of a road movie, *West Side Story*, and Italy's most famous melodrama, *Assunta Spina* (Gustavo Serena, 1915).

Youth Music, Cinema, and Technology

In the late 1950s and early 1960s, music became the soundscape of youth and leisure, and the stereotypical "singing Italians" on their way to modernization were often captured by Italian cinema. All kinds of movies, both high and low, came to exhibit the new musical rituals made possible by new technologies: small transistor radios (Japanese and yet "American," they were carried everywhere, characteristically to follow the live coverage of sacred Sunday soccer); the *mangiadischi*, literally, "record-eater" (a tiny, battery-operated, "all-terrain" designer's object, it was a teenager's magic-religious fetish, perfect for beach rituals); the new, large home turntable (a piece of furniture that topologically replaced the radio in the sitting room before the advent of the television set), the cheap portable record player (one had to kick it to start playing records, as Stefania Sandrelli knew well in *Io la conoscevo bene*); the sophisticated equipment of recording studios (hi-fi tape recorders often reinforced by the record presses); and of course the jukebox (the perfect totem for youths on vacation).

Jukeboxes had made it to Italy in 1956, two years after 45 rpm records, "the great emancipators," had been introduced. Their numbers rocketed from five hundred to twelve thousand at the beginning of 1960. The location of jukeboxes in noisy public places required something completely different from soft-voiced crooning. Screamers and shouters, the *urlatori*, came of age, often out of their professional experience as saloon singers (*cantanti da balera*); one needed a loud voice (or a good pitch, or the ability to gulp) in an era when sound systems were rudimentary or simply absent. In 1958 the song "Jukebox," by Beretta-Malgoni, celebrated consensus around those automatic machines: it skillfully adapted Eddie Cochran's "Sittin' in the Balcony": "The jukebox is a magic invention / jukebox is to listen to a song with you / … the record machine is on." In the boom year 1959, Gaber was drowning his love blues in "Rhum e jukebox" (Drinking while Rocking), while Celentano recorded "I ragazzi del jukebox" (The Jukebox Boys) by Pirro Bonagura-Sciorilli.[29] The title of the latter song was quickly turned into a movie by Lucio Fulci.

The film, *I ragazzi del juke-box*, opened on a talking jukebox, which served as a voice-over narrator. It used metaphors suggested by the Italian title *Gioventù bruciata* (Burnt Youth), given to Nicholas Ray's *Rebel Without a Cause*: "Well, my name does not appear in the credits, but I am the real protagonist of this story. Yes, me, the jukebox, the automatic dispenser of the musical dreams of this age; me, the pinball's cousin, a putative father to all burnt, roasted, toasted youths of the modern era." The film was released in 1960, the same year as Mauro Morassi's own *Jukebox—Urli d'amore* (Jukebox—Cries of Love). Once again, Italian critics blamed the jukebox for its Americanness. Pier Paolo Pasolini, for one, defined Rome's jukeboxes (along with pinball machines) as America's continuation of the war with other means.[30] What Peter Handke has claimed in his recent book on the transnational jukebox seems to hold for the memories of many Italians as well. Like Handke, they associate its early diffusion with the American hits it hypnotically played, notwithstanding the traditional, local tunes that made up large sections of the playlists.[31]

Speeding to an End

The direct imitation, adoption, and reproduction in Italy of American models was eventually limited and even erased; as Sophie Body-Gendrot has put it, "modulation [won] over modelization."[32] In the wake of creolization, the practices of covering turned a controversial influence into creative modulation. Covering proved essentially counterhegemonic and stimulated fiction-making and the effective staging of identity.

Once captured on film, the wild summers of Italian youths modernized by "American" music turned into adult fantasies of eternal youth and carnival. In 1965 Antonio Pietrangeli's extraordinary movie *Io la conoscevo bene* (I Knew Her Well) staged this process on the screen. The end of the film coincides with the end of the record that the young protagonist Adriana, played by Stefania Sandrelli, is listening to.[33] The end of the music, with the record's continuing scratches, also marks the end of Adriana's youth and life. That was more than just a symbolic disappearance: the status of being young was taken out of historical context, transferred to a mental state, and turned into an option—a choice that, so the market promised, one could buy. Even though the idea of a youth problem would persist with sociopolitical tinges after the Italian student upheavals of 1968–69, the mass media now marketed youth as part of a search for longevity/eternity. Advertising packaged youth for the society of spectacle, as in the jingle for one brand of mineral water ("We are the youngest youths / a surfing army") or in the "yellow flag" emblem of Gianni Pettenati's "Bandiera gialla" used to sell tomato sauce ("You'll know / when the yellow flag is on / that young is beautiful / and time will fly"), which equated revolution with the imperatives of having fun and never growing up.

In the leisure economy, youth had become "the ideological sign of pleasure because it is a time of irresponsibility, possibility, change; young people are envied and feared and so feature in the organization of consumption as a recurring adult fantasy."[34] Upon closer examination, in the late 1950s and early 1960s, most Italian juvenile films and songs—even when they appeared to target youth as consumers—proved to be more adult projections than actual teenage fantasies. These products revealed the gaze of aging directors, with a curiosity bordering on voyeurism.

The new accelerated lifestyles were dictated by the economic boom and the "electric" excitement of technology. In his first hit, "24mila baci," Celentano managed to "Taylorize" and speed up a lazy and insomniac Italy by explicitly evoking various metaphors and collocations for love (sex) and speed (cars): "With 24,000 kisses / now you will know why love / requires 1,000 kisses per instant / why 1,000 caresses per hour." Youth music, the sexual allure of youth, and fast cars as a display of male power were also the main constituents of two great Italian movies—*Il sorpasso* (The Easy Life, Dino Risi, 1962) and *La voglia matta* (Crazy Desire a.k.a. This Crazy Urge, Luciano Salce, 1964). These movies associated institutions and straight, conventional individuals with lack of speed and enthusiasm on the one hand, and young, impetuous "rebels" with wild and unrestrained behavior on the other. By depicting an ultimate chaos, they also warned against the risks of going too fast and spinning out of control. In the former film, a quintessential male-bonding road movie, Bruno, played by Vittorio Gassman, is a reckless driver who feels good only at the wheel of his fast Lancia Spider. His fortuitous association with Roberto, a deliberate young law student played by Jean-Louis Trintignant, ends with the death of the latter, who had just been awakened to the pleasures of a freewheeling life. In *La voglia matta*, Ugo Tognazzi, a member of Italy's Automobile Club, finds himself, in his Alfa Romeo Spider ("as a matter of principle, I never drive over 60 mph"), in continuous, dangerous acceleration, with Catherine Spaak's teenage foot pressing his and the accelerator pedal.[35]

The myth and symbol of "dancing the night away" stayed alive in Italian cinema, with its pretentiously modern, international appeal, as in Fellini's *La dolce vita.* Italian hot summer nights appeared ripe with voluptuous sexual promise, although the nightclub culture of the *Italietta del boom*, with its familiar characters—petty rotarians (*commendatori*), social climbers, and irresponsible types—more often exposed its provincial and vulgar message instead. And while adolescent rock was covering and creolizing American music, Italian movie screens and televisions continued to be dominated by inferior swing music and unlikely South-Americanesque mambos and cha-chas. What Italians witnessed was a grotesque soundtrack for the disjunction between the prosperity promised by the new consumer culture boom and all the stories of problematic adaptation.

In the end it is no surprise that the most appropriate examples of youth music of the age were songs that inaugurated the serious, explicitly political vein of the *cantautori* (singer-songwriters destined to flourish in the 1970s). They were directly inspired by both European existentialism and American vernacular musical traditions (jazz, with its particular bebop attitudes, and folk). But these interpreters were never (rhetorically) young, nor did they claim they were; maybe they grew up too fast, like everyone else, in those days.

Notes

1. Rob Kroes, *If You've Seen One, You've Seen the Mall: Europeans and American Mass Culture* (Urbana and Chicago, 1996), 163.
2. Modugno's victory at the Festival della Canzone Italiana di Sanremo is considered a landmark in Italian musical culture, due in part to the international success of "Volare"; as the only record to originate in Italy and top the American charts, it was *Billboard*'s no. 1 in the week of 18 August 1958, and returned to the top on 1 September, staying there for five more weeks. It also won three Grammys for Best Male Vocal Performance, Song of the Year, and Record of the Year. Ten versions were recorded almost immediately by various artists, among them Dean Martin (whose version reached no. 12), Nelson Riddle, Jesse Belvin, Umberto Marcato, Alan Dale, and Linda Ross. In 1960 Bobby Rydell took the song to no. 4, and Al Martino still charted with it in 1975. The foreign, mostly American, singers featured in the momentous 1964 edition of the Festival di Sanremo were Gene Pitney, Frankie Laine, Paul Anka, Bobby Rydell, Frankie Avalon, and Peggy March.
3. The phrase is used by Zygmunt G. Baranski and Robert Lumley in their introduction to *Culture and Conflict in Postwar Italy: Essays on Mass and Popular Culture* (London, 1990), 1.
4. Dick Hebdige, *Hiding in the Light* (London, 1988), 73 (especially the chapter "Towards a Cartography of Taste 1935–1962").
5. See *Eh, Paisano!* (Rhino, 1997), an interesting compilation of "Italian-American classics" featuring Dean Martin, Domenico Modugno, Connie Francis, Louis

Prima, Jerry Vale, Lou Monte, Al Martino, Julius La Rosa, Jay and the Americans, The Three Chuckles, Keely Smith, Tony Reno and the Sherwoods, and Emilio Pericoli.

6. See Omar Calabrese, "Appunti per una storia dei giovani in Italia," in *La vita privata. Il Novecento*, ed. P. Ariès and G. Duby (Bari, 1988), especially 91–92.

7. See Stephen Gundle, *I comunisti italiani tra Hollywood e Mosca. La sfida della cultura di massa (1943–1991)* (Florence, 1995), 239–50.

8. See Umberto Eco, "Il modello americano," in U. Eco, R. Ceserani, and B. Placido, *La riscoperta dell'America* (Bari, 1984), 3–32.

9. See Adriano Mazzoletti, *Il jazz in Italia: Dalle origini al dopoguerra* (Bari, 1983), 326.

10. See Riccardo Schwamental, "Postfazione sul periodo fascista," in Mike Zwerin, *Musica degenerata: Il jazz sotto il Nazismo* (Turin, 1993), especially 185–95; Mike Zwerin, *La tristesse de Saint Louis: Swing under the Nazis* (London, 1985).

11. See Gianni Borgna, *Storia della canzone italiana* (Bari, 1985), 84.

12. See Umberto Eco, "Verso una civiltà della visione?" *Rivista Pirelli* 1 (February 1961), quoted in Aldo Grasso, *Linea allo studio: Miti e riti della televisione italiana* (Milan, 1989), 106.

13. See Gianfranco Baldazzi, *La canzone italiana del Novecento* (Rome, 1989), 96.

14. See Vito Pandolfi, "Rock 'n' roll al night club," *Cinema Nuovo* (1956).

15. In 1958, 45 rpm's outsold 78 rpm's for the first time (10,493,200 against 4,989,800) in Italy, and in 1959 they reached boom figures (15,311,000 items out of a total record sale of 18,332,000). See data in *Musica e dischi* 225 (March 1965). As to the magnitude of the practice of covering in the record industry in the timespan under consideration (1958–64), suffice it here to say that surveys of early 1960s Top 30 charts show a symbolic more than an extensive presence (the trend would be reversed in the late 1960s). Nevertheless, small record companies, those unlikely to make it to the top, generously benefited from covering.

16. This phrase can be found in Peter Wicke, *Rock Music: Culture, Aesthetics and Sociology* (Cambridge, 1990), 48.

17. This notion perfectly suits the historical progression of the reception of America in Italy: as word first, then image, and finally object. See Guido Fink and Franco Minganti, "La vita privata italiana sul modello americano," in *La vita privata*, 351–80.

18. Umberto Fiori, "Rock Music and Politics in Italy," *Popular Music* 4 (1984): 272.

19. See Alessandro Portelli, "L'orsacchiotto e la tigre di carta. Il rock and roll arriva in Italia," *Quaderni Storici* 58, no. 1 (April 1985): 135–47.

20. Fiori, "Rock Music and Politics in Italy," 272.

21. A long line of examples would stretch from Pippo Starnazza's mild Futurism to the 1950s of Renato Carosone, Fred Buscaglione, and Adriano Celentano, to name but a few.

22. Umberto Fiori, "Tra quaresima e carnevale: pratiche e strategie della canzone d'autore," *Musica/Realtà* 3 (1980): 111–25 (my translation).

23. In this guise, we could reconsider the whole parable of the uses of English in Italian pop song lyrics: from a "progressive insertion" (some Renato Carosone's Anglo-Neapolitan routines, or Adriano Celentano's hybridation and mix in the cover of Paul Anka's "You Are My Destiny": "You are my destiny, sei tutti i sogni miei") to nonsensical, mock-English lyrics (again, Celentano's "Prisencolinensinainciusol," or else Lucio Dalla's improvised "stomps" of the 1970s, his signature encores in live concerts).

24. Vespas and Lambrettas would soon invade teenage movies and advertising, namely television's *caroselli*, Italy's peculiar commercials. These scooters were subconsciously experienced as a threat to the motorcycle, the masculine element

of road culture; Italy was learning to detect symptoms of the feminization of the public domain and of the growning aestheticization of everyday life.

25. In the early 1960s one could find a significant number of explicit titles referring to the inconveniences of growing up: "Non è facile avere 18 anni" (It's not Easy to Be 18), "Non ho l'età (per amarti)" (I'm Under Age for Love), "Quelli della mia età" (Those My Age), "Mes amis, mes copains" (My Friends, My Pals)–the last two being French covers.

26. See Piergiorgio Bezzi, "La corsa del 45giri nel 1958 e dintorni," in *Il disco e la sua copertina: Stili e mode musicali negli anni '50 e '60*, ed. P. Bezzi and F. Gabici (Ravenna, 1988).

27. It is important here to note that Italian copyright laws have until recently been quite peculiar. In the 1960s, they allowed the "authors" of the Italian cover (i.e., both the musicians responsible for the arrangement and the lyricists responsible for the adaptation) to share the royalties with the original authors. See Franco Fabbri, "Traduzioni milionarie," in *Il suono in cui viviamo* (Milan, 1996), 138–42.

28. *Yé-yé* came from France, where it referred to Anglo-American music, while "beat" had just vague echoes and faint reminiscences of the Beat Generation: it literally meant the rhythm, and referred primarily to the Beatles. Once again, America reached Italy only as a secondhand, barely comprehensible allusion.

29. The lyrics were: "Happiness costs a dime / to the jukebox boys. / Youths buy it for only 50 *lire*, nothing more. / Sweet blues and a song / are enough for the jukebox boys. / Dancing around / everyone finds their great happiness. / 'Come on, rock with me! / Come on, hug me! / Kiss me ardently!' / Happiness costs a dime / to the jukebox boys. / Youths buy it for only 50 *lire*, nothing more.... In a dime there lies the illusion / there lies the obsession of the jukebox boys."

30. Pasolini quoted in Peter Handke, *Versuch über die Jukebox* (Frankfurt a.M., 1990). My reference, here, is its Italian translation: *Saggio sul juke-box* (Milan, 1992), 33.

31. See Handke, *Saggio sul juke-box*, 47. Interestingly, Handke focuses on the "little rituals and habits" of both the "jukebox players" (this is how he defines the active role of those who select music, spending their dimes for it) and the robotic machines (their liturgic noises: clicks, search whizzes, scratches, etc.).

32. See Sophie Body-Gendrot, "Una vita privata dei Francesi sul modello americano," in *La vita privata*, 321 ("the 'American model' is erased by the appropriation process: modulation wins over modelization").

33. It is an instrumental number, likely a B side or at least a reference to "Letkiss," a foolish dance instruction song by Le Gemelle Kessler, two German bluebell twins popularized by television, that Sandrelli danced to earlier in the movie.

34. Simon Frith, "Frankie Said: 'But What Did They Mean?'" in *Consumption, Identity, and Style: Marketing, Meanings, and the Packaging of Pleasure*, ed. Alan Tomlinson (London and New York, 1990), 180.

35. It is useful to recall that Italy's 1960s car culture, clustered on the Fiat/highway collocation, came to solidify around music (and advertising) in the quiet convoy of the Cantagiro, an itinerant summer song festival that traveled by car around Italy, covering a large territory with concerts every night. This modern "miracle" tried hard to take the attention off the tabloid papers that morbidly recounted popular singers' automobile accidents. After Fred Buscaglione's tragic death, various artists (Ricky Gianco, Gino Paoli, Edoardo Vianello, Isabella Iannetti, and Roby Crispiano) suffered serious accidents, which were, of course, amplified by certain "coffin" songs.

– Eight –

THE SOCIAL PRODUCTION OF DIFFERENCE

Imitation and Authenticity in Japanese Rap Music

Ian Condry

> …Japanese rap is the real thing.… For us, raised in a different envi-
> ronment and different language, Japanese rap by rappers raised in
> the country is much more 'real' (*riaru*) than American rap.
>
> – Ben the Ace, Japanese DJ[1]

> No matter how much one likes black music and culture, both were
> born from the situations blacks faced, and the burden of their history
> and fate. In some ways, it was a brutal process (resistance against
> whites, the need to be proud of their own identity, their unique labor
> in the midst of poverty, etc.). If you consider this, I can't help but
> question the shallow, superficial imitation (*mane*) of us Japanese.
>
> – Reader's letter to a Japanese hip-hop magazine[2]

As American hip-hop artists devote themselves to "keeping it real,"
Japanese rappers and fans debate what exactly "real" means in a
locale far removed from rap's origins. In Japan, the second largest
music market in the world, what started as a dance fad and a style of
singing in the early 1980s has grown to become what some call a
"hip-hop culture" that encompasses fashion, break dance, graffiti,

and rap music. In the mid-1990s, Japanese rappers even produced their own million-selling hits. What happens when rap music is appropriated by Japanese musicians? How do they overcome contradictions involved in bringing hip-hop across cultural and linguistic boundaries? A lively local debate over whether it is possible for Japanese to produce "real" hip-hop, or whether it is all simply imitation, provides an intriguing example of ways that global popular culture is forcing a reconsideration of the relationship between locality and identity. In particular, the discourse surrounding rap music in Japan shows how constructions of class, ethnicity, and gender are influenced by the appropriation of American mass culture.

This speaks to an enduring question: How does one evaluate the local influence of foreign culture? Whether as "diffusion," "cultural imperialism," or "domestication," a recurring problem is how to analyze such phenomena without essentializing either the local or the foreign culture.[3] Analyses are likely to begin with the notion that there are such entities as "Japanese culture" or "hip-hop" and then set out to explore their interaction. But the images from American hip-hop also contribute to Japanese youths' understanding of what Japan is, and conversely Japanese rap may be altering hip-hop as well. In this situation, Akhil Gupta and James Ferguson urge anthropologists to explore "the processes of *production* of difference in a world of culturally, socially, and economically interconnected and interdependent spaces."[4] Hip-hop music in Japan offers a useful vehicle for this type of analysis. In the genre's marketing, its representation in the media, and in the efforts of local rappers to produce an indigenous version of the style, the assertion of "authenticity" contributes to the social construction of class, ethnicity, and gender. For some, hip-hop is above all an outgrowth of black culture, born from the challenges faced in the ghettos of the United States. But for many Japanese youth, rap offers a way of distinguishing themselves from mainstream Japanese, especially as a kind of generational protest. Due to space limitations, I am less concerned here with the reception of rap music. Instead, this essay focuses on the perspectives of Japanese rappers as they try to interpret hip-hop into an authentic Japanese idiom.

There are concurrently processes of production of sameness. In Japan, the 1980s was perhaps the decade of "internationalization" (*kokusaika*), but the catch phrases of the 1990s—"borderless world" and "globalization"—suggest a new conceptualization of links around the world. In regard to music as well, the idiom of a "global hip-hop culture" is promoted by record companies and print media, as well as American and Japanese rappers. The "B-Boy" fashion of droopy, oversized pants, baseball caps, and Nike sneakers is currently a leading style for teenage boys in the fashionable Tokyo districts of Shibuya and Harajuku.[5] It is a style recognizable to anyone familiar with American high school students. Specialty record shops in Tokyo provide the same twelve-inch record releases as are available in New York City within a couple weeks of their U.S. release. Also available in Japan are magazines reporting on the latest rap music trends, both in English (*The Source, Vibe, Rap Pages*, etc.) and in Japanese (*Blast* [formerly *Front*], *Black Music Review, Remix*, etc.). Satellite and cable broadcast of American MTV as well as Japanese music channels offers a chance to study the latest gestures, dance styles, and images of popular rappers. Contrasting their sense of a dearth of information in the 1980s, Japanese DJs and rappers note that nowadays they can experience the latest sounds and news in "real time" (*riaru taimu*), thus collapsing the sense of distance between the Tokyo scene and the rap scene in the United States.

Still, one wonders what exactly is conveyed through this extended media and music industry network. In what sense can there be a "global" hip-hop culture? What is shared? What differences are elided? By what processes are new boundaries and new interconnections being produced through the diffusion of this style? One might think that with such global flows, the question of "authenticity" would disappear as people come to accept the playful pastiche of contemporary music. But if anything, the question of what is real seems as important as ever. During twenty months of fieldwork in Tokyo between 1994 and 1997, I found that the most common reaction to my project on Japanese rap was, "Isn't it merely imitation?" (*mane dake jya nai no ka*). Whether it was Japanese adults looking askance at youthful exuberance towards hip-hop, or record company representatives leery of investing in a genre they worry will not sell, or music magazine editors believing that only African-Americans produce rap, or even Japanese rappers themselves observing the efforts of other rap groups, everyone was quick to use the idiom of imitation as their main criticism of the music. At one level, "imitation" can be interpreted as a gloss for "I don't like the music," but deeper probing reveals that the discourse of authenticity relates to central assumptions about the relationship between music and identity.

In this essay, I discuss the identity politics surrounding rap music in Japan with particular attention to class, ethnicity, and gender. Rap music's origins in black, urban America make it an instructive case. It is tempting to interpret hip-hop music as the voice of marginalized blacks, but this approach falls into a trap: we would have to decide who, among the cacophony of voices, is the authentic representative—and of whom. A similar pitfall appears if one interprets Japanese rap as the voice of that country's youth. Instead, I suggest following Simon Frith's assessment that "we should be asking not what does popular music *reveal* about 'the people' but how does it *construct* them." He adds:

> The most misleading term in cultural theory is, indeed, "authenticity." What we should be examining is not how true a piece of music is to something else, but how it sets up the idea of "truth" in the first place—successful pop music is music which defines its own aesthetic standard.[6]

This idea of truth is closely related to the discourse on imitation and authenticity. With regard to rap music in Japan, how are the lines drawn? What do the distinctions tell us about how popular music is used in the social construction of identity in Japan? In the next section, I discuss how rap's association with lower-class Americans gives the music a particular authority among middle-class Japanese. Then I discuss race and ethnicity in Japan, and the current appeal of "black culture." Finally, I examine how gender is related to different types of Japanese rap music. In conclusion, I explore the issue of globalization and how popular culture constructs and transcends social boundaries.

Class: Ghetto, Street, and Club

Many academic treatments of hip-hop emphasize its emergence from an ethnically marked, lower-class context. Tricia Rose, for example, gives the following definition:

> Hip hop is an Afro-diasporic cultural form which attempts to negotiate the experiences of marginalization, brutally truncated opportunity and oppression within the cultural imperatives of African-American and Caribbean history, identity, and community. It is the tension between the cultural fractures produced by postindustrial oppression and the binding ties of black cultural expressivity that sets the critical frame for the development of hip hop.[7]

Other histories of hip-hop focus on musical influences[8] or African traditions,[9] but in each case the genre is linked to a history of collective experience. Rap music and black culture become entwined and mutually construct each other at least partly, one could assume, in a (laudable) effort to valorize the identity of a marginalized people. A theoretical problem arises, however, when one tries to explain the development of hip-hop outside of the "critical frame" that Rose identifies. How are we to understand the development of hip-hop in Japan?

Hip-hop's appropriation in Japan is not easily mapped by class distinctions. Rather, the music appealed to people, especially youth, who were dissatisfied with the current range of music options. One Japanese writer explains:

> Although hip-hop was born as a street level music of underclass blacks, when it crossed the ocean to the East it was consumed as the "most up-to-date trend." This discovery was linked to a certain timing, because New Wave music was losing steam and in decline. Hip-hop grabbed the attention of the people who were searching for the new style of rock. So naturally, immediately after it was imported it was never established as music rooted in street culture.[10]

In Japan, rap is always represented as "street" (*sutoriito*) music, an implicit reference to class. But while some of the early Japanese hip-hoppers were lower middle class, in general it was not people on the margins who took to the new style. Hence, hip-hop was never rooted in "street culture," but is better considered club music, which in 1980s Tokyo meant all-night discos. In this context, the style offered a certain degree of cultural capital.

Break dancing, hip-hop's striking visual aspect carried through movies and live shows, was what first inspired emulation in Japan. In 1982, a low-budget hip-hop movie called *Wild Style* was shown in Tokyo theaters. Performers who appeared in the movie, such as the New York City break dance team Rock Steady Crew, came to Japan at the same time and performed in Tokyo discos. Although the ghetto origins were poorly understood by the audience, the toughness and originality of the style clearly offered some of those present a challenging recreation and a way to show off. Crazy-A, one of the earliest and most successful break dancers in Japan, says hip-hop offered him an alternative to his bad-boy teenage ways.

> After all, hip hop has an aspect of battle in it. So, instead of fighting, I started with hip hop, and quit the violence. You see, you can fight and get stronger, but—how can I put it?—in the end, nothing of substance remains inside you. It's not as if there are brawling tournaments or anything, so nothing lasts. But with dance, there are competitions and a sense of accomplishment stays with you. You can say, I'm number one, and appeal to an audience. And that gives you something lasting.[11]

Every Sunday, Crazy-A and other break dancers could be found performing in Tokyo's street-musician haven Yoyogi Park right alongside rock 'n' roll dancers and punk bands. MC Bell, another rapper who started as a break dancer, says that as a teenager he learned the moves in a disco from a black American serviceman stationed in Japan.[12] Break dancing offered a sharp contrast to the Eurobeat and disco styles then the norm, and ensured that he would stand out in a nightclub. Thus, class figured in several ways with rap's origins in Japan. On the one hand, fans needed money to buy the expensive and rare rap albums in the early days. On the other, some of today's Japanese rappers were lower-middle-class teenagers who had skipped school and spent a lot of time in nightclubs.

Over time, rap music's association with lower-class African-Americans became more widely known. Now the style offers Japanese youth a way to set themselves apart from what they see as the country's homogeneous mainstream. Every year, the prime minister's survey announces again that 90 percent of Japanese consider themselves middle class.[13] Ideal typifications of what this middle-class lifestyle means are also widely shared: rice-winner father, education mama, and two samurai school children.[14] Rap music's link with black Americans from the ghetto gives it particular strength. Similar to white suburban youth who revel in the gun-toting, drug-slinging fantasies of gangsta rappers, Japanese youth far removed from violence in the streets admire the gritty "reality" espoused by hip-hop's toughs. Even so, it is not the pithy analysis of police brutality or clever turn of phrase that explains the appeal. The various meanings of rap lyrics are mostly lost on Japanese listeners. Instead, the angry attitudes, the swear words (also learned from American movies), and the recorded sirens and gunshots all promote images of what it means to be from the projects. For Japanese fans, the music sounds cool (*kakkoii*), it has a good groove (*nori ga ii*), and when it is good, it is "seriously bad" (*maji yabai*). Spectacular live shows promote an image that American rappers are from a completely different (and more exciting) world. When Cake-K, one of the earliest Japanese rappers, recalls attending a Public Enemy concert in 1989, he mentions the security guards standing on stage, dressed in military fatigues and armed with fake automatic machine guns. At one point, the security men feigned spraying the audience with gunfire. "It was amazing!" (*sugokatta*), he says, "I'd never seen anything like it."[15] In the late 1980s, all Japanese rap groups had their own "security" striking imposing postures on stage.

Initially, Japanese rappers' main worry was not that they were from a too different class setting to produce rap, but that the Japanese language was hopelessly ill-suited to the style. In interviews during 1994, rappers complained that since Japanese was unaccented (English is accented), it was exceedingly difficult to give their lyrics the rhythmic bounce necessary to rap. Some groups even tried rapping in English, though these experiments were abandoned in light of limited audience appeal. Rappers also complained that the grammatical structure of the language made it difficult to produce engaging rhymes. Japanese sentences are generally subject-object-verb, and, with the limited number of verb endings, rhyming options appeared lacking. Musicians experimented with enjambment (splitting a sentence into several lines) and adding English phrases. They also artificially added stress to Japanese to make it "sound like English."

Language is a central idiom for identity, and perhaps particularly so in Japan, given the conservative tendency of so-called "Japan theory" (*nihon-ron*) arguments that the Japanese are unique in part because of the Japanese language.[16] One often hears in Japan that everyone speaks the same language, but this assertion disguises an underlying diversity. Along with regional dialects, there is a wide range of slang associated with generational cohorts and gender. Japanese rappers in effect create a new dialect by rapping Japanese with a punctuated rhythm, and adding English words to make compelling rhymes. These linguistic features may add to the shock value of Japanese rap, but what is more important, they work to produce social difference by setting apart youthful rap musicians and fans from mainstream Japanese.

By 1996, complaints about the limitations of the language had largely disappeared, as a growing number of Japanese rap releases were deemed successful. Ineffective "flow," as an individual's vocal style is called, is now blamed on the rapper, not the language. Indeed, there is a definite pride in clever uses of Japanese. Rappers say that the main defining feature of Japanese rap is that it is in Japanese. During live shows, what little English was used is gradually disappearing.[17] Contemporary Japanese rappers also laugh embarrassedly that they imitated the security guards of American rap groups. They are clearly rethinking rap's relation to the Japanese context. With the recent explosion of available information about hip-hop's origins,[18] however, fans who want to feel they are a part of "hip-hop culture" are faced with a dilemma. They come to understand the connections between rap music and the lives of American rappers—living in the 'hood, being black and often poor, and growing up with a range of funky music to draw on for samples and lyrical themes. But they also realize they cannot be what the American rappers are. Or can they?

Race and Ethnicity: To Dread or Not

aoi me no eijian, eirian	blue-eyed Asian, alien
chijirekke no eijian, eirian	wavy-haired Asian, alien
eijian wa kokujin ni naritai	Asians want to be black people
eijian wa hakujin ni naritai	Asians want to be white people

> – ECD, "Aoi me no eijian" [Blue-Eyed Asian] from the album
> *ECD* (File Records, 1992, 26MF035D)

One of the most conspicuous features of rap's popularity in Japan is the number of Japanese youth who have adopted "dread hair" (*doreddo heaa*) or "afros," in addition to hip-hop fashion. Some people even frequent tanning salons to darken their skin.[19] In Japanese, the construction "to tan" can be glossed "to become black" (*kuroku naru*), and it seems as if some of these hip-hop fans wish to do just that. To understand why this is considered attractive by some, we need to examine race and ethnicity in Japan, and the way it is related to rap music.

Ethnicity is, of course, a key fault line in the social production of difference. An oft-cited contrast with the U.S., a multiethnic nation, is that in Japan everyone has the same skin, eyes, and straight, black hair. At the level of official government discourse, the notion of Japan as a land of "one people" (*tan'itsu minzoku*) serves to disguise domestic inequality while promoting a harmonious image of the country's economic ascendance. In an infamous 1986 speech, then prime minister Yasuhiro Nakasone praised Japan as a high-level information society, and noted that "in America, there are many blacks, Puerto Ricans and Mexicans, and on the average America's level [of intelligence] is still extremely low."[20] But identifying the Japanese as a single people effectively excludes residents of Japan who have been denied full citizenship, such as the over half-million "Koreans" who were born and raised in Japan, as well as the roughly three million *burakumin*, who are still stigmatized based on links to the former outcast group.[21] It is arguable that women as well are excluded as full citizens—if not under law, at least in official practices. The prevalence of ethnic conflict in the U.S. is well known in Japan, usually in sensationalist terms, as in the coverage of the 1992 Los Angeles riots and the O. J. Simpson trial. While there is a general understanding that racial problems are ever present in the U.S., rappers have a special relationship to those problems: they are the ones speaking openly and forcefully about such issues from a position of marginality. Although the English lyrics are difficult for Japanese listeners to understand, Japanese releases of albums usually contain translations of the songs, and music magazine reviews often describe the themes of the albums.

At the same time, these music magazines represent hip-hop as an African-American genre. In the issue of *Music Magazine* that named their top ten picks of 1994, the albums in the category "rap" were all by African-American artists.[22] American rap-influenced musicians who were not black fared well, but only in other genres. For example, in the category "rock (America)" one writer described the top three albums as "mixture rap" (Beastie Boys), "folk rap" (Beck), and "blues rap" (G. Love and Special Sauce), all of which were produced by white musicians.[23] Similarly, record stores tend to categorize hip-hop as "Western music" (*yôgaku*) and within that as "black music" (*burakku myûjikku*). "Japanese rap" sections have appeared in the larger Tokyo record stores, but they are grouped with Japanese music. In realms closer to the core of devoted hip-hop fans and musicians, however, these boundaries are being redrawn. In specialty record shops that deal only in hip-hop LPs (twelve-inch analog on vinyl), there is no spatial distinction between Japanese and American rap music, and both appear side by side on wall racks. In hip-hop clubs, American rap dominates, but Japanese rap is getting increasing time on the turntables. When American rap groups perform in Japan, there are always Japanese rappers as the front act. In 1996, it was not uncommon for several thousand copies of analog releases of Japanese rap to sell out in less than a week, a sign that for a growing number of rap consumers, Japanese artists have been able to accommodate being both Japanese and hip-hop.

Older Japanese dismiss youthful interest in hip-hop as a simplistic adoration of anything American, but, significantly, rap fans are more likely to point to "black culture," not "American culture," as the source of their fascination. A rapper who calls himself You the Rock draws on black history to explain his appreciation for the music.

> My school took an intensely moralistic approach to education, and from second and third grade of elementary school they were teaching us about Malcolm X, Dr. King, Lincoln, even Uncle Tom. They taught it all. So when I heard BDP and Public Enemy, I understood it. All of it was real (*riaru*). For example with *buraku* discrimination, even though they are people just like us, they can't get jobs, they can't get married. From when I was little, I saw it with my own eyes, and it pissed me off. At that time, there were Japanese [pop] groups like BOØWY and Rebecca, but I just didn't get it. Then one day, on a TV show called "11pm," I saw Run-DMC. I ran to the record store the next day.[24]

Because of its association with black struggle, rap music has an authority that Japanese pop music lacks. But when You the Rock considers oppression in a Japanese context, he does not say he suffered from racial discrimination, but rather that his family was looked down on in the neighborhood because of a chaotic home life (hot-tempered parents, many stepsiblings, and so on).[25] In this way, the social protest aspect of hip-hop is reinterpreted into an idiom of injustice in Japan, most often as a kind of generational protest.

As John Russell notes regarding some characters in recent Japanese literature, "disaffected Japanese youth came to see the African American as a counter to the values of the Japanese establishment, and the black Other was adopted as a symbol of defiance, forbidden fruit, and their own alienation from the Japanese mainstream."[26] For some Japanese hip-hoppers, the style of dread hair is a way to illustrate a desired affiliation with African-Americans, while also defying the authority of their parents and teachers. A rapper who goes by the name of Kreva explained that he had two reasons for his dreads: first, to stand out (*medachitai*); and second, to show respect for black culture (*kokujin bunka ni resupekuto*). Nina Cornyetz argues that for young Japanese fond of hip-hop style "blackness is frequently affixed to an antecedent erotic subtext that fetishizes black skin as symbolic of phallic empowerment."[27] I agree that sex appeal is likely to be a goal for youths who kink their hair at beauty salons and darken their skin. This is at best, however, a limited explanation for Japanese interest in hip-hop, because not surprisingly only a small fraction of the fans go so far as to put chemicals in their hair or to lay under the lamps.

Also, there is considerable debate as to whether changing one's hair is an appropriate sign of respect. In a monthly column aimed at Japanese B-Boys, the rapper Zeebra addresses the issue as part of his response to the second quotation at the opening of this chapter criticizing the "shallow, superficial imitation of us Japanese."

> Imitation is not good, imitation itself. It doesn't necessarily follow, but I often wonder about Japanese who perm their hair into dreads. It's well known that Malcolm X, when he was young and didn't know any better, went so far as to put strong, burning chemicals on his scalp so that he could have straight hair like those he admired: white people living elegant lives. But even so, I'd like you all to consider how similar that is with Japanese forcing their hair into dreads.[28]

Thus, some hip-hop musicians and fans (probably a majority) see the adoption of dark skin and curly hair as a mere superficial imitation that contradicts a key element of keeping hip-hop real, namely, being true to who you are. Another rapper, MC Shiro of the group Rhymester, asserts, "We do not want to be black, although there are lots of Japanese kids that do; we love hip-hop, the music."[29]

Indeed, Zeebra rejects commonsense association of hip-hop with American blacks.

> Also, it is not the case that "black" equals "hip-hop." There are many blacks, so-called "house negros," who despise hip-hop's message. For blacks in the American hip-hop community, in some ways, these people are the enemies, and us hip-hoppers living in Japan are the allies. It may be going too far to say so, but I have black hip-hop friends who feel this way. To fight the chaos together, and with all our hearts to spread hip-hop, I am certain that this is the greatest respect that can be paid to the originators.[30]

Zeebra makes a case that spreading hip-hop, and protesting injustice, is the defining feature of a "hip-hopper" and one that transcends ethnic, national, and cultural boundaries. He is also rebutting the implicit argument that middle-class Japanese kids have no right to appropriate ghetto music by arguing that the greatest form of respect towards the creators is to enlarge the circle of hip-hoppers. At this end of the spectrum, ethnicity is no boundary at all, and the transnational identity of "hip-hopper" becomes a meaningful possibility.

Gender: Party Rap vs. Underground Hip-Hop

In 1995, East End X Yuri (the "X" is read "plus") burst onto the scene with several hit songs.[31] Success in the marketplace signaled a certain kind of authenticity to the decision-makers in record companies and the media, prompting a flurry of label signings and a surge of publicity for the genre that had been largely underground. Some commentators hailed the birth of a new genre they called "J-Rap." At the same time, a debate among hip-hoppers about the relationship between "hip-hop culture" and commercialism began to heat up. In concerts, some groups would make a point of saying they were "not J-Rap" but rather "Japanese hip-hop" (*nihon no hippu hoppu*), prompting raucous cheers from the fans. As it turns out, these cheers were not only about being true to an image of what hip-hop should be, but also about the differences between boys and girls.

Among rap fans themselves there is a sharp difference between what men and women consume. Although it is an overgeneralization, one could characterize two trends in contemporary Japanese rap, namely, party rap and underground hip-hop, both of which share many common features. Japanese rappers and DJs tend to be in their twenties, and with few exceptions they hold part-time or full-time jobs, or are students. Over 90 percent of these hip-hop musicians are male. Although an increasing number of women are becoming active on the scene, most often as DJs and break dancers, there are few female rappers. Two examples are RIM, who aims for an underground sound, and a party rap group called NowNow, reminiscent of early TLC. But with the exception of Yuri, who recorded with East End, female rappers have yet to gain much status. In contrast, 1999 is witnessing a "Japanese R&B" boom, with attractive young women singing melodic songs on top of hip-hop beats (e.g., Misia, Utada Hikaru, Double, and Rima). These women are not rappers per se, but they often release remixes or maxi singles that feature male Japanese rappers. Hip-hop dancers show a more even split (about 60 percent are male). The fans of Japanese rap are generally in their teens and early twenties, and are mostly students and part-time workers (*furiitaa*).

Party and underground styles differ in terms of themes, audience, production, and marketing. Party rap tends to have light, funny lyrics that speak of themes from everyday life (e.g., video games, dating, teenage love songs). The most striking feature is that the audience for party rap is over 90 percent female, even though virtually all of the artists are male. Record company representatives I have interviewed contend that women, especially teenage girls, are the main consumers of pop music in Japan. One A&R spokesperson stated that females make up around 80 percent of the hit song market. Major record labels deal almost exclusively with party rap. Representative groups include Scha Dara Parr, East End X Yuri, and Dassen Trio. Such rappers also seem more sanguine about commercial success as a goal. Their live shows tend to be in larger venues like auditoriums or concert halls. They are also regularly featured in wider circulation teen fashion magazines. In contrast, underground hip-hop tends to be more abstract, darker, and at times in opposition to mainstream Japanese society. The audience is 80 percent male, and independent labels are the main producers of records. Specialty magazines, free papers, and flyers at record stores and clubs are the main sources of information on these rappers. Groups such as King Giddra, Microphone Pager, and Rhymester would fall into this category. Their live shows tend to be monthly events in (literally) underground clubs that hold at most a couple hundred people. Underground rappers tend to emphasize being true to who they are, regardless of whether it leads to pecuniary rewards.

It would be a mistake, however, to view party rap as superficial and (therefore) feminized. In my opinion, some underground rappers have a tendency to take themselves too seriously, posing on-stage in a shallow caricature of toughness. Furthermore, party rappers are often quite insightful about Japanese society, in particular the concerns facing youth. The largest selling party rap song to date, East End X Yuri's single "Maicca," reached number three on the pop charts and sold over a million copies in 1995. What is interesting is that the construction of gender relationships in the song is a sharp contrast to much of the male-centered rap of the United States. "Maicca" is youthful slang that translates roughly as "well, no problem, I guess." The female rapper Yuri sings about a clever, perhaps manipulative, Japanese woman deftly keeping her boyfriend(s) guessing. On a date, first she keeps a boy waiting outside, then falls asleep in the car, and finally, after ordering an expensive sushi meal, gets a call on her cellular phone. She answers, and says, "Oh, I am just having dinner with a girlfriend, I'll be there shortly" and hangs up. When her date asks who called, she replies, "Oh, it was a wrong number." The song returns to the refrain:

maikka ittoke maikka	Well, no problem, just say it, no problem
komatta toki wa saa maikka	When there's trouble, well, no problem
fukaku kangaenai de maikka	Don't think deeply, well, no problem
hiraki naotte maikka	Turn everything around, well, no problem

– East End X Yuri, "Maicca" from the album *denim-ed soul 2*
(Epic/Sony, 1995, ESCB-1590)

Clearly, Japanese hip-hop does not always reproduce the all-too-frequent misogynist aspect of rap music in the States. Indeed, the most popular of the hip-hop groups in Japan seems to be achieving considerable success with songs depicting the Japanese woman who gets what she wants.

Among underground rap groups, the most characteristic is King Giddra. Composed of DJ Oasis and two rappers, Zeebra and K Dub Shine, the group is widely respected for rapping about serious issues in Japan. Both Zeebra and K Dub Shine have spent years in the U.S., and carry a certain amount of authority (and coolness) for this experience. Their songs, interviews, and writings illustrate a conceptualization of Japanese rap that sees it as part of hip-hop culture. Originally, King Giddra was a three-headed monster that comes from outer space to battle Godzilla in a movie. Here is why the group chose that name.

First, we realized Godzilla is an international character that would represent (*repurezento*) an international Japan. But Godzilla himself, he's too much everywhere, so we settled on King Giddra. It's exactly us as a three-person group. Also, in the movie King Giddra is the bad guy, but as a public enemy (*paburikku enamii*) he's doing an extremely positive thing, right? That is, as an enemy of the public, we are an enemy of the system that oppresses us. We see the system as the enemy, and for us, Godzilla is the system. We're like "planetary defense forces" [laughs]. For those who don't understand, we've come to tell the truth.[32]

For these rappers authentic hip-hop must embody opposition to authority. The "system" King Giddra opposes takes various forms. The seductive and destructive power of commercialism is portrayed in the song "The Birth of a Star" (*Sutaa tanjô*), which tells the story of a young woman who comes from the countryside to Tokyo to become famous as a singer, but who is tricked into the sleazy underworld of pornographic films. King Giddra also has sharp words for Japan's education system.

kodomo tachi no yume	The "credentials society" crushes
made hakai	the dreams
shite kita gakureki shakai	of even children,
umaku dekita kai?	that's a good thing?
daigaku dereba	You graduate from college and you
ii shûshoku	get a good job
asameshi mae ni kutta yûshoku	It's the easiest thing in
mae ni kutta	the world,
chûshoku kurai no mono	done even before eating breakfast
kyôiku mama yûrai wa	It's that simplistic thinking that
sono an'i kangae angai	leads to education mamas
kawatte kiteru n jya nai?	But things are changing, aren't they
tada sore damatte	And aren't you just shutting up, and
miteru n jya nai?	watching it happen
kotoshi no daisotsu no koyô	This year's survey of col grads
chôsa	employment
kimaranu yatsu no ôsa sô sa	says that almost a quarter of them
yon'bun no ichi ga mada	still have no job,
maji hanahada okashiku tte	Seriously, that makes it nothing
hanashi ni	more
naranai n da tada	than empty talk
shinjitsu no dangan ga meichû	The bullet of truth makes a direct hit
nôsaibô ni yukkuri shimeichû	Slowly redirecting your brain cells
(x4)	(x4)

    – King Giddra, "Shinjitsu no dangan" [Bullet of Truth] from
        the album *Sora kara no chikara* [The Power from the Sky]
            (P-Vine/BluesInteractions, 1995, PCD-4768)

In contrast to party rap's "don't think too deeply," this song illustrates that speaking out is a defining feature of underground hip-hop's aesthetic.

Of course, there are many other variations, and, indeed, one could say there are as many styles as there are rap groups. Nevertheless, the distinction is important for understanding how the music constructs its own idea of the authentic. Party rap groups tend to take the style of rap vocals and music construction, but reject the notion that one needs to be oppositional, angry, or negative. They would argue that this is simply imitating a style that is out of place in Japan and inappropriate for their carefree audience. For underground hip-hoppers, party rappers take only a superficial view of rap, and ignore the cultural and historical background that gives the music its unique strength and meaning.

Conclusion

To create Japanese rap, musicians need to overcome the tensions entailed in bringing hip-hop from one setting to another. I discussed these in terms of class, ethnicity, and gender. There is no objective measure that can settle the question of whether this or that artist is an "authentic" rapper, but such evaluations offer keys to understanding how popular culture is used to construct and transcend societal boundaries. The two quotations at the opening of this essay offer examples. If rap is defined as an outgrowth of black culture, it constructs that culture at the same time. If Japanese rap is considered real for its youthful Japanese audience, then it too helps construct that audience. Thus, the development of Japanese rap music provides insight into more than simply pop aesthetics. Japanese rappers construct social boundaries through the decisions they make in appropriating hip-hop as their own.

Commercial channels provided the initial introduction of rap music in Japan. In the early 1980s, break dancing came first through the movies, and then appeared on Tokyo sidewalks on weekends. From 1989 on, a growing number of American rappers traveled to Japan to promote their albums, and more Japanese rappers were inspired to try rapping and DJing on their own. Over the years, Japanese DJs have honed their abilities to the point where, for example, DJ Krush has become a cult figure among hip-hop fans worldwide. Groups like Rhymester and EDU have collaborated with famous American producers. Most recently, graffiti has become more common in and around Tokyo, as the idea of the "four elements of hip-hop culture"–rap, DJ, break dance, and graffiti–becomes more widespread. This essay has focused on rap music, but each of these activities has involved moving between notions of

Japaneseness and of hip-hop, that is, between local identity and global pop culture.

In what sense is global pop culture actually "global"? When American rap music is enjoyed by Japanese listeners, it is not the lyrical wordplay or cogent political message that is appealing. It is the "cool" (*kakkoii*) sound, the good groove (*nori*), and the energy of the rapper's delivery. Since the mid-1990s, there is information in Japanese magazines about what American rappers are saying for those who take the time to seek it out. What becomes interesting, however, is the way this mediated information is interpreted and then put into practice as Japanese rap music. These interpretations are undeniably imitations at first, but that is not much different than, say, the second generation of rappers in the U.S., who were introduced to rap music via records and television. In Japan, various styles have emerged over the years. I draw a contrast between the commercially successful party rap and the more socially and politically oppositional underground hip-hop, but in both cases the rappers are speaking to issues close to themselves and the lives they lead. In this sense, I agree with Ben the Ace, whom I quoted at the outset asserting that Japanese rap is more real for Japanese than American rap. To play on a famous slogan, all cultural politics is local. As the multinational entertainment industry disseminates music genres and images to distant places, theorists of cultural and social change face the task of evaluating their uses and effects. Drawing on the insights of Gupta and Ferguson, I argue that one of those key effects is to construct social and cultural boundaries.

Drawing images of the U.S. from American hip-hop, Japanese fans see their country as peaceful and boring, saturated with meaningless pop icons and lacking the excitement and "reality" of dangerous, inner city streets. But perceived similarities between Japanese and American rappers can provide a new perspective on life in Japan as well. George Lipsitz argues that transnational linkages can be formed through popular culture

> to produce an immanent critique of contemporary social relations, to work through the conduits of commercial culture in order to illumine affinities, resemblances, and potentials for alliances among a world population that now must be as dynamic and as mobile as the forces of capital.[33]

The rapper You the Rock mentioned above found in rap music a vehicle for expressing his anger at the discrimination faced by fellow Japanese. The group King Giddra argues that problems in Japan are too often ignored, watched in silence with a sense of resignation. For them, fans of hip-hop need to stare with a cold eye on their surroundings to imagine ways that it could be better, and to learn that speaking up is the most important thing to do. Even the "don't worry, be happy" rhymes of such party rappers as Yuri can be viewed as "message songs" for youth who spend numerous after-school hours in "cram academies." For some, the spectacle of adopting dread hair and dark skin is a sign of respect for the obstacles overcome by black American artists. In these ways, we can see how popular culture, deployed in a new setting, takes on new meanings. As Japanese hip-hop matures, we are seeing more critical perspectives on Japan, including recent songs about homelessness, teen prostitution, and drug abuse. In the end, however, it is not "culture" that is exchanged, but rather expressive idioms that are situated in a new context. These new idioms work to build bridges between societies, and can also provide new meanings for local identity. Thus, rather than asking "what influence does foreign culture have?" we should examine how the ideas of foreign and local are produced through various practices, such as those arising in popular culture. Anthropologists and cultural theorists have a large stake in understanding what role these activities play in producing social differences in an increasingly interconnected world.

Acknowledgments

Research for this project was supported by Fulbright (September 1995–February 1997), and Yale University's Council on East Asian Studies (June–July 1994). I would like to thank Bill Kelly, Heide Fehrenbach, Uta Poiger, and Shuhei Hosokawa for their critical comments. Earlier versions of this paper were presented to the American Ethnological Society Meetings (April 1995, Austin, Texas) and Columbia University's Conference on East Asia (February 1995, New York City).

Notes

1. All translations by the author. Akihito Kobayashi, "Ben the Ace [interview]," *Front* 9, no. 19 (1996): 55.

2. Zeebra, "For the B-Boys Only: *'mane' jya naku 'shōka* ~ *shōka' de aru koto o rikai shiro*" [It's not "imitation" but "absorption ~ enlightenment" that one must understand] *Front* 9, no. 17 (1996): 94.

3. Tobin offers a valuable collection of papers on domestication. Tomlinson analyzes the discourse of cultural imperialism. Joseph J. Tobin, *Re-Made in Japan: Everyday Life and Consumer Taste in a Changing Society* (New Haven, 1992). John Tomlinson, *Cultural Imperialism: A Critical Introduction* (London, 1991).

4. Akhil Gupta and James Ferguson, "Beyond 'Culture': Space, Identity, and the Politics of Difference," *Cultural Anthropology* 7, no. 1 (1992): 14.

5. The term "B-boy" originally referred to "break boy," that is, a break dancer, but more recently it indicates a fan of hip-hop. See S. H. Fernando, Jr., *The New Beats: Exploring the Music, Culture, and Attitudes of Hip-Hop* (New York, 1994), 5. In Japanese, the terms "B-Boy" and "hip-hopper" are used interchangeably.

6. Simon Frith, "Towards an Aesthetic of Popular Music," in *Music and Society: The Politics of Composition, Performance, and Reception*, ed. Richard Leppert and Susan McClary (Cambridge, 1987), 137.

7. Tricia Rose, *Black Noise: Rap Music and Black Culture in Contemporary America* (Hanover, 1994), 21.

8. Fernando, *The New Beats*, chaps. 2 and 3.

9. George Lipsitz, *Dangerous Crossroads: Popular Music, Postmodernism and the Poetics of Place* (London, 1994), 36ff.

10. Atsushi Innami, "Japanese Hip-Hop Scene: *Risōteki na seijuku o togeta nihon no hippu hoppu shiin no jūnen* [10 years of Japan's hip-hop scene and its achievement of ideal maturity]," in *Rap/Hip-Hop*, ed. Kiyomi Matsunaga (Tokyo, 1996), 200.

11. Crazy-A, interview with the author (1996).

12. MC Bell, interview with the author (1997).

13. William W. Kelly, "Finding a Place in Metropolitan Japan: Transpositions of Everyday Life," in *Postwar Japan as History*, ed. A. Gordon (Berkeley, 1993), 195–97.

14. William W. Kelly, "Rationalization and Nostalgia: Cultural Dynamics of New Middle-Class Japan," *American Ethnologist* 13, no. 4 (1986): 604ff.

15. Cake-K, interview with the author (1996).

16. Peter N. Dale, *The Myth of Japanese Uniqueness* (London, 1986), 56–76.

17. For example, over the last couple of years, when rappers encourage the audience to join in some call-and-response, the English "Say ho!" has been replaced by the Japanese "*Ie yo ho!*" and "Now scream!" with "*Sawage!*"

18. Fernando, *The New Beats*, has been translated into Japanese as S. H. Fernando, Jr. *Hip Hop Beats*, trans. Atsushi Ishiyama (Tokyo, 1996). Books by a rapper named ECD and by music critic Matsunaga focus on American rap history and styles: ECD, *Perfect Beats* (Tokyo, 1996); Kiyomi Matsunaga, *Rap/Hip-Hop* (Tokyo, 1996). The first book to focus exclusively on Japanese rap history and styles is Tadashi Fujita et al., *Tokyo Hip-Hop Guide* (Tokyo, 1996).

19. Andrew Jones, "Black Like Me," *Spin* (October 1993): 74–78.

20. Quoted in Marilyn Ivy, "Critical Texts, Mass Artifacts: The Consumption of Knowledge in Postmodern Japan," in *Postmodernism and Japan*, ed. Masao Miyoshi and H. D. Harootunian (Durham, N.C., 1989), 22.

21. George DeVos and H. Wagatsuma, *Japan's Invisible Race: Caste in Culture and Personality* (Berkeley, 1966). DeVos and Wagatsuma refer to the *burakumin* as "Japan's invisible race" because they have no physical characteristics to distinguish them from other Japanese. *Burakumin* face discrimination due to an assumed pollution associated with certain types of occupations (e.g., butchering, executions). This impurity is regarded as inheritable via bloodline, which suggests that what once resembled a caste distinction is now treated more like a racial difference. For a concise history of their meaning and place in Japanese society, see Emiko Ohnuki-Tierney, *The Monkey as Mirror: Symbolic Transformations in Japanese History and Ritual* (Princeton, 1987), 75–100. For an excellent discussion of their political battles against discrimination, see Frank Upham, *Law and Social Change in Postwar Japan* (Cambridge, Mass., 1987).

22. Yoriko Kawachi et al., "Best 10: Rap," *Music Magazine* 27, no. 2 (1995): 68–69.

23. The albums are Beastie Boys, *Ill Communication* (Grand Royal/Capitol, 1994), Beck, *Mellow Gold* (Bong Road/Geffen, 1994), and G. Love and Special Sauce, self-titled (Okeh, 1994). Eiji Ogura, "Best 10: Rock (America)," *Music Magazine* 27, no. 2 (1995): 56.

24. Fujita, *Tokyo Hip-Hop*, 98.

25. Ibid., 97–98.

26. John Russell, "Race and Reflexivity: The Black Other in Contemporary Japanese Mass Culture," *Cultural Anthropology* 6, no. 1 (1991): 20–21.

27. Nina Cornyetz, "Fetishized Blackness: Hip-Hop and Racial Desire in Contemporary Japan," *Social Text* 12, no. 1 (1994): 129.

28. Zeebra, "For the B-Boys Only: *'Mane 'jya naku* [not imitation]."

29. Rhymester, interview with the author (1996).

30. Zeebra, "For the B-Boys Only: *Kaigai to onaji kankaku motteru nara jikoku no shiin ni sanka shiro* [If you have the same sense as those overseas, you have to be part of the scene in your own country]," *Front* 9, no. 15 (1996): 90.

31. "Da.Yo.Ne" sold 992,980 copies and climbed to number seven on the Oricon chart. "Maicca" sold 1,044,720 copies and climbed to number three. Atsushi Innami, "East End X Yuri [Interview]," *Music Magazine* 28, no. 7 (1996): 41. Both singles were released by Epic/Sony. The songs also appear on the album East End X Yuri, *denim-ed soul 2* (Epic/Sony, 1995, ESCB-1590).

32. Ken Kido, "King Giddra [Interview]," *Remix* 55 (1996): 42.

33. Lipsitz, *Dangerous Crossroads*, 16–17.

Part IV

DE-ESSENTIALIZING "AMERICA" AND THE "NATIVE"

– Nine –

LEARNING FROM AMERICA

Postwar Urban Recovery in West Germany

Peter Krieger

Confronted with destroyed cityscapes after World War II, many German urban planners seized the chance to fundamentally change urban patterns.[1] The opportunity to construct new dispersed and open urban spaces, as opposed to the historical fragments of irregular traditional street patterns and building clusters, promised finally to make modern utopia concrete, as it had been radically (if often only virtually) defined since the 1920s by avant-garde planners such as Ludwig Hilberseimer and Le Corbusier. However, postwar efforts to implement modern urban planning schemes faced a number of challenges. Local and regional planning authorities in the Western zones of Germany produced contrasting models of urban recovery in the early postwar period because, unlike in France or many Eastern bloc countries including Soviet-administered East Germany, there was no centralized federal authority for urban planning. As a result, compromises between modernization and tradition, between tabula rasa planning and reconstructing historical patterns, characterized the postwar recovery debates in West Germany.

For a certain period in the early postwar years, all proposals for urban recovery and reconstruction clearly considered the political

dimensions of city planning. Following the demise of the Nazi dicta-
torship, the occupying powers supported attempts to reverse or alter
the consequences of twelve years of Nazi planning. Within a few
years after the war, however, German architects and urban planners
who had been professionally active during the Third Reich successfully passed through the de-Nazification process by pleading technocratic neutrality. The German architectural elite at that time in fact
shared similar biographical backgrounds: they were educated in the
Kaiserreich, trained at the universities during the Weimar period,
unemployed in the early 1930s, and had their first professional successes under the Nazi government. After 1945, they wanted to assume responsibility for postwar urban recovery.[2] In many cases,
those same planners who were engaged in the ideologically laden
monumental and vernacular (*Heimatschutz*) architecture during the
Nazi period now welcomed new urban images for democracy.

In the Western zones of Germany, the military governments of
the United States, Britain, and France enforced a de-Nazification
process that ultimately did little to dissolve the structures of administration, economic power, and architectural business.[3] Albert Speer,
Hitler's architect and urban planner, was punished not for his totalitarian architectural fantasies, but for his political responsibility in
organizing the German military industry and its infrastructures.
Speer's collaborators in urban planning noted this fact and confi-
dently claimed professional "neutrality," or noninvolvement in the
crimes of the Third Reich. With few exceptions, their role in Nazi
Germany was kept hidden from public inquiry until architectural
history research of the 1980s, particularly that of Werner Durth,
investigated and thematized continuities between the prewar and
postwar periods. A postwar consensus in German architecture and
urban planning emerged which relied on an overt visual "de-Nazification" that emphasized a stylistic break with the past. Both Germans and the Allied governments regarded the rebuilding of the
cities according to new aesthetic criteria as visual proof of successful
democratization. Such a simplistic equation of urban with political
structures was based on the fact that reconstructed urban living space
and housing produced optimism among the many bombed-out,
homeless inhabitants. Thus material rebuilding was expected to promote public support for the new democratic order. Urban recovery,
moreover, took on symbolic dimensions as critical postwar public
debates about authoritarian structures of urban planning encouraged
a popular mistrust of strict planning directives in general.[4]

The onset of the cold war between the United States in West
Germany and the Soviet Union in East Germany further intensified

the ideological nature of postwar urban recovery. The two emerging German states, and especially the divided city of Berlin, displayed the prevailing values like a shop window.[5] Both sides were acutely conscious of the propagandistic function of urban and architectural planning. Amplified by a broad range of reeducational measures designed to help the German publics comprehend the "messages" of their cities' recovery, the competition between two world powers was fought on a semiotic field that condensed cultural, social, technological, and economic achievements: the city.

The question of what specific functions urban spaces played in the postwar American-German cultural transfer requires us to consider briefly the political and economic conditions. Probably the most important factor in galvanizing and politicizing the German recovery was the Marshall Plan for Europe.[6] In June 1947, United States Secretary of State and former defense minister George C. Marshall presented his plans for an economic cooperation with Europe. For West Germany, this meant immense financial help—in the first five years more than one billion dollars. Marshall's goal of securing the economically and politically weakened western parts of Germany from a potential Soviet invasion was also clearly a political one. Max Brauer, the Social Democratic mayor of Hamburg in the early postwar period, emphatically pointed out in a booklet about the Marshall Plan that American financial help saved Western civilization and had an immunizing effect against "the communist poison."[7] Hamburg inhabitants understood (and enjoyed the benefits of) such political positions in a very direct way: many housing programs for workers were financed and realized with the help of the Marshall Plan. Max Brauer's biography also reveals some specific and characteristic implications of the American-German relations. As an emigrant, Brauer lived in the United States from 1936 to 1946, where he learned about the "American" way of pragmatic political action, about modern schemes for urban renewal with mass-produced architecture, and even—mediated by his friend Lewis Mumford—about the criticism of reckless urban modernization, all themes that colored the urban debates of the 1950s and 1960s.

In 1950, a West German politician stated in an architectural magazine that Germany's fate would be inseparable from American progress.[8] Yet the flow of cultural influence and technical expertise was not unidirectional, and some experts of architecture and urban planning recalled the important role played by German emigrants, mainly from the Bauhaus, in the development of modern American architecture. After World War II the reimportation of modern architecture to Germany served as the blueprint for a democratic design

FIGURE **9.1** Manhattan skyline in the early 1960s with newly constructed
Chase Manhattan Bank. Designed by Gordon Bunshaft of Skidmore,
Owings & Merrill. (Photo: Erich Locker)

Source: Carol Herselle Krinsky, *Gordon Bunshaft of Skidmore, Owings &*
Merrill (Cambridge, Mass., and London 1988), 123.

drafted by the most influential occupying power. Thus, the successful "Americanization" of architectural and urban design leitmotifs
was rooted in a long history of intense and controversial cultural
exchanges between the two countries.[9]

After World War I, the United States was seen in Germany as a
future-oriented country where traditional values were discarded for
new symbols of technological and economic success. Skyscrapers,
the most striking symbol of this distinctive modernity, provoked
both admiration as well as fears of "Americanism."[10] No other image
achieved the iconic status of the Manhattan skyline (see Fig. 9.1).
German beholders throughout the twentieth century were fascinated
by the technological and cultural innovation of skyscrapers, but felt
threatened by the dense urban contexts of high-rise buildings and

the fact that they were designed with real estate profit, rather than social need, in mind.

By contrast, the collective psychological basis for an Americanization of Germany was never really called into question in postwar West Germany. In terms of architectural development, the contemporary American cultural impact was more important than French and British reeducation efforts. In contrast to their Western competitors, Soviet cultural strategies in East Germany sought to break the influential cultural exchange with the United States.[11] East German architectural ideologues criticized modern American trends in West Germany and advocated the Stalinist doctrine of traditional-style architecture as the only true principle for urban recovery—in spite of the irony that the Moscow skyscrapers of the late 1940s resembled the decorated Chicago and New York skyscrapers of the 1910s.

One of the central projects attesting to the political dimension of modern architectural forms and urban patterns was the United Nations Building in New York, whose planning began in 1947 and was completed by 1952.[12] East German architectural theorists perceived inhumane qualities in the modern, isolated building with its curtain wall of glass and aluminum.[13] The thin rectangular slab, placed in midtown Manhattan on the East River, displayed a new type of urban disposition that emerged more clearly some blocks west on Park Avenue. Here the Lever House (1952) and the Seagram Building (1955) demonstrated the "plaza" pattern: a regular slab in an open space that breaks up the closed front of the neighboring stone row.[14] Worldwide, these three buildings set aesthetic standards for postwar modern architecture and displayed the "Americanization of modernism."[15] The West German architectural press presented them as messages from the "promised land" of modernism. Yet, conservative critics like the German art historian Hans Sedlmayr attacked the worldwide success of modern architecture. And although their political and ideological loyalties differed markedly, West German conservative critics of modern, American-inspired architecture employed arguments similar to those of their East German colleagues: both announced that the United Nations Building represented the "end" of architecture because it seemed to render all traditional aesthetics and ethics obsolete.[16] Nonetheless, such opinions created a cultural atmosphere in which American modernism gained increasing acceptance, for they permitted West German critics to denounce traditional architecture as either recidivist or Stalinist, both serving as a foil for progressive modernism.

In 1948 the New York Museum of Modern Art (MOMA) presented the traveling exhibition "Built in the USA" with the message that modern architecture had triumphed in the United States.[17] Many West German observers believed that the buildings and urban projects presented–some of which were designed by the German emigrants Mies van der Rohe and Walter Gropius–did not represent accurately the typical modern American architectural landscape of mass-produced and traditionally ornamented houses. Nevertheless, many postwar architects in West Germany enthusiastically began adopting the new style of such landmarks of American modernity. The American transformation of Bauhaus avant-garde principles from the 1920s into a pragmatic, profit-oriented "international style" consistent with postwar recovery was welcomed as a sign of the occupying power's permission to build over the remains and rubble of the totalitarian past. Even Albert Speer, once guardian and exponent of megalomaniac neoclassicism and now captive in his Berlin-Spandau prison, recognized the enormous impact of modern American architecture.[18] Modern glass boxes in plaza settings became the successful model for corporate self-representation (see Fig. 9.2). West German builder-owners, developers, and architects proudly sought to copy American leitmotifs in order to advertise the postwar industrial and technological standards of the so-called German "economic miracle." A visual language of highly elaborate machine technology, presented in West Germany as an essential "American" expression,[19] conferred the appearance of economic progress and participation in worldwide American cultural hegemony. Not only modern corporate architecture, but also housing quarters like the Hamburg Grindel-Houses, a series of high-rise apartment buildings,[20] evoked images of the "American lifestyle," although these were identified primarily with the urban conditions of Manhattan and were untypical of the average American city. Such naive reception in West Germany was fostered by American architecture journals, which presented the Grindel-slabs as proof of the new post-Nazi German style.[21]

Although rectangular high-rise buildings with glass curtain walls and grid-structured façades were reduced to an emblem of American progress, contrasting opinions arose. In the early 1950s, some West German architecture critics noted that glass façades would cause tremendous heating costs as well as psychological problems.[22] Others warned that "the appearances of American culture" should not be copied because they contradicted German cultural heritage.[23] One of the most prominent urban planners in West Germany, Rudolf Hillebrecht, stated that while the Manhattan skyline was fascinating, it was no shining example for German cities.[24] Finally, in 1960, after a decade of admiration for American modern architecture, Sibyl Moholy-Nagy, architecture critic and witness of

FIGURE 9.2 Office Building Hamburg-Süd/Condor, Hamburg, West Germany. Designed by Cäsar Pinnau, constructed 1964. (Photo: Peter Krieger, 1995)

the modern movement, scathingly attacked this development. She feared that all observers, ranging from professional architects to students and visitors, would focus on the modern beauty of the Lever House, the Seagram Building, and United Nations Building, and forget the fact that these buildings were surrounded by banal glass architecture built for profit. Moreover, she accused the great masters of architecture of being too busy congratulating each other on this success story to realize the ugliness of the new, modern world.[25]

Such attacks did not, however, undermine the affective images of the Manhattan skyline with its glistening skyscrapers. West German advertising firms used these images in commercials to signify the modernity of products. For example, readers of an architecture journal in 1957 were urged to buy an electric shaver through the persuasive power of a Manhattan skyscraper.[26] Or gas works tried to convince builder-owners to choose a gas heating system by claiming that "Americans prefer gas."[27] This advertisement in a West German architecture journal (see Fig. 9.3) employed a vision of a modern postwar utopia: a graphic simplification depicts a series of high-rise slabs and dispersed smaller buildings on an urban field totally dominated by multistory superhighways. Here, the specific quality of the Manhattan skyline as an affective collective image is transformed into an abstraction for modern urban living conditions as they were imagined to have been realized in American cities. In other contexts—books, photographic collections, architectural documentation—the visual myth of the Manhattan skyline dominated as well. In a booklet of the United States Information Service for West Germany, one author stressed that every European visiting the United States would be impressed by the soaring New York skyscrapers.[28] And most of the photographic portraits of America opened with images of Manhattan streets and skyscrapers on the first pages. Such images cast the United States as an ideal country where technological progress and cultural modernization were unrestricted from the burden of history.

Yet, West German architects and urban planners sought to go beyond image in order to learn from and selectively employ American developments for the recovery of the destroyed cities. In the early postwar years American architectural magazines were sent to West German faculties of architecture; libraries provided planners and other experts with information about and from the United States; and German architectural journals presented lively reports about American experiences and trends. In this way, a whole postwar generation of architects was trained. Not only was printed material used to reeducate West German architects in the American way. Lectures, exhibitions, study trips to the United States, and even new American buildings in West Germany did as well. All these modes and media provoked intense discussions, and therefore diversified the affective and simplified images of a skyscraper modernity.

Exhibitions on American architecture and urban culture played a significant role in the process of ideological reorientation in Germany. The Information Services Division of the American military government soon recognized the political dividends that such a cultural strategy could yield in its competition against the cultural impact of Soviet information campaigns in East Germany. In 1948, when the currency reform set the preconditions for the immense West German recovery boom, two exhibitions were exported from the United States to West German cities in order to introduce standards for future development. An exhibition about the large-scale

Learning from America | 195

FIGURE 9.3 Advertisement "Die Amerikaner bevorzugen Gas [Americans Prefer Gas]," published at the end of the 1950s in various West German architectural magazines.

Die Amerikaner

bevorzugen Gas

Source: *Baumeister* 6 (1962): 646.

planning activities of the Tennessee Valley Authority wartime project instructed West German planners on how to cope with a task as big as the reconstruction of cities and industrial plants.[29] At the same time, a MOMA exhibit about modern architectural trends of the 1930s and 1940s in the United States was presented to the West German public.[30] Some years later, another exhibit by the American Institute of Architects (AIA) showed how the success story of modern architecture continued in the United States after World War II. Entitled "American Architecture since 1947," it provoked heated debates among West German experts.[31] Dispersed spatial schemes for urban planning, an architecture devoted to the direct expression of constructive elements, and trends of so-called "organic architecture" since

Frank Lloyd Wright represented the American architectural vision in West Germany in the early 1950s. This selection, which in fact ignored the American traditions of neocolonial villas, of Hollywood-style hotels, and of architecture without architects, was reinforced by further exhibitions with similar themes and tendencies, all infused with the message that Germany could learn from the modern country. Increasingly, modern prefab technologies and aesthetics, like the panel structures of glass and aluminum curtain walls, dominated the exhibits, along with the question of how to make mass society more humane through architectural and urban planning.[32]

Since his directorship of the Bauhaus, Walter Gropius advocated in his writings and lectures the productive synthesis of modern, effective architectural technology and sensitivity to social concerns. In 1947, he was invited to give a series of talks in several West German cities.[33] As an American citizen and official advisor to General Lucius Clay, Gropius explained the possibilities of fundamental urban reforms in Germany after the bombardments of World War II. Refined by American experience and practice, Gropius preached Bauhaus principles such as the standardization of architectural production and the division of big cities into neighborhood units of 5,000 to 8,000 inhabitants. Some traditionally oriented West German planners rejected those ideas outright for both ideological and practical reasons. Anti-modern and anti-Bauhaus resentments stemming from Nazi architectural ideology still implicitly influenced some German architects. Others were not convinced that the principles that Gropius proselytized could be realized. To a disoriented generation of architects surrounded by urban ruins, Gropius seemed to be far removed from the everyday problems of national and urban recovery.

Other lecturers in the early 1950s pointed out that knowledge of American standards would be indispensable for predicting German developments in the 1960s and 1970s. In most cases, German emigrants naturalized as American citizens came back to West Germany to lecture in their native language about urban and architectural planning.[34] One of the central, often repeated topics of their talks concerned the participation of inhabitants–the idea of urban planning with "common sense." Of course, German emigrants were very sensitive to surviving totalitarian attitudes in postwar German administrative authorities, which they criticized as overly bureaucratic and autocratic. In contrast to such habits, they praised the United States as a country where urban planning was a public theme and a matter of practical political action.

Another very important part of American programs of reeducation and cultural instruction was the study trip to the United States.

Since the early 1950s an increasing number of study trips were offered, at first, mainly for experts from industry and business interested in acquainting themselves with effective American planning methods and technologies. Around the mid-1950s, governmental organizations and industry invited an elite of German architects to study the construction technologies and aesthetics of modern American buildings, in most cases skyscrapers and suburban mass-produced houses. Many of these study trips to New York, Chicago, Detroit, Pittsburgh, and Los Angeles could be described as pilgrimages filled with admiration. Visitors later condensed their impressions of American building production that utilized advanced technology and of large-scale planning strategies into detailed reports for publication.[35] Only rarely did critical comments emerge, as in the report of Rudolf Hillebrecht, one of the leading urban planners in West Germany, who made a private three-month tour of American cities in 1953.[36] One of the planners responsible for the remodeling of Hamburg during the Nazi period, Hillebrecht was influential after the war in stimulating debates about the question of what administrative, legal, and aesthetic elements would constitute democratic urban planning. Upon his return to the Federal Republic, Hillebrecht's subsequent lecture tour attracted substantial audiences in many West German cities. His American study trip report revealed the "backside" of the shining American skylines: he discussed problems of public transport, deserted city centers and urban sprawl, the new shopping centers and Levittown architecture. Amid all of the admiring reports, Hillebrecht's criticism had a strong impact and unique message: that the United States would be a country of unlimited *and* missed opportunities. As an urban planner in a high administrative position (in the city of Hanover after 1945), Hillebrecht knew that the local complexity of urban planning could not be solved by an uncritical application of American models. Some years later, Werner Hebebrand, Hillebrecht's colleague from Hamburg, offered similar criticism on a study trip to the United States; he even insisted on walking and not driving through American cities in order to conduct a closer, more detailed inspection.[37]

Nevertheless, the increasing number of West German architects traveling to the United States, their impressions, and the impact on their work speak to a prevailing positive reception of American architecture. Even those German urban planners who fought for very rigorous restrictions against dense urban structures in German cities often marveled at the skyscraper "canyons" of Manhattan.

In West Germany, new buildings contracted by United States authorities also represented the exemplary "American way." Housing

198 | *Peter Krieger*

FIGURE 9.4 U.S. Consulate, Düsseldorf, West Germany. Designed by Gordon Bunshaft of SOM in association with Otto Apel, constructed in 1954. (Photo: Morley Baer)

Source: Carol Herselle Krinsky, *Gordon Bunshaft of Skidmore, Owings & Merrill* (Cambridge, Mass., and London 1988), 79.

quarters, school buildings, cinemas, and hospitals built for the U.S. army, often in collaboration with West German architects, permitted a "concrete" assessment of how American trends would fit into the cultural setting of West Germany. U.S. consulates probably offer the most impressive evidence for these trends in American modernism: they exhibit a strict planning process, rational construction, and modern expression without unnecessary decoration (see Fig. 9.4). Gordon Bunshaft of the large American architectural firm Skidmore, Owings & Merrill (SOM) together with the German architect Otto Apel planned a series of similar consulate buildings in Berlin, Bremen, Düsseldorf, Frankfurt, Stuttgart, and Munich.[38] Those early postwar embassies and consulate buildings, erected with the explicit mandate of the State Department in the early 1950s to "Go modern!" displayed America's technological standards all over the world. Interestingly, these buildings, by expressing values like discipline, from America" corrected naive views and persistent myths. The Americanization of urban and architectural values, for many years proof of the modernization process, was no longer regarded as a suitable tool to reshape European urban culture. At a time when the recovery of West German cities was nearly completed, critical voices warned of the loss of urban identity through a reckless modernization process.[49] Mere West German copies of corporate America, as embodied in the shining modernity of the New York Lever House, could no longer mask the cultural and psychological problems of standardization, anonymity, and leveling.

In the early 1960s, a book by New York architectural critic Jane Jacobs inspired such criticism in West Germany. Soon after its release in 1961, Jacob's *The Death and Life of Great American Cities* was translated into German and published with high circulation.[50] The impact of American civilization on modern architecture and urban planning, it argued, resulted in a worldwide problem of modern "utopia"—in the original Greek sense of *u-topia*, meaning "no place." A series of boring glass boxes with open plazas perhaps was tolerable in Manhattan on the Avenue of the Americas, but it was less acceptable in the historical centers of West German cities with their complex historical patterns. And many examples of church towers hidden by neighboring office blocks in New York seemed more appropriate to a city characterized by rapid changes and business. It is much more difficult to imagine German cathedrals between highrise buildings with reflecting curtain walls (see Fig. 9.5).[51]

Emerging out of such striking images and imaginations, postmodern criticism gained enormous power.[52] One of the most influential postmodern architectural ideologies, American Robert Venturi's well-known architectural manifesto for "complexity and contradiction" was written in the mid-1960s, but had its strongest impact in the 1980s as a postmodern tract.[53] Impressed by the urban complexity of European historical cities and architecture, Venturi pleaded for a contradictory approach toward architectural planning. His book, translated into German and heartily welcomed in West Germany, attacked modern international style architecture as embodied in the work of Mies van der Rohe. It therefore adds another dimension to the German-American cultural exchange, for the German emigrant Mies, former Bauhaus director and head of the architectural school at the Illinois Institute of Technology, was credited with developing an architectural form that came to be equated with hegemonic American corporate identity. With the help of Venturi, who distinguished himself as the most prominent heretic of the modern movement, many German architects of the 1980s advocated changes in architectural

FIGURE 9.5 Office Building Hamburg-Süd/Condor, Hamburg, West Germany. (Photo: Staatliche Landesbildstelle Hamburg)

Note: In the center is the church tower of St. Katharinen, dating from the thirteenth and seventeenth centuries, and reconstructed after war damage in 1955–57.

ideology. But instead of intellectual complexity, only profitable density and uniformity was achieved when the modern postwar urban spaces in West German cities were remodeled according to postmodern dogma. And instead of contradiction, one-dimensional clichés of regionalism gained influence in the urban debates. It became increasingly obvious that the postmodern version of international corporate style—as invented and produced in the United States—promised to express local identity but in fact enforced a new kind of international business utopia. As a result, Americanization of architecture today means the adoption and application of the aesthetic standards that large American architectural firms develop for multinational business clients.

Ironically, one of the most important American architects who set aesthetic standards for American developers in the 1980s was the German-born Helmut Jahn. Raised in Nuremberg and trained in Chicago, he became a transatlantic ambassador, who in the early 1990s left his distinctive mark in Frankfurt, the most Americanized German city. In contrast to his Frankfurt success, Jahn failed in his hometown of Nuremberg where his architectural project was rejected for its lack of structural consideration of one of the most "traditional" German cities.[54]

For different reasons, both cases reveal the uncertainties and clichés of cultural learning and transfers in a globalized economy. The architectural and urban language of corporate hegemony constitutes itself beyond national borders. For nearly five postwar decades, urban and architectural developments in the United States have served as a laboratory and object of study for German planners.[55] In the future, however, the global problems of urban planning will no longer be discussed under the rubric of Americanization but, as the New York architect Peter Eisenman has suggested, under that of "Singapurization."[56]

Acknowledgments

This article presents aspects of my research project on American-German cultural transfer in architecture and urban planning debates after 1945. The research has been generously supported by the Elliot Wilensky Fund of the Municipal Art Society of New York; by a grant from the Getty Research Institute for the History of Art and the Humanities, Santa Monica; and by travel grants from the Hansische Universitätsstiftung and the Graduate Program Political Iconography, both at the University of Hamburg. I also want to thank Dore Ashton, Stanton L. Catlin, Dennis Crow, Kurt W. Forster, Susan Kassouf, Carol Herselle Krinsky, Jeffrey Kroessler, Dietrich Neumann, Anthony M. Tung, Scott Wolf, John Zukowsky, along with many other colleagues, and, of course, the editors and publisher of this book.

Notes

1. Essential for this research topic: Werner Durth and Niels Gutschow, *Träume in Trümmern. Planungen zum Wiederaufbau zerstörter Städte im Westen Deutschlands 1940–1950*, 2 vols. (Braunschweig and Wiesbaden, 1988); other important publications: Jeffry Diefendorf et al., *Rebuilding Europe's Bombed Cities* (London, 1990); Klaus von Beyme et al., eds., *Neue Städte aus Ruinen. Deutscher Städtebau der Nachkriegszeit* (Munich, 1992); Axel Schildt and Arnold Sywottek, eds., *Modernisierung im Wiederaufbau. Die westdeutsche Gesellschaft der 50er Jahre* (Bonn, 1993); Gerhard Rabeler, *Wiederaufbau und Expansion westdeutscher Städte 1945–1960 im Spannungsfeld von Reformideen und Wirklichkeit. Ein Überblick aus städtebaulicher Sicht*, Schriftenreihe des Deutschen Nationalkomitees für Denkmalschutz, vol. 39 (Bonn, 1990); Jürgen Paul, "Der Wiederaufbau der historischen Städte in Deutschland nach dem zweiten Weltkrieg," in *Die alte Stadt: Denkmal oder Lebensraum?* ed. C. Meckseper and H. Siebenmorgen (Göttingen, 1985), 114–56; Hartmut Frank, "Trümmer. Traditionelle und moderne Architekturen im Nachkriegsdeutschland," in *Grauzonen. Farbwelten. Kunst und Zeitbilder 1945–1955*, ed. Bernhard Schulz (Berlin, 1983), 43–83.

2. Werner Durth, *Deutsche Architekten. Biographische Verflechtungen 1900–1970*, 2d ed. (Munich, 1992).

3. Durth, *Deutsche Architekten*; Klaus von Beyme, *Der Wiederaufbau. Architektur und Städtebaupolitik in beiden deutschen Staaten* (Munich, 1987); for a political perspective, Norbert Frei, *Vergangenheitspolitik. Die Anfänge der Bundesrepublik und die NS-Vergangenheit* (Munich, 1996).

4. See Otl Aicher, "Planung in Misskredit. Zur Entwicklung von Stadt und Land," in *Bestandsaufnahme. Eine deutsche Bilanz 1962. Sechsunddreissig Beiträge deutscher Wissenschaftler, Schriftsteller und Publizisten*, ed. Hans Werner Richter (Munich, 1962), 398–420.

5. Andreas Schätzke, *Zwischen Bauhaus und Stalinallee. Architekturdiskussion im östlichen Deutschland 1945–1955* (Braunschweig and Wiesbaden, 1991).

6. Gerd Hardach, *Der Marshall-Plan. Auslandshilfe und Wiederaufbau in Westdeutschland 1948–1952* (Munich, 1993).

7. *Hamburg Heute. Bilder vom Wiederaufbau*, ed. Freie und Hansestadt Hamburg (Hamburg, 1950).

8. *Deutsche Bauzeitung* 10 (1950): 405ff.

9. Peter Krieger, "Types, Definitions, Myths and Ideologies of US-American Modernity in West Germany after 1945," in *Arte, Historia e Identidad en America: Visiones Comparativas*, ed. Gustavo Curiel, Renato Gonzalez Mello, and Juana Gutierrez Haces (Mexico, D.F., 1994), vol. 3, 829–40.

10. Jean-Louis Cohen, *Scenes of the World to Come: European Architecture and the American Challenge, 1893–1960* (Paris, 1995); Dietrich Neumann, *"Die Wolkenkratzer kommen!" Deutsche Hochhäuser der zwanziger Jahre. Debatten, Projekte und Bauten* (Braunschweig and Wiesbaden, 1995).

11. Kurt Liebknecht, "Fragen der Deutschen Architektur," in *Fragen der deutschen Architektur und des Städtebaus. Referate gehalten anlässlich des ersten Deutschen Architektenkongresses in Berlin, Dezember 1951*, ed. Deutsche Bauakademie (Berlin, 1952). A variety of East German anti-American booklets was presented in June 1995 at an exhibition of the Staats- und Universitätsbibliothek in Hamburg entitled "Kalter Krieg und kleine Schriften."

12. George A. Dudley, *A Workshop for Peace: Designing the United Nations Headquarters* (Cambridge, Mass., and London, 1994).

13. Peter Krieger, "Spiegelnde Curtain walls als Projektionsflächen für politische Schlagbilder," in *"Philosophia Practica"* – *Architektur als politische Kultur*, ed. Hermann Hipp and Ernst Seidl (Berlin, 1996), 297–310.

14. Lever House, New York, 1952, design by Gordon Bunshaft of SOM; Seagram Building, New York, 1956, design by Mies van der Rohe in cooperation with Philip Johnson. Those two buildings fostered the change of the New York Zoning Law in 1961. Concerning their impact on the West German debate, see: *Handbuch moderner Architektur* (Berlin, 1957), 313; Krieger, "Types, Definitions, Myths," 837f.

15. Joan Ockman (with the collaboration of Edward Eigen), *Architecture Culture 1943–1968: A Documentary Anthology* (New York, 1993), 16.

16. Hans Sedlmayr, *Die Revolution der modernen Kunst* (Reinbeck, 1955), 66; idem, *Verlust der Mitte. Die bildende Kunst des 19. und 20. Jahrhunderts als Symptom und Symbol der Zeit* (Frankfurt a.M. and Berlin, 1988; 1st ed. 1948); see Krieger, "Spiegelnde Curtain walls," 304.

17. Elizabeth Mock, ed., *In USA erbaut. 1932–1944* (Wiesbaden, 1948), 8. [German translation of the MOMA-catalogue "Built in USA: 1932–1944" (New York 1944)].

18. Albert Speer, *Spandauer Tagebücher* (Frankfurt a.M., 1975), 82, 417.

19. Mary Mix, "Die Amerikanische Architektur der Nachkriegszeit," in *Amerikanische Architektur seit 1947*, ed. AIA (Stuttgart, 1951), 8.

20. Grindel-Wohnhochhäuser, Hamburg, 1946–56, various architects; cf. Axel Schildt, *Die Grindelhochhäuser* (Hamburg, 1988), 168.

21. Peter Blake, "Country Rebuilds in Modern Style," *Architectural Forum* [unidentified vol.; see Getty Center for the History of Art and the Humanities, Special Collections, #850194, Box 9, Germany].

22. *Baumeister* 3 (1951): 188.

23. *Deutsche Bauzeitung* 3 (1951): 117f.

24. Rudolf Hillebrecht, "Neuaufbau der Städte," in *Handbuch moderner Architektur* (Berlin, 1957). The exact quotation is: "Sicher bietet die Skyline amerikanischer Städte, so erregend und eindrucksvoll sie auch ist, kein Vorbild; denn sie ist das Abbild einer geistigen Verfassung, die nicht erstrebenswert ist."

25. Lecture "Architektur – Kunst oder Konstruktion?" presented by Sibyl Moholy-Nagy, New York, at various West German universities; *Bauwelt* 1 (1959): 4ff.

26. *Baumeister* 5 (1957): 346.

27. *Baumeister* 6 (1962): 646.

28. Erich Dombrowski, *Blitzlichter aus Amerika*, ed. US-Informationsdienst Bad Godesberg [no date of publication].

29. Exhibition "Landesplanung in Amerika," on the occasion of the inauguration of the Berlin U.S. Information Center in 1948; reviewed in *Baumeister* 2, no. 3 (1948): 119.

30. "In USA erbaut, 1932–1944"; see footnote 17.

31. *Amerikanische Architektur der USA seit 1947*, ed. AIA (Stuttgart, 1951); traveling exhibition in Stuttgart, Berlin, Munich, 1950/51, afterwards to other West European countries; reviewed in *Bauwelt* 35 (1950): 567; *Baumeister* 4 (1951): 262.

32. For example, AIA Exhibition "100 Jahre amerikanischer Architektur," National Gallery in Washington, presented in West Germany, reviewed in *Bauwelt* 52 (1958): 1272.

33. Gropius gave lectures in Berlin, Frankfurt, and Munich in July and August 1947; see Hartmut Frank, "Un salto costruttivo per uscire dal caos," *Rassegna* 15 (1983): 88f.

34. Lectures of Albert C. Schweizer, director of Civil Administration Division for Bavaria, and Hans Blumenfeld, urban planner in Philadelphia; reviewed in *Baumeister* 2 (1949): 87, and *Bauwelt* 6 (1950): 92.

35. Rationalisierungs-Kuratorium der Deutschen Wirtschaft (RKW), Auslandsdienst, *Bauen in USA. Reisebericht einer deutschen Studiengruppe,* Heft 22 (Munich, 1954).

36. Hillebrecht's travel report and his public lecture were reviewed in *Bauwelt* 27 (1953): 535.

37. *Neue Heimat Monatshefte* 2 (1957): 80.

38. Carol Herselle Krinsky, *Gordon Bunshaft of Skidmore, Owings & Merrill* (Cambridge, Mass., and London, 1988), 47ff., 78f.; Ron Robin, *Enclaves of America: The Rhethoric of American Political Architecture Abroad, 1900–1965* (Princeton, 1992), 138f., 145.f.; Krieger, "Types, Definitions, Myths," 834.

39. The sources quoted here are selected out of the systematic data-based analysis of the German architectural magazines *Baumeister, Bauwelt, Baukunst und Werkform, Bau-Rundschau, Deutsche Bauzeitung,* and *Neue Heimat Monatshefte.* The results of my research will be prepared for publication.

40. Ernst Egli, *Die neue Stadt in Landschaft und Klima. Climate and Town Districts: Consequences and Demands* (Zurich, 1951), 59.

41. As an exemplary study on the impact of modern high-rise buildings on urban planning in postwar West Germany, see Peter Krieger, "Wirtschaftswunderlicher Wiederaufbau-Wettbewerb – Architektur und Städtebau der 1950er Jahre in Hamburg" (Ph.D. diss., Universität Hamburg, 1995); a general overview is provided by Rabeler, *Wiederaufbau und Expansion westdeutscher Städte 1945–1960.*

42. Rationalisierungs-Kuratorium der Deutschen Wirtschaft (RKW), Auslandsdienst, *Bauen in USA,* 124; for critical voices toward urban renewal, see Peter Blake, *No Place Like Utopia: Modern Architecture and the Company We Kept* (New York, 1993), 180f.; Manfredo Tafuri and Francesco Dal Co, *Gegenwart,* Reihe Weltgeschichte der Architektur (Stuttgart, 1988), 71.

43. Hillebrecht's opinion (see footnote 37), articulated in *Bau-Rundschau* 9 (1953): 334f.

44. *Bauwelt* 46 (1961): 1317.

45. To West German beholders in the 1950s, the Boston Fitzgerald Expressway was probably the most impressive example for double-tiered highways. The best West German example of such an urban highway aesthetic can be found in the city center of Düsseldorf.

46. Public lecture of an urban planner in Munich, reviewed in *Deutsche Bauzeitung* 5 (1953): 185.

47. Dietmar Klemke, "Freier Stau für freie Bürger," in *Die Geschichte der bundesdeutschen Verkehrspolitik 1949–1994* (Darmstadt, 1995).

48. Lewis Mumford, *The Highway and the City* (London, 1964), 176ff.

49. Heide Berndt, Alfred Lorenzer, and Klaus Horn, *Architektur als Ideologie* (Frankfurt, 1968); Alexander Mitscherlich, *Die Unwirtlichkeit der Städte. Anstiftung zum Unfrieden* (Frankfurt, 1969, 1st ed. 1965).

50. Jane Jacobs, *Tod und Leben großer amerikanischer Städte* (Berlin, Frankfurt a.M., and Vienna, 1963), U.S. ed., *The Death and Life of Great American Cities* (New York, 1961).

51. See Robert Jungk, *Die Zukunft hat schon begonnen. Amerikas Allmacht und Ohnmacht* (Stuttgart and Hamburg, 1953), 197.

52. The most influential and prominent example is HRH The Prince of Wales, *A Vision of Britain: A Personal View of Architecture* (London, 1989); see Krieger, "Spiegelnde Curtain walls."

53. Robert Venturi, *Komplexität und Widerspruch in der Architektur* (Braunschweig, 1978), U.S. ed., *Complexity and Contradiction in Architecture* (New York, 1966).

54. Messeturm Frankfurt, 1988–91, Helmut Jahn with Murphy; Project Augustinerhof, Nuremberg, design by Helmut Jahn, canceled in 1993.

55. Dieter Hoffmann-Axthelm, "Der Weg zu einer neuen Stadt," *Arch+* 115 (1992): 114–16.

56. Peter Eisenman introduced this term at the "4. Internationales Architekturforum" in Dessau, West Germany, 1994; see *Bauwelt* 24 (1994): 1306.

– Ten –

THE FRENCH CINEMA
AND HOLLYWOOD

A Case Study of Americanization

Richard F. Kuisel

One of the major interpretive issues that has emerged from the study
of Americanization is whether or not this process is producing global
uniformity. Does Americanization create uniformity and convergence
or does the host culture assimilate American mass culture and sustain
divergence?[1] Some of those who have studied the phenomenon stress
the seemingly irresistible and transformative power of American cultural exports. America, from this perspective, has been the initiator,
the model, the disseminator, and the continuing force behind a process that is so potent that it is homogenizing the globe. Those who
receive American mass culture merely import it to the detriment of
native culture. This is the thesis of global "Coca-Colonization" or
"McWorld" or, in its more invidious formulation, of cultural imperialism. Other scholars have emphasized the assimilative capacity of the
receiving cultures. They contend that those who import American
cultural products adapt or domesticate them so that national differences survive or are even reinforced. In this second interpretation the
Europeans, among others, have appropriated American mass culture
and made it their own. In this vein, some have employed the phrase
"creolization" as an alternative to "Coca-Colonization."

In this essay I shall use the case of the French cinema to examine the issue of conceptualizing Americanization. At a theoretical level, scholars will have to find a balance between the convergence/divergence approaches to best conceptualize the process. We need to achieve a theoretical middle ground between the transmission model, which in its crudest formulation is equated with "cultural imperialism," and the assimilationist view, dear to anthropologists, that can exaggerate the capacity of local culture to domesticate imports. To find this balance, Americanization should be theorized so that America remains central to a process that is transforming the globe, but it must also be framed so that the exports of American images, sounds, and values are shown as blended and transformed by the indigenous society. Nowhere, at least in Europe, was America merely imitated. In my view, the French case is more typical than it is exceptional.

A first step in conceptualizing the process of Americanization must be to maintain the centrality of America's role. One must grant that American mass culture has the power to make all cultures more similar. The famous quip that "the only culture the 320 million people of Europe have in common is American culture" rightly suggests the pervasiveness of America. Even if America's hegemonic position may be fading, as some think, it is necessary to historicize the phenomenon and grant America its prodigious contribution throughout most of the twentieth century. Non-American producers of mass culture have emerged, but during most of the postwar period and even in the 1990s America still occupies the central place in the invention, production, and global dissemination of popular culture. The international success of films like *Schindler's List* or *Titanic* or of rap music are suggestive here. And Americanization involves not just addition, but change. The entry of McDonald's and American fast food, for example, has contributed to changes in certain French eating practices, such as the leisurely family meal at midday.[2]

A second step is to avoid the mistake of "McWorld" theorists, who stress the irresistible quality of Americanization and miss the adaptive aspects of the phenomenon. Recent work on the problem affirms the capacity of host cultures to transform or domesticate American imports and make them their own. If, for example, the format of television news in France appears American, the serious manner in which news is presented and the absence of entertainment is French. It is at once French and American. French and European cultures have been resilient and have resisted homogenization.

A third step in thinking about Americanization is to recognize the emergence of transnational cultural forms that transcend America. The cinema—especially Hollywood, but also French film—has evolved in the direction of globalized entertainment. Other icons of mass culture that originated in the United States, such as Coca-Cola, McDonald's, and Disney, have made the same transition as the film and now are seen as both American and global products. Transmission, appropriation, and transnationalism are all features of Americanization, and all appear in the history of the French cinema.

The Example of the French Cinema

The confrontation between Hollywood and the French cinema illuminates the complexities of Americanization. Since the two film industries began their competitive struggle with the birth of the cinema a hundred years ago, French movie screens have been increasingly dominated by images made-in-America. And this direct conquest of the French market has been accompanied by French appropriation of cinematographic forms, production techniques, distribution arrangements, and marketing. But there has also been stiff resistance. If the French cinema has both lost much of its market to Hollywood production and been transformed by the way America makes and markets films, the industry has survived. It has been partly Americanized.

At the most basic level, Americanization has occurred in the form of Hollywood's acquisition of an enormous share of the French market. This process, dating back to the days of the silent film, accelerated after World War II and has assumed the form of market domination in the last two decades. Quantitative trends of production and distribution are, from a French perspective, depressing.

The Americanization of French audiences had been in the making long before the dramatic surge of the last twenty years. It should be remembered that French filmmakers pioneered this cultural form in the 1890s, and once, in the era of the nickelodeon, they even controlled the American market. But the French began to relinquish their hold over American audiences even before 1914, and from World War I on they began to lose the contest for global markets. While the French continued to produce films for local consumption, some of which were widely admired for their aesthetic qualities, the American studios were winning the international competition. Even at home the French could only staunch the invasion of Hollywood imports by erecting protectionist barriers during the 1920s and 1930s. World War II closed the door to Hollywood imports, but by 1946 it was open again. After the war, a kind of standoff occurred between the two industries, but these postwar decades concealed long-term French decline vis-à-vis Hollywood.

During the last two decades, American movies have captured a majority of French screens.

Although the beginnings of this contest date back to the 1920s, I want to limit my discussion to the postwar years. The statistics are unassailable. From the early 1950s through the 1970s, French films attracted about 50 percent of local audiences whereas American films averaged about 35 percent. This French advantage applied to screen time as well as box-office receipts. Moreover, since only 35 percent of the films in circulation were French (compared to 27 percent for American movies), it is clear that the French preferred seeing their own films.[3] As late as 1983, American box-office share was 35 percent—the same proportion as in 1953. But this rather stable pattern that persisted for thirty years was maintained, in part, artificially and concealed problems. The French film industry was able to retain its market share thanks to an elaborate system of protectionism aimed against American imports. Despite such barriers, by the early postwar years Hollywood had already monopolized entire film genres such as musicals, children's movies, and spectaculars. Disney's animated movies proved to be as popular in France as they were in the United States. Meanwhile, French and European film audiences drastically dwindled in size after the late 1950s, and became increasingly dominated by young people. There was also the distressing appearance of American blockbusters that captivated audiences. Moreover, elsewhere in Western Europe Hollywood came to overwhelm domestic movie production as in countries like Belgium, Italy, Germany, and Britain. Then in the mid-1970s a surge of American megahits like *Jaws* and *Star Wars* signaled the end of the steady 50:35 audience ratio in France. In the early 1980s Hollywood took charge. Box office for American films jumped from 35 percent to 57 percent between 1980 and 1993, while the share of the domestic market for French films fell in almost exactly the same proportion.[4] The rivals traded places. Films like *Basic Instinct* were runaway hits, outdistancing any French competition. American movies, as well as other kinds of American programming, also came to dominate French television screens. Not only did the French become ever more eager consumers for Hollywood productions and make actors like Mickey Rourke stars, but their government honored Americans. French officials gave awards to actors like Jack Nicholson and Sharon Stone, and French directors adopted Woody Allen and Robert Altman as their own.

The French love affair with American mass culture has not been confined to films and television. Thus Euro Disney, despite the invective aimed by a handful of intellectuals against the theme park outside Paris that opened in 1992, attracted almost four million French visitors in its first year of operation. The French public ignored the warnings against the dangerous "cultural Chernobyl" voiced by a prominent theater director, and the protest by the guardians of French cultural purity, when compared to earlier incursions of American products like Coca-Cola, was anemic.

At the same time French films were unable to penetrate the American market. In the early 1950s French imports were confined to a few large cities and college towns in houses typically called "art theaters." In the following decade, the work of a few New Wave filmmakers like François Truffaut, Jean-Luc Godard, and Alain Resnais or a director like Jacques Tati drew crowds, but from a restricted audience. Only a few risqué movies like those starring Brigitte Bardot won mass attention. There was little progress in the subsequent decades. A not untypical comparative example occurred when the French film *Blue* opened in two theaters in New York and Los Angeles in 1993 and grossed $40 thousand, while *Wayne's World 2* opened at the same time in two thousand theaters and grossed over $16 million. French films accounted for about one-half of 1 percent of the American box office in the early 1990s, which prompted the French government to launch a huge effort to penetrate the American market—so far without much success. The French became ardent consumers of American films while the Americans have not returned the compliment.

Searching for remedies for this relative noncompetitiveness has obsessed both the French film industry and government. After 1945, with pathetic regularity, the Fourth and Fifth Republics launched investigations into this problem, issued reports, and then introduced new measures to reverse, or at least arrest, the trend. In the end, all they could do was to rely on quotas and subsidies to protect their industry. Little could be done to stop Americanization of French tastes. Nothing could be done to make the Americans watch French films.

This survey of the quantitative trend toward Americanization raises two analytical issues. First, there is the question as to how Hollywood succeeded in winning a majority of the French audience. Answers here are to be found in comparing such features as industrial structures and cinematic styles. A second question asks how Hollywood influenced French filmmaking and marketing. This aspect of Americanization raises the appropriation side of cinematographic exchange and looks to the various ways the process was diluted so that the phenomenon appears far more complex than simple transmission. My analysis of these questions will concentrate on the postwar era, especially the recent years when American films both made dramatic gains in the French market and modified French cinematographic practices.

Among the most compelling reasons for the decline of the international competitiveness of the French cinema has been the limitation imposed by language.[5] The advent of the talking picture in the late 1920s represented an enormous setback to the industry's global pretensions. The relatively narrow base of the Francophone world, when compared to that for English speakers, set strict limits to the audience for French cinema. Neither subtitles nor dubbing, at least for Americans, proved to be a successful antidote. The French tried dubbing in the 1960s with potentially popular films like *A Man and a Woman*, but the response at the box office was disappointing. And today American moviegoers continue to turn away from foreign films because they dislike subtitles. The subtitled version of *Trois Hommes et un couffin* (Three Men and a Baby) earned a mere $3.5 million in the United States while its Hollywood remake grossed $170 million. New, and supposedly improved, attempts at dubbing have not converted American tastes. Test screenings of a dubbed version of *The Visitors,* a comedy that earned $90 million in France, were so disastrous that the distributor scrapped the half-million dollar experiment and reverted to subtitles. As American English continues to spread and become the world's lingua franca, the audience for French language film diminishes.

Comparative industrial structure is a second reason for French market losses. The business structure that framed how films were made and distributed in France, compared to that in the United States, has been feeble. French cinema has been notorious, at least since the1930s, for its fragmented, "artisanal" structure and its undercapitalization. Both production and distribution have suffered from small-scale operations. For example, in any given year during the 1950s over two-thirds of French companies produced one film per year and most of the others produced only two.[6] There was no vertical integration among producers, distributors, and exhibitors, and financial support, despite state subsidies, was precarious. Advertising via the star system during the 1950s remained backward. In contrast, Hollywood at this time enjoyed large-scale production units (even after the breakup of the studio system), vertical integration, rich financial resources, an enormous home market, and dynamic marketing strategies, including the star system that dated from the era of the silent film. Moreover, American filmmakers had learned how to produce films for cross-class, transnational viewers which made their films appealing to non-American audiences. And given Hollywood's power over foreign distribution systems, its leverage with the United States government, the monopolistic powers of the Motion Picture Association of America (MPAA), and its ability to amortize costs domestically, the industry had become a juggernaut that overwhelmed global markets after 1945. The Blum-Byrnes agreement of 1946, which allowed the MPAA, with Washington's help, to pry open the French domestic market that had closed during the war, is an example of this power.[7] In this case, the French government, concerned about winning American economic aid, bowed to pressure from the MPAA to show large numbers of Hollywood films on French screens.

Historically, the Americans and the French have also held different conceptions of filmmaking and marketing. The elite of French cinematographers have believed for decades that they turn celluloid into art, which by definition does not attract a mass audience. Critics point out that French filmmakers have a predilection for producing moody, actionless, introspective, sometimes impenetrable human dramas that have little box-office appeal. In the 1950s, for example, when the French industry was trying to widen its access to the American market, it created a distribution and promotion office in New York City and purchased a marquee theater to showcase French films. When ticket sales flagged, the officials in New York pondered the alternative of dubbing. But they rejected this strategy because, they contended, it would turn away the high-brow audience that had been their faithful customers.[8] The French refused to stoop to crass commercial criteria.

Such a conception of cinema has always hampered the French film industry, especially when it has sought global markets. It would be a mistake to exaggerate here, though, for the French have produced their share of commercial cinema before, during, and after the war. A commercial mainstream that has tried to please large audiences by relying on crime thrillers, slick literary adaptations, comedies, and stars has always existed. But much of this production has been for local audiences. In the first postwar decade, the cinema that was later dubbed the "tradition of quality" produced movies like *Le Rouge et le noir* and *Caroline chérie* with stars like Gérard Philipe and Martine Carol, that exploited French traditions and ignored foreign markets.[9] Then in the late 1950s and early 1960s the so-called *auteur* films associated with the New Wave took precedence. Even if this genre of self-consciously artistic and experimental cinema gradually merged into the commercial mainstream of French cinematography in the later 1960s and 1970s, for foreign audiences it became identified with French filmmaking.

When Americans refused to flock to such bleak French imports in the 1960s as Alan Resnais's *Last Year at Marienbad*, the French industry tilted its collective nose. Yankee audiences, it was said, were too infantile for sophisticated Gallic wares. Recently the head of Unifrance, the French export marketing office, grumbled that:

> ... Americans don't even know what the word "cultural" means. Hardly 10 percent of them are educated in the sense that we use the term in Europe. A film like *The Visitors* is just too complicated for them. It contains references to the Middle Ages that the average American would absolutely not understand: he doesn't imagine a past that existed before him.... In fact their cinema has become a kind of giant video game where the family amuses itself.[10]

But this same official also attacked French filmmakers for their vanity and blind pride in making only artistic or experimental films that ceded the global market to the Americans. As one critic complained, young French directors are satisfied if they reach an audience of three hundred and receive a review in *Le Monde*.[11] The French, connoisseurs say, have been waiting for a new New Wave that never crested. Only in the 1990s did the French launch a major effort using grand spectacles, action films, and comedies to win the rich American market.

Some critics extend the aesthetic argument to artistic creativity. They argue that the French cinema, since the New Wave, has lost its creative edge—that other cinemas, like that of the Americans or the Italians, have become superior. Sophie Marceau, a prominent French actress, fled to Hollywood recently because she found French moviemakers out of touch with the modern world. She told an American journalist: "It's painful to see so few people attending French films, but it's our own fault because we have not been making films that are relevant to people's lives."[12] This criticism may or may not be valid, but in this case there is little consensus among experts about assessing collective artistry.

Yet another interpretation blames government protectionism for the decline of the industry vis-à-vis Hollywood. Protectionism has been, and continues to be, the French way to keep Hollywood at arm's length. But the intricate web of support may have also harmed the industry by nurturing a kind of dependence and an unwillingness to face the demands of the market. One recent study concludes that state subsidies have created an elitist, inbred network that rewards *auteur* films at the expense of more commercial films that would have a global appeal.[13] Other scholars believe the selective subsidies introduced in the 1950s have actually helped bring new blood into the industry.[14] Whatever the case, state protectionism, at best, slowed down the cross-Atlantic invasion from the end of the war to the 1970s, but in the last twenty years the barriers have ceased to provide effective deterrence.

Meanwhile, the French government has never pursued a consistent policy toward Hollywood. While trying to protect the local industry from the California invaders with quotas and subsidies, it has also honored them. In 1926 the Third Republic gave the Legion of Honor to the Hollywood mogul Marcus Low, who had bought a French distribution network, while simultaneously trying to shut the door on American films.[15] It was no different in the early 1980s when the Fifth Republic's minister of culture denounced American cultural imperialism and then officially celebrated American actors like Sylvester Stallone. Such contradictory policies amuse outsiders and perplex insiders.

A final reason for Hollywood's success may be found by looking at French audiences. Some experts complain that French taste in films has descended to the infantile level of Hollywood productions. In 1992 a prominent film producer observed, "What works in Chattanooga now works in the sixth arrondisement of Paris. It's a little sad."[16] One statistical study correlates the growing popularity of American films in the 1980s with a shift in audience.[17] As the typical moviegoer frequented the theater less often, that is, attended less than one movie per month, the appetite for diversion and spectacle, in which Hollywood excels, grew. Other shifts in the profile of the audience, such as increasing youthfulness, may also have contributed to the popularity of American blockbusters.

Whatever the cause or causes—be it language, industrial structure, Hollywood's marketing, cinematic style, aesthetic creativity, the government, or the audience—the result is that the French film industry has been losing the contest with the Americans. Americanization of the cinema, in the sense of Hollywood's winning more than half of the French box office, has succeeded. This conclusion seems even more obvious if the sample is extended from France to Western Europe, where approximately 80 percent of the market has fallen into American hands. But Americanization in the narrow sense of the box office is only one aspect of this transatlantic rivalry. Americanization has also emerged in the broader sense of French appropriation of Hollywood's cinematographic style and its production, distribution, finance, and marketing techniques.

It would be simplistic to view the celluloid contest between America and France as a zero-sum game in which the former's gains have been the latter's loss. Rather, the recent evolution of the cinema—whose history resembles that of French popular culture in general–has been marked by adaptation as well as importation. The French have not simply imported the American film at the expense of their own productions. There has been both appropriation and resistance. At one level, the two cinemas have merged by borrowing from each other. Thus the French cinema may have become less national and less distinct while Hollywood has become increasingly transnational. At another level, there has been resistance. The French postwar cinema has not passively succumbed to Hollywood; it has, rather, Americanized itself, and it has resisted.

The evolution of the French cinema has been toward a kind of hybridization that blurs, without entirely obliterating, a "national" style. In an aesthetic sense, the French learned from Hollywood, the most obvious examples being the conscious borrowings by filmmakers like Jean-Pierre Melville and especially by New Wave directors like François Truffaut and Claude Chabrol from Americans like Howard Hawks, Orson Welles, Sam Fuller, and John Ford. Truffaut's generation incorporated Hollywood genres like the crime thriller into their creations. Jean-Paul Belmondo's homage to Humphrey Bogart in Jean-Luc Godard's *A bout de souffle* (Breathless) vividly illustrates this transatlantic influence. French film companies also heavily engaged in coproduction. In the 1950s coproductions, mainly Franco-Italian, generated about 40 percent of receipts for French producers.[18] And in time the French came to coproduce with Americans, creating a genre of film called Euro-American art cinema. By the 1960s coproductions often outnumbered strictly national productions. At the end of his career in the 1970s, René Clément coproduced thrillers using Hollywood stars like Charles Bronson. In a desperate effort to remain competitive, the French were even willing to make English-language films as a way of broadening their influence in a world that increasingly relied on English, while French television companies either coproduced with American filmmakers or financed films like *Terminator 2* and *J.F.K.* French producers have also tried to imitate American formulae with action films like *La Femme Nikita* or with science fiction spectacles like *The Fifth Element*. Today U.S. film studios and communications giants are investing heavily in European television as it goes commercial. This process is as much one of globalization as it is Americanization.

Cinematographic influences have also moved west, as well as east, across the Atlantic. Hollywood has spoken with a French accent for a long time.[19] From the prewar years when actors like Charles Boyer and Maurice Chevalier worked in California to the postwar era that featured stars like Leslie Caron and Yves Montand to today when Gérard Depardieu appears in comedies like *Green Card,* French actors have made films in the United States. Directors, from Jean Renoir and René Clair to Louis Malle and Bernard Tavernier, have also worked in Hollywood. Couturiers like Coco Chanel and Hubert de Givenchy have contributed, for example, in dressing Audrey Hepburn. And Paris or the Riviera have been favorite locales for American films, like *An American in Paris* or *Funny Face* in the 1950s and 1960s. Hollywood borrowed from France to portray a kind of sensuality free from puritanism, as played by Maurice Chevalier in *Gigi.* In the 1990s so many French filmmakers, not to mention French actors and actresses, moved to Los Angeles that they have formed an informal group called the "French Hollywood Circle."[20] They argue that the United States is a better place to make films. Here they have bigger budgets, fewer regulations, and a huge domestic market to recoup costs. In recent years Hollywood has also purchased French films, like *Trois Hommes et un Couffin, La Cage aux folles, Le Retour de Martin Guerre,* and remade them for American audiences (*Three Men and a Baby, The Birdcage,* and *Sommersby* respectively). Today nine out of ten Hollywood "remakes" were originally French. And Disney has continuously delved into French literary classics, like *Sleeping Beauty, Beauty and the Beast,* and Victor Hugo's *Notre Dame de Paris* for scripts.

What has been happening is an acceleration of a long-term trend that began with the inception of the cinema and is moving toward a kind of hybrid transnational film. "Hollywood" is more and more a metaphor for a kind of globalized entertainment rather than a synonym for a national cinema. Hollywood films, and in some respects French films too, have been "neutered" or "denationalized." A Warner Brothers label means rather little when the stars are British, French, and Italian; when the director is Dutch; and when the film is shot on location in Israel. What nationality is a film like *The Piano?* It was produced with French money, but it featured an American actress and an Australian director, and was filmed in New Zealand. Even the Cannes Film Festival has stopped selecting movies by country of origin because it is too difficult to identify them by a single nationality.

The transnational film represents the globalization of the cinema. The overseas market has become so important that Hollywood now insists on some measure of international appeal for its productions. The inevitable result, according to critics, has been more formulaic movies depending on special effects that will sell in the global market. Those in France who have voiced opposition to the Americanization of their cinema have recognized this trend. Their complaint about Hollywood is not aimed so much at an "American cinema," as it is against a kind of standardized image–which they are quick to add is either vulgar or barbaric. Whatever the qualitative judgment, the attack is against a cinematographic product that has no specific nationality and destroys cultural pluralism. Soon, the French warn, the movie screens of the world will present just one image.[21]

Cinematographic hybridization, as has been pointed out, is occurring in France as well as in Hollywood. But, one should not exaggerate this transnational trend because, in many ways, a distinctive French national cinema persists. Gallic habits and tastes remain. In recent years, when the French industry tried to gain access to the global market with big budget films, they relied on the old formula of using literary or historic scripts like *Germinal, Madame Bovary, Cyrano de Bergerac,* and *Indochine.* The French, along with other European filmmakers, have proudly asserted that they have preserved cinema as an art form. It can be argued that a certain kind of French national style survives in a world of transnational filmmaking. Recent French films like the series *Blue, White,* and *Red,* or *La Gloire de mon père,* or *La Belle Noiseuse,* or *Un Coeur en Hiver* display this continuity of "Frenchness." What constitutes a national film is difficult to define and historically it has been utilized as a means of cultural resistance. But just as German film critics in the 1920s struggled to define and defend "German cinema" against Hollywood, so the French film industry and its protectors have insisted that there is a "French cinema" worth preserving.[22] What constitutes any national style is a construction of an imaginary homogeneous entity. Defenders claim the French film is a vehicle for the expression of human emotion, human dilemmas, and ideas. There is, they argue, a kind of Gallic approach to subject, plot, and dialogue and a certain seriousness of purpose that is at odds with pure entertainment. The French film, as its advocates construct it, features lengthy and sophisticated dialogue, complex narration, introspective protagonists, social and political commentary, and a certain philosophical pessimism. Whatever the validity of this claim for a unique national cinema, it is evident that a substantial part of French audiences prefer the local product. The full houses of the 1950s and the lesser crowds of the 1960s and 1970s still made local films their choice. Even in the mid-1990s at least a third of the audience continued to prefer French productions, though most of these films were commercial products like comedies and not art films.

Thus, when the French film industry and the government evoke the argument of cultural defense, when they insist–as the former minister of culture Jack Lang did–that "cinema is a national art which expresses a country's history and imagination," when they proclaim that they are defending art against commerce, there is a certain resonance.[23] What is unusual about French cinema is that it has sustained its level of film production, whereas most European cinemas have not and some have totally succumbed to Hollywood's invasion. France maintains Europe's largest movie industry, making about 150 films annually.

A kind of defiant opposition has been a historic feature of the Gallic response to Hollywood. Leading this resistance has been the French cinema industry, its intellectual Praetorian guard, and the government. Apprehension about American mass culture and Hollywood in particular is hardly new in France. Film interests began warning against a Hollywood takeover during the days of the silent movie. Between the wars, intellectuals ridiculed American movies. In the most popular treatise on America of the time, entitled *America the Menace,* Georges Duhamel belittled Hollywood films as vapid escapism: "I assert that any people subjected for half a century to the actual influence of the American movie is on the way to the worst decadence." Duhamel predicted that Americans would be so stupefied by celluloid inanities that one day they would find themselves "incapable of doing any task that requires sustained resolution." [24] Such shrill attacks have continued over the decades. Régis Debray, writer and former adviser to President Mitterrand, recently declared: "What's good for Columbia and Warner Brothers is good for America. O.K.; the question now is whether it's good for the rest of the world. The American empire will pass, like the others. Let's at least make sure it does not leave irreparable damage to our creative abilities behind it."[25]

Gallic resistance assumed the form of a stout defense as well as pointed attacks. The French film industry, from the inception of the sound picture, has enjoyed some form of government protection against Hollywood. As early as the interwar years, the film industry employed various protectionist techniques, such as quotas, to guard their cultural terrain. The Fourth Republic added an elaborate system of direct and indirect subsidies as a way of helping the industry recover from the war. Unhappy with the Blum-Brynes accord of 1946, which opened French borders to American imports, French actors, directors, and technicians in 1947–48 staged large demonstrations to force the government to modify the agreement and raise barriers against Hollywood. In the postwar era, import quotas and subsidies to domestic producers, distributors, and exhibitors have been the main form of defense. The financial history of the industry indicates that the French cinema would not have survived as long as it has except for government assistance. Subsidies have been lavish–running at about

$350 million per year currently—and they have been effective in keeping the industry running. Today, taxes on box-office receipts, over half of which are generated by American films, subsidize French film and television production—much to the distaste of Hollywood.

French protectionism, however, faced a direct assault from the world, led by the MPAA, in the Uruguay round of the General Agreement on Tariffs and Trade (GATT) negotiations in the early 1990s. The United States tried to include the audiovisual sector as part of a general reduction of trade restrictions, but the French resisted. They insisted on a "cultural exception." One might ask why the French government put at risk its relations with the United States, its partnership with Germany, and its standing in Europe by threatening to stop the Uruguay round? To be sure, the audiovisual sector involved huge profits, but French officials subordinated such economic issues and treated the problem as a matter of protecting Europe from the Americanization of culture. Jack Lang warned that the time had come to declare "war" in order to defend the nation's culture, while French movie producers, directors, and actors demanded protection, as they had in the late1940s, against Hollywood. When a settlement was reached, Lang boasted that the exclusion of the audiovisual sector was "a victory for art and artists over the commercialization of culture."[26]

Opposition to GATT's opening of the audiovisual sector was presented to the French not only as a matter of protecting art, but also—on an even grander scale—as an issue of defending cultural pluralism and national identity. Lang's successor as minister of culture, Jacques Toubon, argued that "French identity" was threatened by films such as *Jurassic Park*.[27] It is too easy to dismiss such posturing as an attempt to hide motives of economic protection or political gain behind the rhetoric of culture and identity. In this case, warnings about identity evoke popular fears. What is striking, for example, is the anxiety expressed by French parents about the influence of American culture on their families. Some worry that if the Yankee invasion continues they might not be able to recognize, in a cultural sense, their own children.

Complexities of Americanization

The postwar history of the French cinema in its response to Hollywood illustrates the complexities of Americanization. Alongside the direct conquest of the French market by American imports, there has also been appropriation and the emergence of transnational forms. In order to compete in global markets, the French have, to a degree, Americanized the way they make films. However, the French have also openly resisted. Thus, there has been national cinemato-graphic survival so that, to date, images made-in-Hollywood have not completely engulfed French screens.

The French encounter with Hollywood helps refine the concept of Americanization. Americanization itself is a complicated historical process that has little to do with the crude notion of cultural imperi-alism. It also is more helpful in conceptualizing contemporary trends than some forms of globalization theory, which tend to underesti-mate the central role of America in this history of cultural exchange. The thesis of Americanization, if properly nuanced, is a useful way to approach the cultural history of the twentieth century.

Returning to the question of global uniformity, this case study points to some level of convergence as the most likely outcome of a process that began with the diffusion of American mass culture early in this century. Even if Europeans, and other non-Americans, have become increasingly independent of America in producing mass cul-ture and even if they have been able to domesticate American imports, Americanization has advanced. Speaking only of Europe in the post–cold war era, it appears that the Continent has become either Americanized, or globalized, or semi-Americanized–that, whatever conceptualization one prefers, there is some measure of convergence via a transnational culture.

Notes

1. Some recent studies that introduce the general issues of Americanization and globalization, especially from a European perspective, are: *Cultural Transmis-sions and Receptions: American Mass Culture in Europe*, ed. Rob Kroes, Robert W. Rydell, and Doeko F. J. Bosscher (Amsterdam, 1993); *Modernity and Its Futures*, ed. Stuart Hall, David Held, and Tony McGrew (Oxford, 1992); David Morely and Kevin Robins, *Spaces of Identity: Global Media, Electronic Landscapes and Cul-tural Boundaries* (London, 1995); *Hollywood in Europe: Experiences of a Cultural Hegemony*, ed. David W. Ellwood and Rob Kroes (Amsterdam, 1994); John Tom-linson, *Cultural Imperialism: A Critical Introduction* (Baltimore, 1991); Rob Kroes, *If You've Seen One You've Seen the Mall: Europeans and American Mass Culture* (Urbana and Chicago, 1996); Benjamin R. Barber, *Jihad vs. McWorld: How the Planet Is Both Falling Apart and Coming …* (New York, 1995); Richard Pells, *Not Like Us: How Europeans Have Loved, Hated and Transformed American Culture since World War II* (New York, 1997). I wish to thank David Ellwood and Robert Har-vey for their counsel in writing this essay.

2. Rick Fantasia, "Everything and Nothing: The Meaning of Fast-Food and Other American Cultural Goods in France," *Tocqueville Review* 25, no. 2 (1994): 57–88.

3. Françis Bordat, "Evaluation statistique de la pénétration du cinéma américain en France," *Revue française d'études américaines* 24/25 (1985): 227–43. Comparable data are in Colin Crisp, *The Classic French Cinema, 1930–1960* (Bloomington, 1993), 82–83.

4. *Le Nouvel Observateur*, 23–29 September 1993, 63. Similar data can be found in *L'Express*, 7 October 1993, 73.

5. For an insightful anthology of essays on the history of Europe's response to the American film, see David Ellwood and Rob Kroes eds., *Hollywood in Europe*. For the critical account of an insider, see David Puttnam, *The Undeclared War* (London, 1997).

6. Crisp, *The Classic French Cinema*, 87.

7. The Blum-Brynes agreement has provoked a seemingly endless debate about its intentions and its consequences. This debate can be found in: Jean-Pierre Jeancolas, "L'Arrangement: Blum-Byrnes à l'épreuve des faits," *1895, Revue de l'Association française du cinéma* 13 (December 1993): 3–49; Irwin Wall, " Les Accords Blum-Byrnes," *Vingtième Siècle* 13 (January–March 1987): 45–62; Michel Margairaz, "Autour des accords Blum-Byrnes," *Histoire, économie, société* 3 (1982): 429–70.

8. Centre des Archives Contemporaines (Fontainebleau), Archives of Unifrance, file no. 760010, carton no. 73, Voyage de M. Cravenne, 1953.

9. Alan Williams, *Republic of Images* (Cambridge, Mass., 1992), 278ff.

10. Daniel Toscan du Plantier, head of Unifrance, quoted in *Télérama*, 6 October 1993, 14.

11. *New York Times*, 14 January 1996.

12. *The Washington Post*, 19 March 1995.

13. Harvey B. Feigenbaum, "The Culture of Production and the Production of Culture," George Washington University, unpublished paper, 1995, 19.

14. Crisp, *The Classic French Cinema*, 78.

15. Jacques Portes, "Hollywood et la France, 1896–1930," *Revue française d'études américaines* 59 (1994): 33.

16. *New York Times*, 9 August 1992. See also Mario Vargas Llosa in *Libération*, 2 December 1992.

17. Claude Forest, "Histoire économique de l'exploitation cinématographique française," in Ecole Polytechnique, *Programme de recherche du premier siècle du cinéma: histoire économique du cinéma français, année 1993–1994* (Paris, 1995), 54–55.

18. Crisp, *The Classic French Cinema*, 80.

19. Joseph Fichett, "Lights, Camera, Accents," *France Magazine* 28 (1993): 24–27; Dominique Lebrun, *Trans-Europe Hollywood* (Paris, 1992).

20. *New York Times*, 22 October 1995.

21. *Le Monde*, 18 September 1993.

22. See the discussion of a German national cinema in Thomas J. Saunders, *Hollywood in Berlin: American Cinema and Weimar Germany* (Berkeley, 1994), 196–220, and the analysis of a national cinema in Morley and Robins, *Spaces of Identity*, 90–91.

23. Quoted in *Le Nouvel Observateur*, 23–29 September 1993, 63.

24. Georges Duhamel, *America the Menace*, trans. Charles Miner (Boston, 1931), 35.

25. Quoted in the *New York Times*, 2 January 1994.

26. Quoted in the *New York Times*, 15 December 1993.

27. Quoted in *Le Nouvel Observateur*, 23–29 September 1993, 62.

– Eleven –

WAITING FOR GODZILLA

Chaotic Negotiations between Post-Orientalism
and Hyper-Occidentalism

Takayuki Tatsumi

In the wake of cyberculture, multiculturalism, and postcolonialism in
the 1980s, we cannot help but notice the tremendous impact of
"hyperreality"–that is, of a media-saturated reality in the sense of
Jean Baudrillard–upon the discursive status of "Orientalism" as a
Western stylization of the East and of "Occidentalism" as an Eastern
stylization of the West. Multinational cybermedia have helped to blur
the distinction between reality and fiction as never before, and, at the
same time, the Western concept of a logocentric reality has proven to
be no more than a dominant narrative. Let me illustrate this point by
reconsidering the recent relationship between the United States and
Japan, exploring the three stages in the development of "mimicry":
first, the essentialist myth of originality and imitation; second, the late
capitalist synchronicity between different cultures; and third, the multicultural and transgeneric poetics of chaotic negotiation.

The Essentialist Myth of Originality and Imitation

There is no doubt that, since its reopening to the outside world in the
early Meiji Era during the 1850s, Japan has persistently Westernized, modernized, and especially "Americanized" itself by closely

"imitating" Anglo-American styles and obediently following the example of modern, white Western civilization. And yet, until recently, few critics have fully examined the political nature of Japanese mimetic desire. Recent postcolonial theory can help us in this project. Japan was of course never formally colonized by a Western nation—indeed, it became a colonial power itself. However, Japan's status as one of the objects of Western, including American Orientalist, imaginations and Japan's efforts to emulate Western and American examples make it useful to draw on concepts developed in postcolonial theory, such as mimicry, in order to understand the complex interactions between Japan and the United States. As Homi Bhabha points out, it is in the comic turn from the high ideals of the colonial imagination to its low mimetic literary effects that "mimicry" becomes visible as "the desire for a reformed, recognizable Other, as a subject of a difference that is almost the same, but not quite."[1] It has long been assumed that although the colonized respond to colonial domination via a complex "mimicry," this mimicry can never succeed in effacing the difference between the Western original and the colonized copy. Western thinking on Japan has much in common with attitudes towards the (formerly) colonized. Thus, Westerners have both admired and denigrated the Japanese as adept mimics, who are good at copying but lacking in originality.

Postcolonial theorists, however, have exposed the very concept of originality as a Western ideological invention, and in turn see mimicry not as a failed attempt to achieve originality, but as a counterstrategy that radically problematizes the very origin of "originality." Using these insights, Marilyn Ivy, in her provocative book *Discourses of the Vanishing*, has explained the myth of "imitation" with regard to Japan:

> It is no doubt Japan's ... entry into geopolitics as an entirely exotic and late modernizing nation-state instead of as an outright colony that has made its mimicry all the more threatening. As the only predominately nonwhite nation to have challenged western dominance on a global scale during World War II.... Japan, in its role as quasi-colonized mimic, has finally exceeded itself: now it is American companies, educators, and social scientists who speak of the necessity of learning from Japan in the hope of copying its economic miracles, its pedagogical successes, its societal orderliness.[2]

Following Ivy, an innovative reconsideration of mimicry can thus provide us with a powerful device for analyzing U.S.-Japanese relations from a postcolonial perspective.

Ivy's reformulation of Japanese mimicry has direct and persuasive applications for literature. Modern Japanese writers, whether prewar or postwar, started their careers by imitating and assimilating the works of Anglo-American precursors. One example is *The Legends of Tono* (1910), an apparently original collection of Japanese traditional myths, legends, and folklore, that was compiled by the father of Japanese nativist ethnology, Kunio Yanagita. The work focused on the town of Tono in the deep north of Japan, where people still encountered difficulty in telling fact from fiction and the actual from the imaginary (just like the inhabitants of Sleepy Hollow in Washington Irving's tale). Yanagita carefully stylized what he collected orally from one of the young native informants named Kizen Sasaki, a walking "database" of Tono narratives. Yanagita modeled his work on Lafcadio Hearn, whose naturalized name, Yakumo Koizumi, is more familiar to the Japanese. Hearn had made the legends and tales of an unknown culture, Japan, a part of American literature around the turn of the century. In Japan, these ghost stories of Lafcadio Hearn/Yakumo Koizumi have long been taught to every schoolchild as part of Japanese literary history. Thus, it was not the Japanese nationalist Yanagita, but the multinational author Hearn/Koizumi who established a Japanese sensibility for folklore at the turn of the century. While Yanagita himself believed his naturalist anthology to be antithetical and even "antidotal" to modern Westernization, his project was in fact not imaginable without the Western Orientalism of Hearn.[3] In a sense, the search for "originality" turned out to be the result of "imitation," revealing how problematic both concepts are.

In the 1950s and the 1960s, it became almost inevitable for Japanese writers to adopt much from the latest translated Anglo-American fiction and to follow American examples produced in the Pax Americana climate. Thus the Japanese tried to import a huge amount of Anglo-American cultural products and unwittingly misread their own Occidentalism as a genuine internationalism. Japan's excessive Occidentalism has sometimes gone so far as to simulate the most canonical discourse of Western Orientalism.

Representations of the ethnic "other," whether correct or incorrect, have long enchanted talented writers who are ambitious to incorporate the most avant-garde images into their fiction. Just as Anglo-American representations of the Japanese still seem to derive from the stereotypes of Fujiyama-geisha-sushi-harakiri, so the Japanese (including intellectuals) have long modeled America upon the stereotypes of Kennedy-Apache-Gone-with-the-Wind. In her provocative essay "Imaging the Other in Japanese Advertising Campaigns," Millie Creighton carefully analyzes the way in which advertisements in Japan invoke foreigners of several sorts, especially white Occidentals, who are referred to as *gaijin*.

In ways parallel to Western orientalism, Japanese occidentalism also involved a sexual projection of the other, particularly the allure of the occidental woman. However, as a response to the increasing impact of Western culture on Japan, Japanese occidentalism involved more than attraction to and exoticization of the Western other. The creation of gaijin as a social construction of Japanese Occidentalism also mirrored a need to assert control over the moral threat of an intruding outside world.[4]

Japanese commercials of the mid-1990s are perfect examples of such an Occidentalist strategy for domesticating and naturalizing the other. In a Kirin beer campaign, Harrison Ford is depicted not as a glamorous celebrity but as an ordinary "salaryman" working for a typical Japanese company. As David Lazarus reports, a number of A-list Hollywood stars still pitch Japanese products in more traditional I-use-this-and-so-should-you endorsements: "Jodie Foster sells cars. Madonna and Sean Connery sell liquor. Arnold Schwarzenegger sells energy drinks.... Demi Moore sells shampoo. Sharon Stone sells cosmetics. And, of course, there's Sylvester Stallone, who seems a particularly apt choice for commercials that sell ham."[5] Thus, the traditional discourse of Japanese Occidentalism has at once exoticized and domesticated *gaijin*; it has tried to overcome its hidden Anglophobia, which is caused by the essentialist myth of originality and imitation. The result has been a certain synchronicity of Japanese Occidentalism and American Orientalism.

One significant aspect of postwar Japanese history has been the metamorphosing of masochistic imitation into the principle of techno-capitalist recreation. In his splendid book *Suicidal Narrative in Modern Japan*, Alan Wolfe has described the sensibility that shaped thinking on postwar Japan: "If there is a metaphorical paradigm that best characterizes historical writing about the 1940s in Japan, it is that of death and rebirth.... The resulting combination of marginal deprivation (buffeted by American rations and black marketeering) and relative freedom seemed to produce a mood of heady optimism and expressive vitality."[6]

The way the Japanese responded to the disastrous earthquake that struck the Osaka-Kobe district on 17 January 1995 (at the beginning of the fiftieth anniversary of the end of World War II) illustrates how a distinct form of memory has developed out of the postwar history of reconstruction. This form of memory represents, assimilates, and domesticates the earthquaking "other." Just as economic disaster in the 1980s seduced Americans to revive the discourse of Japan-bashing, so the Osaka-Kobe earthquake carried some Japanese religious fanatics to renewed anti-Americanism. Immediately after the earthquake, Shoko Asahara, the charismatic leader of the doomsday religious cult Aum Shinrikyo (The True Teaching of Aum), attributed the disaster to a conspiracy by the United States, whose "mysterious Great Power had set off the earthquake either with a small, distant nuclear explosion or by 'radiating high voltage microwaves' into the ground near the fault line."[7] No matter how fanatic this death cult is, its response to disasters is typically Occidentalist and has a longer history. In the 1950s, for example, the monster Godzilla represented the similarly sinister effect of nuclear devastation brought about by the United States. The figure of Godzilla as the ultimately disastrous other helped the postwar Japanese to reconstruct a national identity by making themselves into victims of and resistors against an outside threat. The Occidentalist Godzilla of the 1950s helped postwar Japanese writers develop the prophetic imagination of creative masochism based on what William Kelly has designated as "the absence of moral panic."[8]

Godzilla was followed by similar images in the 1970s. Shozo Numa's futuristic speculative fiction *Kachikujin Yapuu* (Yapoo the Human Cattle) of 1970 recharacterized the Japanese people not as Homo sapiens but as "Simias sapiens."[9] Isaiah Ben-Dasan's *Nihonjin (Nipponjin) to Yudayajin* (The Japanese and the Jew), published that same year, attempted a highly inventive comparison between Judaism and "Nihonism." In 1973 these works were followed by Sakyo Komatsu's four-million bestseller *Nippon Chimbotsu* (Japan Sinks),[10] in which an apocalyptic earthquake causes the whole land of Japan to sink, so that the Japanese people are forced to enact the example of the Jewish diaspora.[11] Komatsu radically reconfigured the very notion of diaspora into a powerful engine of Japanese capitalism during the high growth period of the 1970s. Although some reinterpret this novel in the late 1990s as a highly accurate prediction of the devastating Osaka-Kobe earthquake, in the 1970s *Japan Sinks* helped popularize diaspora as the ideal Occidentalist form of internationalism. The blurb for the first Kobunsha edition of the novel designated Sakyo Komatsu as an "international literary figure," and referred to *Japan Sinks* as a work "having been awaited internationally." The novel in turn encouraged contemporary Japanese businessmen or "salarymen" to go abroad as volunteer exiles, and to develop Japanese economic hegemony. *Japan Sinks* thus symbolized the "econo-internationalist" spirit of the high growth period of the 1970s and 80s.

This concept of a postmodern diaspora has been further developed by recent "virtual reality" narratives, such as Goro Masaki's *Venus City* (1992) and Alexander Besher's *RIM* (1994).[12] In both, the erasure of Japan or Tokyo is scheduled to take place not in geospace but in cyberspace. The advent of the post-bubble economy in the mid-1990s has apparently made it easier for the Japanese to accept other creative masochistic concepts like "creative defeat" (Shigeto Tsuru), the "mental history of failure and defeat" (Masao Yamaguchi), and "the strategy of being radically fragile" (Seigo Matsuoka).[13] Japanese intellectuals thus have gradually systematized a self-reflexive form of Occidentalism, which I would like to call the hyper-Occidentalist philosophy of creative masochism. This Occidentalism does not simply imitate Anglo-American precursors but radically transforms the potentially humiliating experience of an imagined Japanese diaspora into the techno-utopian vision of construction.

The Late Capitalist Synchronicity between Different Cultures

Insofar as literature is concerned, Japan has been a country of excessive importation, not excessive exportation. This "kingdom of translation" is very good at translating and popularizing foreign cultures; however, Japan itself is largely invisible to other nations because it is not translating and exporting many of its own national literary fruits. As a result, Japanese literature is nearly invisible abroad, where it constitutes a minor culture or what Samuel Delany would call "paraliterature." Like women's fiction, black fiction, gay fiction, experimental fiction, or romance novels and mysteries, Japanese literature abroad is undoubtedly marginal.[14] However, situated on the margin, paraliterature has recently become a model for literature itself. At the same time, in Japanese postmodern fiction, the logic of imitation has been replaced by "synchronicity"—synchronicity between American and Japanese works.

This paradigm shift from the logic of imitation to the logic of synchronicity is especially evident in the artistic development of Haruki Murakami, one of the most famous postmodern Japanese writers known in English-speaking countries. Murakami started writing in the late 1970s by imitating the literary style of H. P. Lovecraft, F. Scott Fitzgerald, and Kurt Vonnegut. More recently, the deeper sense of the past that is characteristic of his 1990s trilogy *Wind-Up Bird Chronicle* has coincided with the historical consciousness apparent in the work of a young American video artist David Blair, who stormed Japan with his avant-pop masterpiece *WAX: A Discovery of Bee Television* in 1991, and who is now completing a hyperhistorical romance called *Jews in Space (Israel in Manchuria)*.[15] These examples suggest that the more often cultural transactions and transpositions occur between any two cultures, the more synchronic these cultures and their narratives become.

Indeed, it has become more difficult to determine who is the precursor and who is the latecomer. The American writer Paul Auster's *Moon Palace* (1989) and the Japanese writer Masahiko Shimada's *Higan-Sensei* (Master Otherside, 1992)[16] are two typically "avant-pop" novels: both skillfully displace the boundary between literature and paraliterature, and both use a Chinese restaurant, Moon Palace, in New York City as the central setting. Their plot structures are likewise similar as they weave their exemplary "orphan" narratives. Shimada, who wrote *Master Otherside* without having read Auster, narrates a story of an orphan-seeking father, who contrasts strikingly with a father-seeking orphan in Auster's *Moon Palace.*

In another example of synchronicity, Greek-American woman writer Eurudice in *f/32* (1990) and Japanese woman writer Rieko Matsuura in *Apprenticeship of Bigtoe-P* (1993) have both produced typically "cyborg-feminist" novels that radically mock the boundary between patriarchal literature and feminist paraliterature.[17] Both writers characterize genitals as independent protagonists, either male or female. While Eurudice describes a woman's vagina running away from her body in a Gogolian way, Matsuura tells us of a woman's big toe, which metamorphoses into a penis in Kafkaesque fashion.

In addition to such an intercultural synchronicity, the 1980s saw another revolutionary paradigm shift. For the first time, Anglo-American writers imitated and reappropriated "Japanesque" images, that is, images that at once draw on and distort Japanese culture. At the same time, their Japanese counterparts came to realize that writing subversive fiction in the wake of cyberpunk meant gaining an insight into the radically "science-fictional" aspects of Japan. Of course, while American representations of Japan have become attractive in the United States precisely due to their distortions of Japanese culture, they have often given rise to heated controversy on the part of the Japanese audience. I remember one of my friends from Chiba City reacting angrily when he read the first chapter of William Gibson's *Neuromancer,* "Chiba City Blues," which seemed to him to represent the Chiba people pejoratively.[18]

In another appropriation of Japanese images, the American avant-pop writer Mark Jacobson became so fascinated by Godzilla the famous Japanese "gangster" that, in his first novel *Gojiro* (1991), Jacobson "re-Orientalized" Japan by making the friendship between Godzilla and a Japanese boy, Komodo, its central topic. By the 1980s Godzilla had undergone a transformation in Japan. The image of Godzilla the oversized public enemy in the 1950s[19] was displaced with that of Godzilla the national superhero in the economic high-growth period. While Godzilla the radioactive green monster of the 1950s revived the fear of Moby Dick the white whale, he now encourages not only Japanese screenwriters but also American novelists to recreate the postnuclear romance between Japan and the United States. The more synchronic the two cultures become, the more accepting the Japanese are—even to the rise of postmodern Orientalism.

The Multicultural and Transgeneric Poetics of Chaotic Negotiation

In the late 1990s, the two cultures have thus entered a new phase of interactions. Now chaotic and transculturally infectious negotiations occur between Orientalism and Occidentalism; between the Western belief in eternity and the Japanese aesthetics of the moment; between a Western productionist and idealist sensibility and a Japanese high-tech-consumerist and posthistorical mentality; or even between the science-fictional Japan of the American imagination and Japanese science fiction.

One example of such a chaotic negotiation between the discourse of Japanese hyper-Occidentalism and that of North American post-Orientalism is William Gibson's latest novel *Virtual Light* (1993). While Sakyo Komatsu had developed the postwar Occidentalist imagination and described a tremendous earthquake in *Japan Sinks*, Gibson speculates in *Virtual Light* upon the significance of the 1989 San Francisco earthquake and predicts a Japanese earthquake in the near future, which he nicknames "Godzilla." Unlike Komatsu's hyper-Occidentalist invitation to diaspora in the heyday of internationalist politics, Gibson—from the viewpoint of multinational aesthetics—re-Orientalizes the disasters that the Japanese people have long identified with the radical other. *Virtual Light* brilliantly envisions the near future as a junk-artistic atmosphere on the post-earthquake San Francisco Bay Bridge in 2005. By that time, California has split into two states—SoCal and NoCal. In the wake of "the Godzilla," the devastating earthquake in Japan, another huge earthquake, "the Little Grande," has helped close to traffic the Bay Bridge that links San Francisco and Oakland. Ex-hippies and homeless people have stormed the bridge and have built themselves a new self-governing community. What makes the situation so intriguing is that these post-flower children, called "bridge people," have completely redesigned the whole bridge.

Their dadaist and "tree house"-like architecture has been named "Thomasson" by the character Yamazaki, a Japanese sociologist from Osaka University, who is conducting research on the formation of the bridge culture.

It is through Gibson's own personal transactions with Japanese subcultures that he must have picked up the otherwise incomprehensible term "Thomasson," which signifies the latest phase of the Japanese neo-dadaist movement championed by Genpei Akasegawa from the 1960s through the 1990s. In the novel, Yamazaki explains the origins of the term:

> Thomasson was an American baseball player, very handsome, very powerful. He went to the Yomiuri Giants in 1982, for a large sum of money. Then it was discovered that he could not hit the ball. The writer Genpei Akasegawa appropriated his name to describe certain useless and inexplicable monuments, pointless yet curiously artlike features of the urban landscape. But the term has subsequently taken on other shades of meaning. If you wish, I can access and translate today's definitions in our Gendai Yogo no Kisochishiki, that is, The Basic Knowledge of Modern Times.[20]

Genpei Akasegawa is not an imaginary figure created by Gibson, but a real person born in 1937 in Yokohama, who is well known in Japan as a neo-dadaist and a mainstream writer. While Euro-American dadaism, however avant-garde, often presupposed a work of art designed and authorized by an individual genius or a group of collaborators, Japanese neo-dadaism radically displaces the conventional notion of a "work of art," completed by an individual artist, with the revolutionary idea of "Hyper-Art Thomasson," which refers to junk-art-like junk objects scattered all over the cityscape. It becomes an alternative "art" by being discovered and authorized as an "art" by ordinary urban strollers, "flaneurs" in Charles Baudelaire's term, and not by the artists. Thomasson, then, transgresses not only the boundary between junk and art, but also the difference between self-proclaimed dada artists and the anonymous urban strollers. Akasegawa radically Occidentalized and comically "Japanized" French dadaist Marcel Duchamp as the near-precursor of Thomasson, who "unluckily could not attain Thomassonian perfection," but whose sense of "non-art" brilliantly "corresponded with the Japanese heritage of the tea ceremony" in which the natural world has persistently been considered full of "ready-made" objects.[21]

Gibson gets direct access to postmodern Japanese vocabulary through his wife Deborah, who teaches English to Japanese businessmen in Vancouver, and through Bruce Sterling, his cyberpunk colleague deeply versed in Japanese underground cultures, and it is therefore no wonder that he picked up some information about the great Japanese neo-dadaist Genpei Akasegawa. In *Virtual Light,* Gibson seems to have imitated and reappropriated the avant-pop aesthetics of Japanese art, as well as the ultrapragmatic ethics of Japanese high-tech industry. In sharp contrast to the way the Japanese were "semi-Americanized" in the postwar years, Gibson in the 1990s was so radically "semi-Japanized" that he succeeded in negotiating the distance not only between city and suburb, diaspora and utopia, San Francisco and Tokyo, but also between Occidentalism and Orientalism.

While ultraconservative Western essentialists might dismiss this kind of chaotic transcultural negotiation as being nothing but "trash," this "trash" in fact has complex meanings. As Donald Kuspit points out, "Capitalism joins forces with trash culture to destroy human dignity, indeed, to eliminate the very idea and possibility of it."[22] By the term "human dignity" Kuspit seems to mean Western white "phallogocentric" dignity. An Australian journalist reappraised the prophetic nature of Sakyo Komatsu's *Japan Sinks* after the Osaka-Kobe earthquake by saying: "At a time when government white papers are laughable, perhaps it should not be surprising that trash can make sense."[23] If one redefines the term "trash" as applying to invisible culture and paraliterature per se, it becomes applicable not only to popular fiction in the United States, but also to all non-Western literary discourses, including Japanese literature. While non-Western artists started their careers by imitating Western works of art, their art of "mimicry" has domesticated and even outgrown the Western other. They paved the way not only for the late capitalist synchronicity between different cultures, but also for the highly chaotic and splendidly creative negotiations between Western and non-Western cultures that have recently occurred.

Conclusion

We can confirm the creative potential of "mimicry" by tasting the multicultural artistic fruit of "miscegenation" and metamorphic cross-fertilization between Western and non-Western cultures. Examples include Yoshishige Yoshida's Orientalization of Emily Brontë's novel *Wuthering Heights* (1988), David Henry Hwang and Philip Glass's collaborative libretto *The Voyage* (1992) on the life of Christopher Columbus, Wayne Wang's film *Smoke* (1995), as a visual adaptation of Paul Auster's tale, and Hollywood's remake of *Godzilla* (1998). These contemporary films and performances reveal the ways that Asian and Asian-American directors adopt and adapt Euro-American texts, but also the ways that Euro-American directors reappropriate Asian narratives. The history of Godzilla is emblematic of the history of these interchanges. In the 1950s Godzilla started his career as a typically Occidentalist adaptation of Hollywood's dinosaur-like creature movies. In the 1990s, after a multimillion dollar deal between Japan's Toho Studios and America's Tri-Star Films, Godzilla has achieved his present status of international superhero.[24] Although Roland Emerich's 1998 film *Godzilla* has aroused heated controversy on the radical transformation of the original Godzilla, this superhero will undoubtedly continue to entertain us as a multicultural, transgeneric, post-Occidentalist, and post-Orientalist monster of postmodern representation. Therefore, one could agree with Mark Jacobson that "the green of Gojiro (Godzilla)" is not the color that God splashed upon the spectrum, but that of men—"the green we have created"[25] in the postcolonial age. Godzilla's is the greenness of the whole earth radically refigured in the chaotic negotiations between post-Orientalism and hyper-Occidentalism.

Notes

1. Homi Bhabha, "Of Mimicry and Man: The Ambivalence of Colonial Discourse," *The Location of Culture* (London, 1994), 85–86.
2. Marilyn Ivy, *Discourses of the Vanishing: Modernity, Phantasm, Japan* (Chicago, 1995), 7.
3. See Bon Koizumi, *Minzokugakusha Koizumi Yakumo* (Tokyo, 1995).
4. Millie Creighton, "Imaging the Other in Japanese Advertising Campaigns," in *Occidentalism: Images of the West*, ed. James Carrier (Oxford, 1995), 144.
5. David Lazarus, "Harrison-San! You're Late for Work!: Gaijin Celebrities in Japanese Ads," *Mangajin* 54 (April 1996): 58.
6. Alan Wolfe, *Suicidal Narrative in Modern Japan : The Case of Dazai Osamu* (Princeton, 1990), 167.
7. Murray Sayle, "Letter from Tokyo: Nerve Gas and the Four Noble Truths," *New Yorker*, 1 April, 1996, 68.
8. I came to note William Kelly's theory of "the absence of a moral panic," at the conference "The Impact of American Culture on Postwar Italy, France, Germany, and Japan," Brown University, April 1996.
9. Shozo Numa, *Kachiku-jin Yapuu* [Yapoo the Human Cattle] (Tokyo, 1972; first published in 1970), and *Kachiku-jin Yapuu: Kanketsu-hen* [The Definitive Sequel to Yapoo the Human Cattle] (Tokyo, 1991).
10. Sakyo Komatsu, *Japan Sinks*, trans. Michael Gallagher (New York, 1976, first published in Japanese in 1973).

11. Isaiah Ben-Dasan explains the analogy and the difference between Judaism and Nihonism (Nipponism) as follows: "More than anything else, the Diaspora forced the Jews into an intensified sense of identity and, perhaps, excessive consciousness of being part of a particular religious faith. Scattered over many parts of the globe, yet united by the idea of the synagogue and by rabbinical tradition, Jews could not avoid comparing themselves with the peoples among whom they lived. In doing so, they discovered their own traits, from which evolved an awareness of a unique thing called Jewishness. The Japanese, never having undergone such dispersal, are less aware of the forces that unite them, especially of that great binding faith which I have called Nihonism. It has so permeated the minds of its followers that it is taken for granted, a remarkable fact when one considers that it is as valid a religion as Judaism, Christianity, or Islam." Ben-Dasan, *The Japanese and the Jews,* trans. Richard L. Gate (New York, 1972, first published in Japanese in 1970), 106–7.

12. Goro Masaki, *Venus City* (Tokyo, 1992); Alexander Besher, *RIM* (New York, 1994).

13. See Shigeto Tsuru, *Japan's Capitalism: Creative Defeat and Beyond* (Cambridge, 1993); Seigo Matsuoka, *Fragile* (Tokyo, 1995); Masao Yamaguchi, *Zasetsu no Showa-shi* (Tokyo, 1995); Yamaguchi, *Haisha no Seishinshi* (Tokyo, 1995).

14. Samuel Delany, *Silent Interviews: On Language, Race, Sex, Science Fiction, and Some Comics* (Hanover, N.H., 1994), 212–13.

15. Haruki Murakami, *Nejimaki-dori Kuronikuru* [Wind-Up Bird Chronicle] (Tokyo, 1995); David Blair, *WAX: A Discovery of Bee Television* (1991; Tokyo, 1993).

16. Paul Auster, *Moon Palace* (New York, 1989); Masahiko Shimada, *Higan-Sensei* (Tokyo, 1992).

17. Eurudice, *f/32* (Boulder, Colo., 1990); Rieko Matsuura, *Oyayubi-P no Shugyo-Jidai* (Tokyo, 1993). See Takayuki Tatsumi, "Matsuura Rieko's *The Apprenticeship of Big-toe-P*," *Japanese Literature Today* 20 (June 1995): 68–73; Donna Haraway, "A Manifesto for Cyborgs: Science, Technology, and Socialist Feminism in the 1980s." *Socialist Review* 15, no. 2 (1985): 65–108.

18. William Gibson, *Neuromancer* (New York, 1984). See Stephan Tanaka, *Japan's Orient: Rendering Pasts into History* (Berkeley, 1993).

19. Joseph Anderson and Donald Richie explain how *Godzilla* was exported to the United States: "He [President Kobayashi of Toho M.P.Co.] allowed such films as Akira Kurosawa's *Seven Samurai* and Mikio Naruse's *Late Chrysanthemums* [Banbiku], and cemented American-Japanese ties by selling an American film company Japan's first science-fiction film, *Godzilla* [Gojira], as well as Toho's first color-period film, *Musashi Miyamoto.* The former played all over America after being remade in Hollywood as *Godzilla, King of the Monsters*; the latter made somewhat more of a splash by winning an Academy Award as *Samurai*." Joseph Anderson and Donald Richie, *The Japanese Film: Art and Industry* (Princeton, 1982), 247. See also David J. Skal, *The Monster Show: A Cultural History of Horror* (New York, 1993).

20. William Gibson, *Virtual Light* (New York, 1993), chapter 6, "The Bridge," 64–65.

21. Genpei Akasegawa, *Geijutsu Genron* [The Principles of Art] (Tokyo, 1988), 249–59. See also Paolo Polledri, ed., *Visionary San Francisco* (San Francisco, 1990).

22. Donald Kuspit, "Art and Capital: An Ironic Dialectic," *Critical Review* 9, no. 4 (Fall 1995): 478.

23. However, taking for granted the prophetic nature of Sakyo Komatsu's *Japan Sinks,* Peter Hartcher seems more amused by the author's acute observation on the conservative sensibility of Japanese bureaucrats in general : "… what is particularly striking as an insight from Komatsu's book was the Government's reluctance

to act in the face of impending disaster.... To get the Government to act, the scientists are obliged to use a circuitous route of private introductions and personal backdoor contacts.... At a time when government white papers are laughable, perhaps it should not be surprising that trash can make sense." Peter Hartcher, "Trashy Novel Was a Sign of Things to Come," *Financial Review* (28 August 1995): 11.

24. According to a recent issue of *Asian Trash Cinema*, "Presumably, with Godzilla coming to make movies in the States, his tenure at Toho has ended." Thomas Weisser and Yuko Mihara Weisser, "Godzilla vs. the Destroyer," *Asian Trash Cinema* 11 (1995): 5.

25. Mark Jacobson, *Gojiro* (New York, 1991), 110.

SELECT BIBLIOGRAPHY

Anderson, Benedict. *Imagined Communities: Reflections on the Origin and Spread of Nationalism.* Rev. ed. New York, 1991.

Ang, Ien. *Watching Dallas: Soap Opera and the Melodramatic Imagination,* trans. Della Couling. London, 1985.

Appadurai, Arjun. "Disjuncture and Difference in the Global Cultural Economy." *Public Culture* 2, no. 2 (1990): 1–24.

Armes, Roy. *French Cinema.* New York, 1985.

Bailey, Beth, and David Faber. *The First Strange Place: The Alchemy of Race and Sex in World War II Hawaii.* New York, 1992.

Baranski, Zygmunt G., and Robert Lumley, eds. *Culture and Conflict in Postwar Italy: Essays on Mass and Popular Culture.* New York, 1990.

Barber, Benjamin R. *Jihad vs. McWorld: How the Planet Is Both Falling Apart and Coming Together and What This Means for Democracy.* New York, 1995.

Bathrick, David. "Max Schmeling on the Canvas: Boxing as an Icon of Weimar Culture." *New German Critique* 51 (Fall 1990): 113–36.

Bauschinger, Sigrid, Horst Denkler, and Wilfried Malsch, eds. *Amerika in der deutschen Literatur: Neue Welt–Nordamerika–USA.* Stuttgart, 1975.

Ben-Ghiat, Ruth. "Envisioning Modernity: Desire and Discipline in the Italian Fascist Film." *Critical Inquiry* 23 (Autumn 1996): 109–44.

Bennett, Tony, ed. *Rock and Popular Music: Politics, Policies, Institutions.* New York, 1993.

Berghahn, Volker R. *The Americanisation of West German Industry, 1945–1973.* New York, 1986.

Bhabha, Homi. "Of Mimicry and Man: The Ambivalence of Colonial Discourse." *October* 28 (1984): 125–133.

Bigsby, C. W. E., ed. *Superculture: American Popular Culture and Europe.* Bowling Green, Ohio, 1975.

Biskind, Peter. *Seeing Is Believing: How Hollywood Taught Us to Stop Worrying and Love the Fifties.* New York, 1983.

Bordat, Francis. "Evaluation statistique de la pénétration du cinéma américain en France." *Revue francaise d'études américaines* 24–25 (1985): 225–48.

Brantlinger, Patrick. *Bread and Circuses: Theories of Mass Culture as Social Decay.* Ithaca, N.Y., 1983.

Bridenthal, Renate, Atina Grossmann, and Marion Kaplan, eds. *When Biology Became Destiny: Women in Weimar and Nazi Germany.* New York, 1984.

Burleigh, Michael, and Wolfgang Wippermann. *The Racial State: Germany, 1933–1945.* New York, 1991.

Campbell, David. *Writing Security: United States Foreign Policy and the Politics of Identity.* Minneapolis, 1992.

Carrier, James, ed. *Occidentalism: Images of the West.* New York, 1995.

Carter, Erica. "Alice in the Consumer Wonderland: West German Case Studies in Gender and Consumer Culture." In *Gender and Generation,* ed. Angela McRobbie and Mica Nava, 185–214. London, 1984.

Chapple, Steve, and Reebee Garafalo. *Rock 'n' Roll Is Here To Pay: The History and Politics of the Music Industry.* Chicago, 1977.

Cohen, Jean-Louis. *Scenes of the World to Come: European Architecture and the American Challenge, 1893–1960.* Paris, 1995.

Collier, James Lincoln. *The Reception of Jazz in America: A New View.* Brooklyn, 1988.

Cooper, Frederick, and Laura Ann Stoler, eds. *Tensions of Empire: Colonial Cultures in a Bourgeois World.* Berkeley, 1997.

Corber, Robert J. *In the Name of National Security: Hitchcock, Homophobia, and the Political Construction of Gender in Postwar America.* Durham, N.C., 1993.

Cornyetz, Nina. "Fetishized Blackness: Hip Hop and Racial Desire in Contemporary Japan." *Social Text* 12 (1994): 113–39.

Costigliola, Frank. *Awkward Dominion: American Political, Economic, and Cultural Relations with Europe, 1919–1933.* Ithaca, N.Y., 1984.

———. *France and the United States: The Cold War Alliance since World War II.* New York, 1993.

Crisp, Colin. *The Classic French Cinema, 1930–1960.* Bloomington, 1993.

Culbert, David. "American Film Policy in the Re-education of Germany after 1945." In *The Political Re-education of Germany and Her Allies after World War II,* ed. Nicholas Pronay and Keith Wilson, 173–202. London, 1985.

D'Attorre, P. P., ed. *Nemici per la pelle. Sogno americano e mito sovietico nell'Italia contemporanea.* Milan, 1991.

Dale, Peter N. *The Myth of Japanese Uniqueness.* London, 1986.

De Grazia, Victoria. "Mass Culture and Sovereignty: The American Challenge to European Cinemas, 1920–1960." *Journal of Modern History* 61 (March 1989): 53–87.

———. "Nationalizing Women: The Competition between Fascist and Commercial Cultural Models in Mussolini's Italy." In *The Sex of Things: Gender and Consumption in Historical Perspective,* ed. Victoria de Grazia, 337–58. Berkeley, 1996.

De Grazia, Victoria, ed., with Ellen Furlough. *The Sex of Things: Gender and Consumption in Historical Perspective.* Berkeley, 1996.

Dean, John, and Jean-Paul Gabilliet, eds. *European Readings of American Popular Culture.* Westport, Conn., 1996.

Denning, Michael. "The End of Mass Culture." *ILWCH* 37 (Spring 1990): 4–18.

Diefendorf, Jeffry M., ed. *Rebuilding Europe's Bombed Cities.* New York, 1990.

Diefendorf, Jeffry M., Axel Frohn, and Hermann-Josef Rupieper, eds. *American Policy and the Reconstruction of West Germany, 1945–1955.* New York, 1993.

Diner, Dan. *America in the Eyes of the Germans: An Essay on Anti-Americanism,* trans. Allison Brown. Princeton, 1996.

Doering-Manteuffel, Anselm. "Dimensionen von Amerikanisierung in der deutschen Gesellschaft." *Archiv für Sozialgeschichte* 35 (1995): 1–34.

Douglas, Susan J. *Where the Girls Are: Growing Up Female with the Mass Media.* New York, 1994.

Dudziak, Mary. "Desegregation as a Cold War Imperative." *Stanford Law Review* 41 (November 1988): 61–120.

Duignan, Peter, and L. H. Gann. *The Rebirth of the West: The Americanization of the Democratic World, 1945–1958.* Cambridge, 1992.

Ellwood, David W. *Rebuilding Europe: Western Europe, America and Postwar Reconstruction.* London, 1992.

Ellwood, David W., and Rob Kroes, eds. *Hollywood in Europe: Experiences of a Cultural Hegemony.* Amsterdam, 1994.

Ermath, Michael, ed. *America and the Shaping of German Society 1945–1955.* Providence, R.I., 1993.

Fantasia, Rick. "Everything and Nothing: The Meaning of Fast-Food and Other American Cultural Goods in France." *Tocqueville Review* 25, no. 2 (1994): 57–88.

Fehrenbach, Heide. *Cinema in Democratizing Germany: Reconstructing National Identity After Hitler.* Chapel Hill, N.C., 1995.

———. "Rehabilitating Father*land*: Race and German Remasculinization." *Signs: Journal of Women in Culture and Society* 24, no. 1 (Fall 1998): 107–27.

Forest, Claude. "Histoire économique de l'exploitation cinématographique française." In Ecole Polytechnique, *Programme de recherche du premier siècle du cinéma: histoire économique du cinéma français, année 1993–1994,* 46–56. Paris, 1995.

Frith, Simon, and Andrew Goodwin, eds. *On Record: Rock, Pop, and the Written Word.* New York, 1990.

Frith, Simon. *Sound Effects: Youth, Leisure, and the Politics of Rock 'n' Roll.* New York, 1981.

Garofalo, Reebee, ed. *Rockin' the Boat: Mass Music and Mass Movements.* Boston, 1992.

Gassert, Philipp. *Amerika im Dritten Reich: Ideologie, Propaganda und Volksmeinung 1933–1945.* Stuttgart, 1997.

Gentile, Emilio. "Impending Modernity: Fascism and the Ambivalent Image of the United States." *Journal of Contemporary History* 28 (1993).

Giddens, Anthony. *The Consequences of Modernity* (Stanford, 1990).

Gilroy, Paul. *The Black Atlantic: Modernity and Double Consciousness.* Cambridge, Mass., 1993.

——. *There Ain't No Black in the Union Jack: The Cultural Politics of Race and Nation.* London, 1987.

Gimbel, John. *The American Occupation of Germany: Politics and the Military, 1945–1949.* Stanford, 1968.

Gluck, Carol. "Entangling Illusions–Japanese and American Views of the Occupation." In *New Frontiers in American-East Asian Relations,* ed. D. Borg and W. I. Cohen. New York, 1983.

Gordon, Andrew, ed. *Postwar Japan as History.* Berkeley, 1993.

Grimm, Reinhold, and Jost Hermand, eds. *Blacks and German Culture.* Madison, Wisc., 1986.

Grossberg, Lawrence, Cary Nelson, and Paula A. Treichler, eds. *Cultural Studies.* New York, 1992.

Grossmann, Atina. "*Girlkultur* or Thoroughly Rationalized Female: A New Woman in Weimar Germany?" In *Women in Culture and Politics: A Century of Change,* ed. Judith Friedlaender et al., 62–80. Bloomington, 1986.

Guback, Thomas H. "Shaping the Film Business in Postwar Germany: The Role of the US Film Industry and the US State." In *The Hollywood Film Industry,* ed. Paul Kerr, 245–75. New York, 1986.

——. *The International Film Industry: Western Europe and America since 1945.* Bloomington, 1969.

Gupta, Akhil, and James Ferguson, "Beyond 'Culture': Space, Identity, and the Politics of Difference." *Cultural Anthropology* 7 (1): 6–23.

Hall, Stuart, David Held, and Tony McGrew, eds. *Modernity and Its Futures.* Oxford: 1992.

Hall, Stuart. "Notes on Deconstructing the Popular." In *People's History and Socialist Theory,* ed. Raphael Samuel. London, 1981.

——. "The Local and the Global: Globalization and Ethnicities." In *Culture, Globalization, and the World System,* ed. Anthony D. King, 19–39. Albany, 1991.

Hansen, Miriam. "Of Mice and Ducks: Benjamin and Adorno on Disney." *South Atlantic Quarterly* 92 (Winter 1993): 27–61.

Hartenian, Larry. "The Role of Media in Democratizing Germany: United States Occupation Policy, 1945–1949." *Central European Studies* 20 (June 1987): 145–90.

Hebdige, Dick. "Toward a Cartography of Taste 1935–1962." In Hebdige, *Hiding in the Light: On Images and Things,* 45–76. New York, 1988.

Herf, Jeffrey. *Reactionary Modernism: Technology, Culture and Politics in Weimar and the Third Reich.* New York, 1984.

Hermand, Jost. *Kultur im Wiederaufbau: Die Bundesrepublik Deutschland 1945–1965.* Munich, 1986.

Hobsbawm, Eric, and Terence Ranger, eds. *The Invention of Tradition.* Cambridge, Mass., 1983.

Hogan, Michael J. *The Marshall Plan: America, Britain, and the Reconstruction of Western Europe.* New York, 1987.

Hollander, P. *Anti-Americanism: Critiques at Home and Abroad 1965–1990.* New York, 1992.

Horkheimer, Max, and Theodor W. Adorno. *Dialectic of Enlightenment,* trans. John Cumming. New York, 1972.

Huyssen, Andreas. *After the Great Divide: Modernism, Mass Culture, Postmodernism.* Bloomington, 1986.

Iriye, Akira. *Cultural Internationalism and World Order.* Baltimore, 1997.

———. *Power and Culture: The Japanese-American War, 1941–1945.* Cambridge, Mass., 1981.

———. "Culture." In "A Roundtable: Explaining the History of American Foreign Relations." *Journal of American History* 77 (June 1990): 99–107.

Iriye, Akira, ed. *Mutual Images: Essays in American-Japanese Relations.* Cambridge, Mass., 1975.

Ivy, Marilyn. "Critical Texts, Mass Artifacts: The Consumption of Knowledge in Postmodern Japan." *Postmodernism and Japan,* ed. Masao Miyoshi and H. D. Harootunian, 21–46. Durham, N.C., 1989.

———. *Discourses of the Vanishing: Modernity, Phantasm, Japan.* Chicago, 1995.

———. "Formations of Mass Culture." In *Postwar Japan as History,* ed. Andrew Gordon, 239–58. Berkeley, 1993.

Jameson, Frederic. *Postmodernism: Or the Cultural Logic of Late Capitalism.* Durham, N.C., 1991.

Jarausch, Konrad, and Hannes Siegrist, eds. *Amerikanisierung und Sowjetisierung in Deutschland.* Frankfurt a.M., 1997.

Jarvie, Ian. *Hollywood's Overseas Campaign: The North Atlantic Movie Trade, 1920–1950.* New York, 1992.

Kaplan, Amy, and Donald E. Pease, eds. *Cultures of United States Imperialism.* Durham, N.C., 1993.

Kaplan, Wendy, ed. *Designing Modernity: The Arts of Reform and Persuasion, 1885–1945.* New York, 1995.

Kater, Michael H. *Different Drummers: Jazz in the Culture of Nazi Germany.* New York, 1992.

Kellerman, Henry. *Cultural Relations as an Instrument of U.S. Foreign Policy.* Washington, D.C., 1978.

Kelley, Robin D. "Notes on Deconstructing 'The Folk.' AHR Forum." *American Historical Review* 97 (December 1992): 1400–1408.

Kelly, William W. "Rationalization and Nostalgia: Cultural Dynamics of New Middle-Class Japan." *American Ethnologist* 13, no. 4 (1986): 603–18.

Koschmann, J. Victor. "The Nationalism of Cultural Uniqueness." *American Historical Review* 102, no. 3 (June 1997): 758–68.

Kroes, Rob. *If You've Seen One You've Seen the Mall: Europeans and American Mass Culture.* Urbana and Chicago, 1996.

Kroes, Rob, and Marten van Rossem, eds. *Anti-Americanism in Europe.* Amsterdam, 1986.

Kroes, Rob, Robert W. Rydell, and Doeko F. J. Bosscher, eds. *Cultural Transmissions and Receptions: American Mass Culture in Europe.* Amsterdam, 1993.

Krüger, Heinz-Hermann, ed. *"Die Elvis-Tolle, die hatte ich mir unauffällig wachsen lassen": Lebensgeschichte und jugendliche Alltagskultur in den fünfziger Jahren.* Opladen, 1985.

Kuisel, Richard. *Seducing the French: The Dilemma of Americanization.* Berkeley, 1993.

Lacorne, Denis, Jacques Rupnik, and Marie-France Toinet, eds. *The Rise and Fall of Anti-Americanism in Modern Times,* trans. Gerry Turner. Westport, Conn., 1978.

LaFeber, Walter. *The Clash: A History of U.S.-Japanese Relations.* New York, 1997.

Laqua, Carsten. *Wie Micky unter die Nazis fiel.* Reinbek bei Hamburg, 1992.

Lazarus, David. "Harrison-San! You're Late for Work!: Gaijin Celebrities in Japanese Ads." *Mangajin* 54 (April 1996): 58–59.

Lazere, Donald, ed. *American Media and Mass Culture: Left Perspectives.* Berkeley, 1987.

Lebrun, Dominique. *Trans-Europe Hollywood.* Paris, 1992.

Le Mahieu, D. L. *A Culture for Democracy: Mass Communication and the Cultivated Mind in Britain between the Wars.* Oxford, 1988.

Lhamon, W. T. *Deliberate Speed: The Origins of a Cultural Style in the American 1950s.* Washington, D.C., 1990.

Liebes, Tamar, and Elihu Katz. *The Export of Meaning: Cross Cultural Readings of Dallas.* New York, 1990.

Lipset, Seymour Martin. *American Exceptionalism.* New York, 1996.

Lipsitz, George. *Dangerous Crossroads: Popular Music, Postmodernism and the Poetics of Place.* London, 1994.

Lowe, Lisa. *Immigrant Acts: On Asian American Cultural Politics.* Durham, N.C., 1996.

Lüdtke, Alf, Inge Marßolek, and Adelheid von Saldern, eds. *Amerikanisierung: Traum und Alptraum im Deutschland des 20. Jahrhunderts.* Stuttgart, 1997.

Luger, Kurt. *Die konsumierte Rebellion: Geschichte der Jugendkultur 1945–1990.* Vienna, 1991.

Maase, Kaspar. "'Amerikanisierung der Gesellschaft': Nationalisierende Deutung von Globalisierungsprozessen?" In *Amerikanisierung und Sowjetisierung in Deutschland,* ed. Konrad Jarausch and Hannes Siegrist, 219–41. Frankfurt a.M., 1997.

———. *Bravo Amerika: Erkundungen zur Jugendkultur der Bundesrepublik in den fünfziger Jahren.* Hamburg, 1992.

Maier, Charles S. "Between Taylorism and Technocracy: European Ideologies and the Vision of Industrial Productivity in the 1920s." *Journal of Contemporary History* 2 (1970): 27–61.

Marcus, Greil. *Mystery Train: Images of America in Rock 'n' Roll Music.* New York, 1982.

Martin, Linda, and Kerry Segrave. *Anti-Rock: The Opposition to Rock 'n' Roll.* Hamden, Conn., 1988.

Mattelart, Armand, Xavier Delcourt, and Michelle Mattelart. *International Image Markets.* London, 1984.

May, Elaine Tyler. *Homeward Bound: American Families in the Cold War.* New York, 1988.

May, Larry, ed. *Recasting America: Culture and Politics in the Age of the Cold War.* Chicago, 1989.

McAlister, Melani. *Staging the American Century: Race, Gender, and Nation in U.S. Representations of the Middle East, 1945–1992.* Berkeley, forthcoming.

McCormick, Richard W. *Politics of the Self: Feminism and the Postmodern in West German Literature and Film.* Princeton, 1991.

McRobbie, Angela. *Feminism and Youth Culture: From Jackie to Just Seventeen.* Boston, 1991.

Milward, Alan S. *The Reconstruction of Western Europe, 1945–1951.* Berkeley, 1984.

Miyoshi, Masao. *Off Center: Power and Culture Relations between Japan and the United States.* Cambridge, Mass., 1991.

Miyoshi, Masao, and H. D. Harootunian, eds. *Postmodernism and Japan.* Durham, N.C., 1989.

Modleski, Tania, ed. *Studies in Entertainment: Critical Approaches to Mass Culture.* Bloomington, 1986.

Morley, David, and Kevin Robins. *Spaces of Identity: Global Media, Electronic Landscapes, and Cultural Boundaries.* New York, 1995.

Mukerji, Chandra, and Michael Schudson, eds. *Rethinking Popular Culture: Contemporary Perspectives in Cultural Studies.* Berkeley, 1991.

Nacci, M. *L'anti-americanismo in Italia negli anni trenta.* Turin, 1989.

Neumann, Dietrich. *"Die Wolkenkratzer kommen!" Deutsche Hochhäuser der zwanziger Jahre. Debatten, Projekte und Bauten.* Braunschweig, 1995.

Ninkovich, Frank. *The Diplomacy of Ideas: U.S. Foreign Policy and Cultural Relations, 1938–1950.* New York, 1981.

Nishi, Toshio. *Unconditional Democracy: Education and Politics in Occupied Japan 1945–1952.* Stanford, 1982.

Nolan, Mary. "Against Exceptionalism." *American Historical Review* 102, no. 3 (June 1997): 769–74.

———. *Visions of Modernity: American Business and the Modernization of Germany.* New York, 1994.

Nowell-Smith, Geoffrey, and Steven Ricci, eds. *Hollywood and Europe: Economics, Culture, National Identity, 1945–1995.* London, 1998.

Pells, Richard. *Not Like Us: How Europeans Have Loved, Hated, and Transformed American Culture since World War II.* New York, 1997.

Pence, Katherine. "The 'Fräuleins' meet the 'Amis': Americanization of German Women in the Reconstruction of the West German State." *Michigan Feminist Studies* 7 (1992–93): 83–108.

Peukert, Detlev J. K. *Inside Nazi Germany: Conformity, Opposition, and Racism in Everyday Life,* trans. Richard Deveson. New Haven, Conn., 1987.

———. *The Weimar Republic: The Crisis of Classical Modernity,* trans. Richard Deveson. New York, 1991.

Pincus, Leslie. *Authenticating Culture in Imperial Japan: Kuki Shuzo and the Rise of National Aesthetics.* Berkeley, 1996.

Pinkus, Karen. *Bodily Regimes: Italian Advertising under Fascism.* Minneapolis, 1995.

Poiger, Uta G. "Rock 'n' Roll, Female Sexuality and the Cold War Battle over German Identities." *Journal of Modern History* 68 (September 1996): 577–616.

———. *Jazz, Rock, and Rebels: Cold War Politics and American Culture in a Divided Germany.* Berkeley, forthcoming.

Pommerin, Reiner, ed. *The American Impact on Postwar Germany.* Providence, R.I., 1995.

Portes, Jacques. "Hollywood et la France, 1896–1930." *Revue française d'études américaines* 59 (1994): 25–34.

Prinz, Michael, and Rainer Zitelmann, eds. *Nationalsozialismus und Modernisierung.* Darmstadt, 1991.

Pronay, Nicholas, and Keith Wilson, eds. *The Political Re-education of Germany and Her Allies after World War II.* London, 1985.

Ramet, Sabrina P., ed. *Rocking the State: Rock Music and Politics in Eastern Europe and Russia.* Boulder, Colo., 1994.

Rauhut, Michael. *Beat in der Grauzone: DDR-Rock 1964 bis 1972 – Politik und Alltag.* Berlin, 1993.

Rentschler, Eric. "How American Is It? The U.S. as Image and Imaginary in German Film." *German Quarterly* (Fall 1984): 603–19.

———. *The Ministry of Illusion: Nazi Cinema and Its Afterlife.* Cambridge, Mass., 1996.

Rogin, Michael. *Black Face, White Noise: Jewish Immigrants in the Hollywood Melting Pot.* Berkeley, 1996.

Rollins, Roger, ed. *The Americanization of the Global Village: Essays in Popular Culture.* Bowling Green, Ohio, 1989.

Rosenberg, Emily S. *Spreading the American Dream: American Economic and Cultural Expansion, 1890–1945.* New York, 1982.

Ross, Kristin. *Fast Cars, Clean Bodies: Decolonization and the Reordering of French Bodies.* Cambridge, Mass., 1995.

Rupieper, Hermann-Josef. *Die Wurzeln der westdeutschen Nachkriegs-demokratie: Der amerikanische Beitrag 1945–1952.* Opladen, 1993.

Rupnik, Jacques. "Anti-Americanism and the Modern: The Image of the United States in French Public Opinion." *France and Modernisation,* ed. John Gaffney, 189–205. London, 1988.

Russell, John. "Race and Reflexivity: The Black Other in Contemporary Japanese Mass Culture." *Cultural Anthropology* 6 (1991): 3–25.

Ryback, Timothy W. *Rock around the Bloc: A History of Rock Music in Eastern Europe and the Soviet Union.* New York, 1990.

Saunders, Thomas J. *Hollywood in Berlin: American Cinema and Weimar Germany.* Berkeley, 1994.

Schäfer, Hans Dieter. "Amerikanismus im Dritten Reich." In *National-sozialismus und Modernisierung,* ed. Michael Prinz and Rainer Zitelmann, 199–215. Darmstadt, 1991.

———. *Das gespaltene Bewußtsein: Über deutsche Kultur und Lebenswirklichkeit, 1933–1945.* Munich, 1981.

Schaller, Michael. *Altered States: The United States and Japan since the Occupation.* New York, 1997.

Schildt, Axel, and Arnold Sywottek, eds. *Modernisierung im Wiederaufbau: Die westdeutsche Gesellschaft der 50er Jahre.* Bonn, 1993.

Schiller, Herbert I. *Mass Communications and American Empire.* Boulder, Colo., 1992.

Schulte-Sasse, Linda. *Entertaining the Third Reich: Illusions of Wholeness in Nazi Cinema.* Durham, N.C., 1996.

Servan-Schreiber, Jean Jacques. *The American Challenge,* trans. Ronald Steel. New York, 1968.

Silverberg, Miriam. "Constructing a New Cultural History of Prewar Japan." *Boundary 2* 18 (Fall 1991): 61–89.

———. "Constructing the Japanese Ethnography of Modernity." *Journal of Asian Studies* 51 (February 1992): 30–54.

Stacey, Jackie. *Star Gazing: Hollywood Cinema and Female Spectatorship.* New York, 1994.

Starr, S. Frederick. *Red and Hot: The Fate of Jazz in the Soviet Union.* New York, 1983.

Stella, Simonetta Piccone. "'Rebels without a Cause': Male Youth in Italy around 1960." *History Workshop* 58 (1994): 157–78.

Storm, J. P., and M. Dressler. *Im Reiche der Micky Maus: Walt Disney in Deutschland, 1927–1945.* Berlin, 1991.

Stovall, Tyler. *Paris Noir: African Americans in the City of Light.* New York, 1996.

Strauss, David. *Menace in the West: The Rise of French Anti-Americanism in Modern Times.* Westport, Conn., 1978.

Swann, Paul. *The Hollywood Feature Film in Postwar Britain.* London, 1987.

Tanaka, Stephan. *Japan's Orient: Rendering Pasts into History.* Berkeley, 1993.

Tent, James F. *Mission on the Rhine: Re-education and Denazification in American-Occupied Germany.* Chicago, 1982.

Thompson, Kristin. *Exporting Entertainment: America in the World Market, 1907–1934.* London, 1985.

Thomson, Charles A., and Walter H. C. Laves. *Cultural Relations and U.S. Foreign Policy.* Bloomington, 1963.

Tobin, Joseph. *Remade in Japan: Everyday Life and Consumer Taste in a Changing Society.* New Haven, Conn., 1992.

Tomlinson, Alan. *Consumption, Identity, and Style: Marketing, Meanings, and the Packaging of Pleasure.* New York, 1990.

Tomlinson, John. *Cultural Imperialism: A Critical Introduction.* Baltimore, 1991.

Treat, John Whittier, ed. *Contemporary Japan and Popular Culture.* Honolulu, 1996.

Trommler, Frank, and Joseph McVeigh, eds. *America and the Germans: An Assessment of a Three-Hundred-Year History.* Philadelphia, 1985.

Tsuru, Shigeto. *Japan's Capitalism: Creative Defeat and Beyond.* Cambridge, Mass., 1993.

Tunstall, Jeremy. *The Media Are American.* London, 1977.

Wagnleitner, Reinhold. *Coca-Colonization and Cold War: The Cultural Mission of the United States in Austria after the Second World War,* trans. Diana M. Wolf. Chapel Hill, N.C., 1994.

Wall, Irwin M. *The United States and the Making of Postwar France, 1945–1954.* New York, 1991.

Wicke, Peter. *Rock Music: Culture, Aesthetics and Sociology,* trans. Rachel Fogg. New York, 1990.

Willet, John. *The New Sobriety: Art and Politics in the Weimar Period.* New York, 1978.

Willet, Ralph. *The Americanization of Germany, 1945–1949.* New York, 1989.

Williams, Alan. *Republic of Images: A History of French Filmmaking.* Cambridge, Mass., 1992.

Woodward, C. Vann. *The Old World's New World.* New York, 1991.

Yonnet, Paul. *Jeux, modes et masses: La société française et le moderne, 1945–1985.* Paris, 1985.

Yoshino, Kosaku. *Cultural Nationalism in Contemporary Japan: A Sociological Inquiry.* London, 1992.

Zwerin, Mike. *La tristesse de Saint Louis. Swing under the Nazis.* London, 1985.

INDEX